Call up the GROUPS!

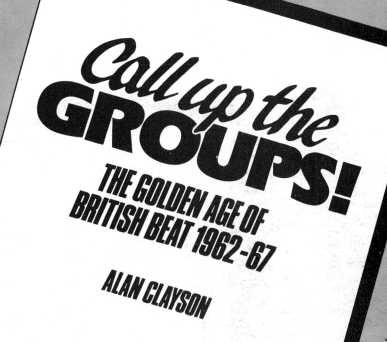

Call up the GROUPS!

THE GOLDEN AGE OF BRITISH BEAT 1962-67

ALAN CLAYSON

Blandford Press
Poole · Dorset

First published in the UK 1985 by Blandford Press,
Link House, West Street, Poole, Dorset, BH15 1LL

Distributed in the United States
by Sterling Publishing Co., Inc.,
2 Park Avenue, New York, NY 10016

British Library Cataloguing in Publication Data

Clayson, Alan
    Call up the groups : the golden age of British
    beat, 1962–1967.
    1. Rock groups—Great Britain—History
    I. Title
    780'.42'0922   ML3492

ISBN 0 7137 1553 7

Typeset by Graphicraft Typesetters Ltd. HK

Printed in Great Britain by R. J. Acford, Chichester

FOR JACK AND HARRY —
IF EVER THEIR TIME COMES.

CONTENTS

BITS AND PIECES

First of all, I wish to express my deepest gratitude to Inese who kept many mundane but harrowing problems at arm's length during the writing of this book. She also weathered my foul temper, artistic pretentions and endless torments above and beyond the call of duty. Hopefully, she will continue to do so.

Next, I am grateful to Stuart Booth and Blandford Press for giving me a break and to Steve Maggs and John Tobler for their faith and very real assistance — particularly as consultants over apparent trivia. I would also like a round of applause for Charles Salt and Garry Jones.

Much of the photography and collage assembly was accomplished through the artistry of Paul Tucker and the craftsmanship of Pete Cox — the noblest Argonaut of them all.

Thanks is also owed in varying degrees to: Sue Allen, Daphne Andrews, Maurice Bacon, Roger Barnes, Dave Berry, Bob Brunning, Roy Burchill, Clive Chandler, Gordon and Rosemary Clayson, Mike Cooper, Tracey Cox, Debi Daniels, Decca International, Dave Dee, Kevin Delaney, Fred Dellar, Peter Doggett, Edsel Records, Tim Fagan, Pete Frame, Herman Hamerpagt, Paul Hearne, Tony Hicks, Graham and Angela Hobbs, Debbie Hodder, Nick Horne, Dave Humphries, Rick Huxley, Allan Jones, Neil Kinnock, Billy J. Kramer, Anne Martin, Phil May, Jim McCarty, Tom McGuinness. *Melody Maker*, Sally Mills, Sandy Newman, John Otway, Andy Pegg, Ray Phillips, John Platt, Terry Pratt, Reg Presley, Alan Price, *Record Collector*, April Relf, Richard Riding, Mike Robinson, George Rowden, Pete Rowe, Mary Russell, Deborah Salt, Paul Samwell-Smith, Steve Stone, Peter Sullivan, Dick Taylor, Gary Thomas, Michael Towers, John Townsend and Ron Watts.

PHOTOGRAPHIC CREDITS

Whilst every effort has been made to contact the original sources or copyright holders of the photographs used in the book this did not always prove possible and the use of any consequently uncredited illustration is acknowledged with gratitude and apologies.

The following are acknowledged with very many thanks for their permission to use photographs on the pages listed:

Stuart Booth (187)
Pete Cox (21, 96, 101, 102, 112, 113, 161, 167)
Decca Record Company (92, 122, 124, 147, 150, 170, 171, 174, 177, 183, 184)
Edsel Records (56, 65, 120, 159, 179)
Herman Hamerpagt (31, 32, 87)
Granada Television (24)
Bill Harry (111)
HMV Records (115)
David John (47)

Belinda Manning (78)
Marshall Arts (39)
Melody Maker (37, 42, 45, 63, 64, 69, 70, 72, 73, 74, 85, 87, 89, 91, 98, 105, 109, 131, 139, 149, 153, 158, 180, 181, 185)
New Musical Express (133)
Office of the Leader of the Opposition (74)
Terry Pratt/Medway Records (25)
Richard Riding (16, 34, 35, 36, 57, 68, 95, 99, 100, 107, 116, 118, 137, 140, 155, 182)
Mike Robinson (54)
George Rowden (29)
Mary Russell (27)
Springboard (58)
Gary Thomas (172)
Michael Towers (26)
Paul Tucker (14, 18, 23, 26, 46, 49, 53, 59, 62, 76, 77, 81, 125, 130, 163, 171, 176, 186)
Yorkshire Television (178)

FOREWORD

It isn't difficult to work out why there was such a big change in music in Britain in the early 1960s. The initial impact of the mid-sixties rock'n'roll had soon been watered down to musical wallpaper with all the Bobbies and Jimmies from white America flooding the U.K. market.

Like most of my fellow sixties artists, I spent my late school days listening to Little Richard, Fats Domino, Gene Vincent and, of course, Chuck Berry. It was at this time that most of us formed our first groups only to find that the rock 'n' roll dream had faded. It was the start of a musical wasteland. Here in Britain, apart from isolated cases like Vince Taylor and Johnny Kidd, no-one had much idea performance-wise.

Around 1960–1, the Cruisers and 1 — in common with other groups — had continued playing rock and blues material, favouring black musicians who recorded on obscure US labels in preference to most of the stuff we heard in the Top Twenty. I remember seeing a blues package show in Manchester at this time which included John Lee Hooker, Memphis Slim and T-Bone Walker. A large percentage of the audience consisted of musicians.

The kids who came to the early gigs were also fed-up with the music in the charts. As happened in 1955, and as would happen again in 1976, the groups built up a tremendous following in their respective cities — in my case, Sheffield — playing the small rock clubs that had sprung up everywhere. Our strength was that we had an audience just waiting for record releases, hence the excitement when our first discs appeared in 1963.

The overall direction of the period is well summarised in the words of Jonathan King: 'We were one big family and have been pleased to see many of our colleagues succeed and become millionaires. Others carved themselves a long term career in music but, sadly, many did not make it at all.'

DAVE BERRY
Derbyshire, 1985

'The cheap music that Arthur loved so much is more versatile than its sniffy detractors often allow. There are not many of us who do not have in our heads, however irritatingly, the remote or even half-forgotten tinkle of a popular song which can instantly carry us back on swift wings to a time, a person, an event significant to us.'

Pennies from Heaven Dennis Potter

FROM ME TO YOU — A PROLOGUE

I knew a Boy Scout called Kevin who sang with the first group I ever saw, the E-Types. He was hovering apprehensively as the others prepared to entertain on 'Open Day' at their Aldershot secondary modern one afternoon in 1965. The lead and bass guitarists both plugged into a 15-watt Rangemaster while Kevin's microphone went through a nameless practice amplifier. The youth on rhythm thrashed a finger-lacerating acoustic guitar as the drummer did likewise on a cheap Gigster kit — kick bass, snare, hi-hat and floor tom.

Authority, complaining of noise from this 'Teddy Boys gala', abruptly terminated the set after twenty minutes of wrong notes, meandering tempos and long pauses between numbers which included *I'm Into Something Good* (twice) and a *Concrete and Clay* in which Beatle-fringed, barrel-shaped Kevin, forgetting the words, mumbled vaguely about 'candy in the moonlight'. Nevertheless, I filed out of the classroom in a daze. That The E-Types had approximated Number One hits placed them beyond criticism. Surely it was only a matter of a year at most before they 'made it'.... READY STEADY GO....TOP OF THE POPS....SUNDAY NIGHT AT THE LONDON PALLADIUM....MADISON SQUARE GARDEN. Imagine the laugh-a-minute recording sessions: the limousine gliding to the sold-out theatre; changing into stage gear fresh from Carnaby Street; David Jacobs announcing you in his BBC voice; everybody screams; wild scenes on the boards and off; police cordons; adoring girls; envious boys; hanging about the Scotch Of St. James with all the other stars.

What would be The E-Types angle? The Stones and Beatles were deadly enemies — everyone knew that. Gerry grinned. Freddie was Clown Prince. Dave Berry was weird. The Merseybeats had frilly shirts. Manfred had a beard. Them were Irish. The Joystrings were religious. The Who smashed up their equipment. Kevin would think of something.

Of course, I had no idea how many groups there were in Aldershot alone. Even our next door neighbour's quiet, nervous elder son turned out to be rhythm guitarist in one. There he was on the Rotary Club float on Guy Fawkes Night duplicating Hilton Valentine's raw arpeggios to *House of the Rising Sun*.

From that moment, it took five years before I made a public appearance with my own group. Much of the delay was interrelated with my C-stream drudgery in a desperate boys' grammar school in Farnborough. Whereas 11-plus exam failures like the E-Types enjoyed their headmaster's neutrality, we A-Types were discouraged from forming time-wasting, intellectually-stultifying 'Pop Groups' though, in fact, a large percentage of top groups came from higher education establishments. Boys in groups were like girls in brothels — you only had to read the newspapers.

A strong enough incentive for any red-blooded adolescent lad to join a group was no matter what you looked like you could still be popular with young ladies. Ringo and his nose, Herman and his spots — all festooned the snow-blinded pages of *Jackie*, *Fabulous* and *Mirabelle*...."ooo, 'e's lovely!'

Boys' reasons for liking groups weren't always musical either. In 1964 I finally transferred my allegiance from Adam Faith to the Dave Clark Five when a Patrol Leader I admired said that they were his favourite group. Taking the mildest censure of them as a personal insult, I supported the Five as others would a football team until tested by a horrified preference for the Yardbirds that I could barely bring myself to articulate.

A more typical memory was tuning into Radio Luxembourg under bed-clothes where the small hours were illuminated by a wrist watch's writhing numerals and the transistor dial. Under these conditions, I first heard *You Really Got Me* — lying awake suffocating in case it was aired again. I studied the music press like the Bible and conducted conversations in song titles and lyric quotes — a Pretty Things B-side being far more meaningful to me than any Euclid theorum or Schleswig-Holstein Question.

After finishing one number, *Pretty Face* by the Beat Merchants pared down to two chords, my first group, Ace and the Cascades, disbanded when the guitarist's mother denied us the use of his bedroom for rehearsals when she heard a Cascade say 'bloody.' She also objected to our kitless drummer flailing about the furniture with sticks sawn-off from a fishing rod.

A most deceitful facade was when groups mimed on TV. With no amp or speaker in sight until READY STEADY GO went 'live' in April 1965, this led to dangerous misunderstandings — such as the time blue smoke curled from a Top Twenty guitar pick-up after I'd contrived to plug it directly into the mains. In the highest tradition of skiffle, I broke a Melodica while trying to rig it up like a Vox Continental organ with the aid of a bicycle pump operated with the knee. The respective owners of both these instruments were most unpleasant about my mistaken ingenuity.

At one of two, school-sponsored, flamenco guitar lessons I attended, the tutor showed us how *not* to play by smashing out a fast blues shuffle. Impressed, I swapped my Spanish guitar's gut strings for metal, stuck a tape recorder mike over the hole and sent it through a Dansette record-player amp. In front or the mirror, I mastered *Money*, *For Your Love* and *Reelin' and Rockin'* for a fourth year group that dare not speak its name. It was nearly 1967. As 'O' Level examinations and *Sergeant Pepper* gave their marching orders to the Golden Age of British Beat, I had a row with the drummer and the group broke up.

Alan Clayson

BIG
TIME
OPERATORS

'Ready Steady Pause' RSG hostess Cathy McGowan (left) and interviewee Sandie Shaw take five as cameras are repositioned during rehearsals.

16

The Animals Bring It On Home

Mark studied at a college down south. He made no bones about his contempt for stuck up southerners as he thickened his Harry Hotspur Geordie accent, swilled Newcastle Brown Ale exclusively and generally came on as the Poor, Honest Northern Lad Trying To Better Himself. The only subject he kept quiet about was that of his father who was a banker. Once Mark rose from a bath to rush dripping to the Common Room when informed that Lindisfarne — allegedly his 'mates' — were on TV. Bill, another student, privately adhered to the widespread opinion that Mark was a bit of a twerp but whenever this feeling was expressed, Bill would swoop unquestioningly to Mark's defence. You see, Bill too was a Geordie.

More than Liverpool, Newcastle — grimy pivot of Victorian enterprise — inspired a fierce sense of regional loyalty and identity à la LIKELY LADS or AUF WEIDERSEHN, PET TV shows. Even sophisticated Bryan Ferry born on the outskirts, claimed to 'feel a great affinity for the area — I try to get back as often as I can'. A group more synonymous with Newcastle than Roxy Music was the Animals who likewise never reneged on their roots. No matter how far their wanderings before and after their disbandment, they still kept in touch via the songs, honouring landmarks of their birthplace — notably Alan Price's last hit *Jarrow Song* — and periodic reunion bashes at Newcastle City Hall. On these occasions, the world revolves round Tyneside — and Edwy of Deira is once again Bretwalda of Angle Land.

The Animals were also true to each other. Though a few old wounds may have been reopened, the lads reassembled in 1976 at Chas Chandler's place in Surrey, near Lingfield racecourse, to reach back over the years with a low profile new album BEFORE WE WERE SO RUDELY INTERRUPTED. And when Hilton Valentine was on the skids, hadn't Eric Burdon found him a job as War's road manager? In kaftan and beads, hadn't Eric been special guest on Alan's BBC TV children's series showing that the sleeve notes he wrote on A PRICE TO PLAY weren't just empty words? In 1973, though Burdon had the cheek to name his American backing trio 'The Animals' he was forgiven because even in the throes of acid fantasy, he'd never forgotten his past.

Born down river in a Walker-on-Tyne tenement, Eric was the son, as he later insisted, of a 'lower working class' family. In adolescence, he slid trombone in a trad jazz outfit before realising his true vocation as a blues singer, having been captivated by the records imported by a seaman who occupied a downstairs flat. With a madcap obsession beyond mere enthusiasm, he ritually inked the word BLUES in his own blood across the cover of an exercise book in which lyrics of the same had been compiled. Luckily, he had a voice to match — a raucous, black, rebel yell. Inability to reach high notes without cracking only compounded passion so deeply felt that Burdon's short, rotund figure was to become one of the most charismatic to grace a British stage.

At Newcastle's College of Art and Industrial Design in 1960, a gifted young bass guitarist in the *ad hoc* relief band was invited to sit in on keyboards with Eric's group, the Pagans. During his first year at Jarrow Grammar, Alan Price had been given a guitar by his big brother John, thus enabling him to join the Black Diamonds skiffle group. Though a guitar was what Presley and Donegan played, Alan was better on piano with which, by the age of fifteen, he was augmenting the Frankie Headley Five. Acquiring an electric organ, Alan formed a trio which in 1960 included drummer John Steel who shared his leader's encyclopaedic knowledge of jazz, and stout bass player Bryan 'Chas' Chandler, whom Price had met when both were members of the Kontors. Becoming The Alan Price Combo that same year, the line-up was swelled when guitarist Hilton Valentine was shanghaied from the Wild Cats — resident rock'n'rollers from Whitley Bay's Club-a-Go-Go. By 1962, Price's Pagan acquaintance, Burdon, relieved him of his duties as lead singer thus allowing a more intense concentration on the ivories.

Alan and Eric greatly admired the jazz-gospel fusions of Ray Charles, and it was his *Hit The Road Jack* that became one of the highlights of the Combo's all-nighters at the Downbeat, a dingy club well-named as it was balanced above a semi-derelict warehouse near the docks. Even nearer was a railway bridge which caused the place to shudder with every passing train.

Yet by the time they graduated to the more up-market Club-a-Go-Go towards the city centre — not Hilton's old coastal haunt — the group were cooking with gas. With coat torn off and shirt hanging out, Burdon's orange peel complexion would pour sweat as a savage Combo drove him through *Smokestack Lightning*, *Pretty Thing* and other urban blues standards. They weren't above good old rock'n'roll either as Eric bawled out *The Girl Can't Help It* and *Shake Rattle and Roll*. Then they'd take it down easy with, say, a shivering *St. James Infirmary* before roaring off into another thrilling crescendo to wind up for the night.

By the end of 1963, it was obvious that they were too hot for Northumberland to hold. The agony and ecstasy of their frenzied sessions had earned them the nickname 'Animals' which they adopted officially — possibly at the suggestion of visiting London bluesman Graham Bond. Freelance record producer Mickie Most may have interpreted the name as a North-East answer to the Beatles as he lent an ear to one of the five hundred privately-pressed E.P.'s of selections from their club set. Immediately impressed, Most hurried to Tyneside to catch The Animals in their natural habitat. Finding no uniform Beatlesque image, Most was sold entirely on their music and untutored stagecraft.

Signed to Columbia, these uncut Geordie rubies issued their debut single in March 1964. *Baby Let Me Take You Home* was a cleaned-up blues called *Baby Don't You Tear My Clothes* which Bob Dylan had reworked on his first L.P. On the same record, Dylan also revived a Josh White number that the Animals and Most taped at their very first session together. Columbia Records executives, however, could not see *The House Of The Rising Sun* setting the hit parade alight on the grounds that it was twice the length of the average single — and 'boring' to boot. Moreover a version by the Sundowners a few months earlier had been frowned upon by the BBC. Wasn't it about

prostitutes or something? (How small are the thoughts of small men?) With leverage provided by *Baby Let Me Take You Home* and its slow infiltration to Number 21, Most demanded that *House Of The Rising Sun* should be next on the agenda.

The song's melodramatic arrangement was attributed to Alan Price, though Burdon asserted to the *Sun* newspaper in 1982 that it had been a communal effort. Certainly Eric's soaring lament as much as Alan's sonorous organ extrapolation contributed to the overall tension, building from Valentine's staggered chording to the swirling high tide of the instrumental break, anchored by a pounding bass drum. Not only did it top the charts on both sides of the Atlantic but it also confirmed Dylan's resolve to hire a backing rock'n'roll group, and jarred the wistfulness from other folk singers like Paul Simon, who wrote *Richard Cory* for a band like the Animals.

Early Animals: there were few moments on the Animals first L.P.'s that approached their live power.

18

Caged in a West London apartment where the group found it more convenient to live, Burdon and Price composed the follow-up. *I'm Crying*, which with Hilton's aggressive riffing to the fore was more representative of the Animals' R'n'B zeitgeist. However, Most considered its comparatively low placing of Number 8 in Britain sufficient reason to relegate all future Animal originals to B-sides and to album tracks.

Most's talent was for putting product in the charts at minimum cost — especially in the USA at a time when L.P.'s containing a hit single song could sell a million — even if the L.P. was short on needle time and stuffed with uncertain first takes, stylised instrumentals and dud songs. (It could be said that the Beach Boys thrived on this for years.) However, attempts to rattle off any Animals codswallop specials were firmly resisted but their Columbia L.P.'s taken as a whole fell wide of the mark compared to their fierce, live power. Perhaps the studio's clinical atmosphere was partly to blame, though many unneccessary errors went unchanged to the pressing plant such as the odd line

'you'll never find another boy to treat me like I used to treat you' on Burdon's turgid 12-bar *For Miss Caulker* also notable for Valentine's aimless twanging solo and Price's valiant attempt at disguising it.

From the first album, their work-outs of *She Said 'Yeah'* and *Around And Around* sound thuggish beside the Rolling Stones' more dulcet blasts — admittedly recorded at Chess studies in Chicago rather than at EMI's London Abbey Road studios. Even *I Ain't Got You* from ANIMAL TRACKS pales against the Yardbirds less ponderous rendering — though heaven knows, Burdon could outsing Mick Jagger and Keith Relf any day. Although Price could crush notes with the best of them, another critical factor was that of his keyboards' fixed tuning and purer tone, sounding at odds with the essential dissonance at the rough guitar-heart of the blues.

Of course, there were good moments too. Significantly receiving more airplay than other album selections, *Bright Lights Big City* developed Jimmy Reed's simple idea intelligently — but again it was a

*Priceless: 1966 Animals (*left to right*) John Steel, Eric Burdon, Hilton Valentine, Chas Chandler and new recruit Dave Rowberry.*

pleasant vibration in the air and only made more tangible on stage at London's famous live venue the Marquee. A change was bound to come when they left Most in 1965.

Nevertheless, with *Don't Let Me Be Misunderstood* and *Bring It On Home To Me* — from Nina Simone and Sam Cooke respectively — splattering the hit parades of the world, Mickie Most was doing his job. The Animals were also immortalised on the silver screen in pop exploitation films like 'GET YOURSELF A COLLEGE GIRL' with the Dave Clark Five — with whom they shared the same agent, fan club secretary, record label and little else. Director Peter Watkins considered Burdon for the main role in 'PRIVILEGE.' A later opportunity to star opposite Rod Steiger likewise came to nought. Another aborted scheme was for an Animals Big Band with brass and a chorus line. Nonetheless, by summer 1965, a *New Musical Express* popularity poll had them breathing down the necks of the Beatles and Stones in the international stakes.

This was achieved in the teeth of much Mod antagonism, deliberately provoked. At 'ease with the grease' even in their early days, the Alan Price Combo had backed not only bluesmen like Sonny Boy Williamson (Alex Miller) and John Lee Hooker but also the old wild men of classic rock — Jerry Lee Lewis, Carl Perkins, Gene Vincent *et al*. The Animals felt privileged to appear shrouded in leather and motor bikes on a British Lewis-Vincent TV spectacular in 1964. Chuck Berry joined them onstage throughout their maiden US tour. On READY STEADY GO — the Mod shop window — Burdon unbuttoned his jacket to reveal the legend 'rock'n'roll lives' scrawled on cardboard across his front. Leaving no doubt where their sympathies lay, it was small wonder that narrow-minded Mods melted Animals records into plant pot holders.

All the same, the group — especially garrulous Eric — became very much the young men about Town, hanging round London clubs like the Flamingo, the Scotch of St. James and In Crowd, watering holes not mentioned on the ad-libbed fade of *Bright Lights Big City*. However, it was on the road that these new pop aristocrats really let go. The most daring of their nocturnal shenanigans was a midnight raid on a girls' Borstal thwarted when a warden woke to find an Animal prowling round her bedroom.

In mid-1965 came trouble in paradise: Alan Price left the group allegedly suffering from nervous exhaustion and a fear of flying. One exuberant lady Juke Box Jurist cited him as 'the greatest organist in the world' but a satisfactory replacement was found in Dave Rowberry

from the Mike Cotton Sound after Mick Gallagher of the Unknowns from South Shields had deputised for a few engagements.

Though Rowberry enforced a stronger melodic emphasis, in general he lacked Price's depth of sound. However this trait was not apparent on the Price-less *We Gotta Get Out Of This Place* which, in hard financial terms, was as big worldwide as *House Of The Rising Sun*. Cynthia Weill and Barry Mann were reportedly shocked at the Animals' overhaul of their creation from which Chandler's stark bass menace to the abrupt unison coda was an anthem of inner city dead end realism, truer to Tyneside smoke than to Big Apple optimism. (Testifying to this interpretation was its rude reawakening in 1979 by another Geordie outfit, the Angelic Upstarts of punk renown.)

As *de facto* Lord of the Rowberry Animals, Burdon took it upon himself to demonstrate disenchantment with Columbia Records' indifference to their musical aspirations by wantonly messing around while miming to the next 45, *It's My Life* on TV. Unsolicited, the pirate station Radio England nodded approval by broadcasting the flip *I'm Gonna Change The World* as the promotion side.

With the group's track record, Decca gave their new acquisitions the red carpet treatment, but only after a bad start when an injunction was filed on the company to delay reissue of the ancient Newcastle E.P. The first single under the new regime was *Inside Looking Out* and although advantaged by *Outcast*, a powerful B-side, it seemed wilfully uncommercial, lacking a discernable melody line to carry its harrowing prison narrative (which when Eric had first tried it during a jam session with Alexis Korner's Blues Incorporated, had the more genteel title of *Rosie*). On the strength of the Animals' reputation, it hacksawed to No. 12 in the UK, though it failed in the USA — home of their new producer, Tom Wilson.

Under Wilson's influence, the group were geared towards a blacker, American sound best heard on the valedictory ANIMALISMS L.P. in which contemporary covers of songs like Joe Tex's *One Monkey Don't Stop No Show* rubbed shoulders with Downbeat Club chestnuts like *Sweet Little Sixteen*. On the final single *Don't Bring Me Down*, increased artistic freedom was detailed by a 2-bar piano drop-in, varying degrees of guitar fuzz and Burdon's calculated, muttering overdub at the end.

Without the autocracy of someone like Most, group policy was blighted by internal discord. Before the last hurrah, Chas Chandler was already making contingency plans to go behind the scenes as a producer-manager while Steel jacked it in altogether to become, eventually, a captain of industry back on Tyneside. With Valentine and a new drummer, Barry Jenkins from the Nashville Teens, supporting Burdon's advocacy of the psychedelic music wafting from California, the Animals went their separate ways after a farewell American tour in September 1966.

By recording and promoting *Help Me Girl* — straight off Tin Pan Alley — Eric polished off the Decca contract before securing a new deal for himself and the New Animals, which included Jenkins and ex-Lord Sutch Savage Danny McCulloch, who the magnanimous Burdon allowed to take a couple of lead

Alan Price is rewarded with author Clayson's autograph as he relives high points of his career in the auditorium of Reading's Hexagon theatre, 1984.

vocals. Pandering to their leader's hippy fixations, the new team still raked in the loot with international chartbusters such as *San Francisco Nights* and the epic *Sky Pilot* before the flowers wilted.

Meanwhile, Alan Price had kept his head above water. After a false start with a reworking of Chuck Jackson's *Any Day Now*, he and his six-piece Set had rung up a handful of UK hits before their dissolution. Without letting his love of Theolonius Monk, Jimmy

Smith and other jazz giants tempt him to overreach himself, Alan's gruff tenor made a better job of Screamin' Jay Hawkins' *I Put A Spell On You* than Eric's rancorous version on ANIMALISMS as well as giving *Hi-lili Hi-lo* a joyous verve reflecting his own good nature. Though Cilla Black was first with *I've Been Wrong Before*, Price did most to familiarise the British public with the works of Los Angeles songwriter Randy Newman. It was Newman's *Simon Smith And The Amazing Dancing Bear*, which, having been rejected by the Fourmost, made the biggest chart splash for Price — together with his own *The House That Jack Built* which also reached Number 4. A vinyl marriage between a Sonny Rollins tune and Price's lyrics, *Don't Stop The Carnival* was the Set's final Top 50 entry.

Since 1968, Alan Price has made only rare excursions into the charts — among these being *Rosetta*, which tipped the iceberg of a musical liaison with Georgie Fame. Other diverse activities included acting and composing soundtracks for films — notably Lindsay Anderson's O LUCKY MAN and BETWEEN YESTERDAY AND TODAY, an exploration of his Northern origins. An intermittent foray into journalism began with his review of Thom Keyes' *All Night Stand* which delved into the seamier side of pop.

This novel naturally included a chapter set in the beat city of Hamburg where Eric Burdon turned up in 1982. Commuting to London, he led the house band through a prodigal salvage of Presley's *Trying To Get To You* on a Channel Four TV pub-rock programme. A buzz in the air suggested that this was no flying visit.

A few months later came the news that the original Animals had reformed for a world tour — centred on the lucrative US market. Most in need of a cash transfusion was Hilton, on the dole back in Newcastle. Meanwhile down in Sussex, Chas, who'd never got his motives confused, left his business affairs to look after themselves. Chandler, Valentine and Steel were a bit out of practice, but the employment of auxiliary musicians — including organist Zoot Money — steered them out of danger. This meant that Price had to be prime mover at rehearsals and in the arranging of the inevitable comeback album, while his malcontented assistant, Eric, looked forward to meeting his estranged daughter, long resident in the USA.

However, any conflicting interests were suspended onstage. There, tempered by maturity, the Geordie boys delivered the goods once again — though not even the most susceptible of their sold-out stadium audiences could pretend that that was what it must have been like in the Downbeat around 1962.

Ask Me Why: Another Opinionated Beatles Memoir

The Bible can prove any religious or moral theory. Similarly, the millions of words chronicling and analysing their every trivial act — to which I am adding — can warp the saga of the Beatles to any purpose. With a certain mental athleticism, it is even possible to deny that they were ever anything special.

Following a few years as nondescript skifflers, they began adhering to the late 1950s 'Somebody and the Somebodies' dictate which differentiated between a star and his backing group. Such a schism was indicated either by appellation e.g. 'Johnny and the Moondogs' or, owing to their glut of guitarists, by showcasing 'featured singers' — Paul McCartney being the prize exhibit though the fragile Stuart Sutcliffe evoked screams with his tremulous warbling of *Love Me Tender*. Eventually, they bowdlerised the name of Buddy Holly's Crickets — their deep admiration extending from copying *That'll Be The Day* on a 1959 demo to McCartney's investment in the bespectacled Texan's publishing rights in the seventies. As they acquired a more professional veneer, they were hired to support solo celebrities like Johnny Gentle and American comedian Davy Jones, who played temporary Cliff Richard to their Shadows.

Though John Lennon later professed to despise the polished stage antics of Hank Marvin and Co., The Beatles' repertoire included Shadows numbers when they made their Hamburg debut in 1960. With one eye on the charts and another on the rough-house they were paid to entertain, they gamely tried gauche requests like Pat Boone's *Speedy Gonzales* and Frank Ifield's *I Remember You*. The Twist craze left its mark mainly with its eight-to-the-bar hi-hat rhythm. Paul even composed a Twist number for drummer Pete Best to sing and demonstrate in a solo spot.

This acute awareness of contemporary trends pervaded when they became famous. Before showtime in theatres and TV studios, the Beatles and others would often light-heartedly jam current hits inevitably absorbing ideas of rivals. Renditions of *The House of the Rising Sun*, for instance, surfaced on two in-person radio programmes during a US tour. A subtler influence emerged in the dentist's drill feedback introducing *I Feel Fine* which echoed its live — though unrecorded — use by the Kinks and Yardbirds. In summer 1965, the same two groups released singles attempting an Indian feel principally by distorting the lead guitar to sound like a sitar. With greater resources and studio time than these less bankable acts, the Beatles exhaled an even bigger breath of the Orient by using the actual instrument on RUBBER SOUL — their Yuletide album of that year.

In front of an audience, even manager Brian Epstein didn't think they were all that great. No Beatle was a virtuoso — though McCartney evolved into an agile bass guitarist. Physically, even his moon-faced similarity to Elvis failed to disguise the group's collective callowness. Before their Parlophone audition, they had already taken their local impact to its limit. If, in a parallel universe, they hadn't sustained record company interest, they may have been superceded in the Merseyside popularity stakes by younger acts such as the Remo Four or the Mojos. The group scene might then have fizzled out bar a handful of brave anachronisms unknown beyond Lancashire, battling through the old *Money — Some Other Guy* routines for the few who still remembered.

Of course, all this obtuse speculation is unfair as it could be applied to virtually any 1960s beat group who also experienced wary ventures from skiffle to amplification, emulation of American idols, punishing schedules in seedy dance halls, holiday camps and violent European clubs — with scuffling for a recording contract a far-fetched afterthought. To just survive, bands had to provide action-packed rock to divert a boozing, flirting, trouble-making clientele. On mercifully rare occasions the Beatles discovered what it was like to get themselves and their equipment smashed up by disgruntled gangs of youths. Many close shaves and remarkable coincidences helped, but it was no happy accident that this group found itself the cream of the crop. Rather it was a real natural aptitude plus unconscious forces within their common background.

George Harrison suggested that the Beatles phenomenon resulted from an English Grammar School interpretation of rock'n'roll. Certainly the band that Allan Williams drove to the Grosse Freiheit were a representative cross-section of an institution of this type. When George brought his £30 guitar to Quarrymen sessions, his friendly overtures were overlooked by John, who exculpated himself from any criticism of hob-nobbing with a younger boy. Nonetheless, both he and Harrison were C-stream hard cases who rejected formal education. Conversely,

Money: among unsolicited Beatle money-spinners pictured here are the very first cover of a George Harrison song, possibly the worst Beatle biography ever written and Freddie Lennon's saga of his life, his soul . . . .his torment.

Was Pete best after all? Ringo wonders if the others are talking about him on Granada's Scene at 6.30, *1963.*

while not quite front row smarmers, Paul, Pete and Stuart complied more clearly with teachers' desires and were rewarded with 'A' level exam results.

Best's dismissal in 1962 was largely through his inability to conform to the mores of his peers — an example of this being his maintenance of a gravity-defying quiff instead of the Hamlet hair style adopted by the others. More serious was his refusal of the amphetamines partaken by the rest, initially to stay awake during their Reeperbahn residencies. Pete's need of natural sleep stressed his isolation as Ringo became first his deputy and later his successor.

With adolescence extended by adulation, the fifth form dance went on. Like many intelligent teenagers, their ideas were more intriguing conceptually than in practice, hence Apple's 'controlled weirdness' and the money wasted on too many Billy Bunters whose postal orders never arrived. Less attractive was a tendency to blurt out what their minds hadn't formulated in simple terms. Much of this behaviour which included psychedelic escapades and comparisons with Christ, was not entirely their fault, obliged as they were to live up to the off-beat expectations of their selfish public.

They could also be exonerated from most of the blame for the decline of Merseybeat in the wake of their success. South Lancashire was not the sole bastion of beat in the early 1960s, but it *was* an organised settlement rather than a mere outpost like Basildon, Cardigan or Aldershot. An earnest enthusiasm for regional music was reflected in the very existence of a hitherto unprecedented journal like Bill Harry's *Merseybeat*. With its venue information and fortnightly accounts of its key personalities' triumphs and tribulations, its three-year run aligned with the rise and fall of a buoyant local scene singled out by the press as a pop centre before being gutted of its major talents by London A & R men. Like Liverpool itself, *Merseybeat* was murdered and the culprits pardoned.

The Beatles peaked as live performers on their first British tour with Helen Shapiro after *Love Me Do* had made Number 18. However, it was only their maiden TV appearance on THANK YOUR LUCKY STARS, when they stole the show from the insipid Mark Wynter, that their career advanced on a national scale. With many rough edges removed, the coherence of their image presented what seemed at first glance to be a single focus for adoration epitomised by uniform stage suits, Scouse intonations and haircuts as distinctive as

Hitler's moustache. This 'Midwich Cuckoo' regularity was balanced by the paradoxical realisation that inevitable differences between them could be displayed by liberal non-conformity within the fundamental structure — Ringo's homely wit proved particularly beneficial to the North American breakthrough. However, John's idiosyncracies were the most distracting. Though his upbringing in Lancashire — as opposed to Liverpool — placed him slightly higher in the British class system than his fellow Beatles, he first became conspicuous by being married. He was also noted as an author, cartoonist and film actor. As token Beatle, it was John who was invited to take part in JUKE BOX JURY several weeks before the whole quartet comprised the panel in a special edition at the Liverpool Empire in 1963.

Though more acephalous than similar organisations, the group and its entourage periodically reaffirmed Lennon's driving force. Less tacitly, the media too elevated him to a commanding position — the *New Musical Express* once referred to him as 'lead singer', much to Paul's chagrin no doubt. In Dick Clark's romanticised 1980 TV film of their early days, John was portrayed as the Beatle most anxious about the group's future. When they played as session musicians for Tony Sheridan in 1961, producer Bert Kaempfert was conscious enough of the Beatle hierarchy to allow John a lead vocal (*Ain't She Sweet*). George's *Cry For a Shadow* instrumental from the same date — though enlivened by Paul's barely audible background yelling — is co-credited to John who had presumably given it his executive clearance.

This opus was the first Beatle composition to be immortalised on vinyl. But the motivational crux of the Beatles — a self-contained songwriting team — was denied to virtually all other beat groups of the time. The possibility of a British band developing musical composition to this extent was unheard of beyond sporadic B-sides of no real artistic value. Even the exceptions like *Move It* and *Shakin' All Over* began as flips of songs imported from America. Instigated by Paul in 1957, the Lennon-McCartney partnership had become formidable by the time the Beatles impinged on national consciousness. As the junior partner, George had, with Bill Harry's encouragement, made tentative songwriting explorations in 1963 but he, along with Ray Davies, Jagger-Richard and other composers with potential, found Paul and John's head start a hard yardstick. As well as adapting visual aspects of the Beatles' format, many famous bands — including the Stones — were launched or stabilised by the gift of a Lennon-McCartney song.

Stylistically, John and Paul covered all waterfronts from schmaltz to avant-garde. This eclecticism was mirrored in the group's perverse choice of non-originals. In the course of a Cavern set, they would veer fitfully from the jokey *Sheik of Araby* to a rocking *Hully Gully* to a torchy *September In the Rain*. Unlike other collaborators of the Rodgers and Hart ilk, where roles of tunesmith and lyricist were plainly designated, the functions of McCartney and Lennon were never cut and dried. Though the sleeve notes for *Beatles For Sale*

Package tour: the Beatles and fellow Epstien clients Billy J. Kramer and Tommy Quickly hit the road.

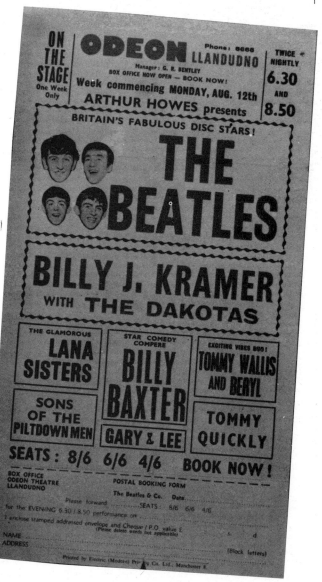

Idol on parade: Private Lennon is eyes right as director Dick Lester drills Roy Kinnear during filming of How I Won the War *in Verden, Germany.*

Queen's Road Palais, on the corner of Perowne Street, where, as evidence in the Aldershot News and Military Gazette *suggests, the Beatles made their post-Hamburg British debut on a midwinter's night in 1960.*

propagate the myth of 'raw John and melodic Paul', it was only their public persona that suggested diplomatic Paul's responsibility for ballads, leaving ravers to rough old John. On the likely conjecture that the principle composer was also lead singer, their most memorable numbers show a fairly even split — for nearly every *Yesterday* there is an *In My Life*; for every *I Feel Fine*, a *Can't Buy Me Love*. Nevertheless, in general, Lennon was the most experimental while McCartney sold more. Though John with good reason ridiculed Paul's 'granny music' in the last desperate months of the Beatles, he was to demonstrate an alarming capacity for tweeness beyond *Her Majesty* or *My Love* throughout his subsequent uxorious career until he was deprived of a hero's death on a New York pavement.

However, back in August 1966 when this seemed more likely, the emotional and musical bonds of the group were loosened when concert tours were abandoned forever. This was exacerbated the following year with the passing of their painfully committed mentor, Brian Epstein. During this transitional period, the Beatles transcended the mere mortals that constituted its personnel. Ceasing to be a popular beat group, they still continued to startle the world while vacillating between the colour supplement Art of SERGEANT PEPPER and vain endeavours to get back to their Merseybeat womb.

In the context of this discussion, the wide perspective of the Beatles' inspiration embraces both the blueprint and flowering of the beat group — its figurehead and its grey eminence. Developing and expanding on frequently opposing tendencies from pop's short history, the Beatles dictated the aspirations of the entire movement.

Did the Five Jive Crush the Beatle Beat?

In 1966, Ginger Baker's tacit sarcasm was not directly obvious to Maureen Street, the Dave Clark Five's fan club secretary, when it was reported that he had been sighted in Soho signing autographs with an official Dave Clark biro. Among the reasons for such ridicule from the pop intelligentsia was the Five's wholesome, sporty image and their use of inane — though ultimately effective — publicity stunts that other groups would disdain. This had been aggravated by Fleet Street's unfair field day when 'Has the Five Jive Crushed the Beatle Beat?' became a prototypical headline as 'Glad All Over — a racket by these North London upstarts — dislodged the Moptop Mersey Marvels from a long reign at Number One'.

A further critical factor was the Five's music. Though a 'classical' session was mentioned in *Fabulous* teen magazine in 1965, there was little indication of any highbrow influences in their short, danceable singles. Though a studio out-take the following year verged on ethereal Pink Floyd regions, they usually stuck to traditional pop structures of verses, choruses, hooklines and middle eights. While Lennon, Jagger and Davies wrote about strawberry fields, nervous breakdowns and dead end streets, the Five's emotional vocabulary hinged on boy-meets-girl-where-the-action-is, albeit more sophisticatedly expressed with time.

There were also spurious claims that drummer Clark did not actually beat the skins on his own records. As late as 1977, journalist Barry Miles named the Lower Third's Phil Lancaster as one Clark changeling. Dave — by his own admission — was no Krupa (no Ginger Baker either), but in 1965 he was to become, second to Ringo, the most famous drummer in the world.

Apparently, seven years earlier, sixteen-year-old Clark had been taking drumming lessons from Laurie Jay (who later enjoyed two minor hits with Nero and the Gladiators). Inspired by such distinguished tutorship, Dave conceived the ambition to also record a chart instrumental with his own band. To this end he and his mate, bass guitarist Chris Walls, advertised in *Melody Maker* for like-minded players.

Soon they were joined by Kentish Town rhythm guitarist Richard Huxley and a singer, doubling on baritone sax, with the stage name Stan Saxon. Adding lead guitarist Mick Ryan, 'the Dave Clark Five featuring Stan Saxon' made its debut at a Harringay youth club. They were an undistinguished though adaptable combo with a bias towards Lord Rockingham/Johnny and the Hurricanes instrumentals. The story goes that the Five raised the cash needed for Dave's rugby team in Tottenham to play an away match in Holland.

By 1960, despite some personnel changes, they had become quite a popular outfit on the ballroom circuit of south-east England. Their set still consisted mainly of instrumentals — particular preferences now being *Peter Gunn*, Link Wray's *Rumble* and Phil Upchurch's *You Can't Sit Down* which were both cited as prototypes for their 1964 chartbusters. They had also introduced their own rather derivative originals which later broadened to embrace modern jazz — such as Clark's Cannonball Adderley-tinged *Time* — as well as bland cinema interlude musak. However, there is sufficient evidence from their later recordings that, had not the Beat Boom placed greater emphasis on vocals, the Five might have developed into one of the great British instrumental acts like the Tornados or Shadows.

Much of their growing vocal repertoire was culled from American imports by the likes of the Contours and Drifters, borrowed from Spinnin' John, the disc jockey at Basildon's Locarno ballroom. Further stimulus came from songbooks of the classic rockers — especially Chuck Berry — and soul stars such as Sam Cooke and Brook Benton. They were unaware that only two hundred miles away the emergent Merseyside bands were under much the same influences.

The Dave Clark Five were to return to these primal sources right to the end of their existence, even plagiarising titles for their own compositions, the prime example being Carl Perkins' *Glad All Over*. By 1965, they began reverting to covers of Locarno crowd-pleasers like *Reelin' and Rockin'* and Bobby Byrd's *Over and Over* to redress the balance after the clever stuff like *Everybody Knows* (the first of two Clark A-sides of that title) and *Try Too Hard* bombed. Their merciless theft of Cat Mother's *Good Old Rock and Roll* medley in 1969 was, to be fair, tailor made for them, utilising as it did vignettes of the showstoppers that got them through rough nights in provincial palais de danses ten years earlier.

The Five's big showbusiness break came in 1961 when, following an audition at the Strand Lyceum in London, they signed a long term contract with the vast Mecca circuit, which had belatedly clasped rock'n'roll to its bosom. Reputations were made with Mecca, who provided a link between youth club bashes and big theatre tours. Leisure corporations held regular promotions in dance halls, town halls, sports centres, and even swimming pools, where the water had to be boarded over for each show. These venues purposely had few seating arrangements, and drifting, shuffling,

and dancing were encouraged within the limits of 'decent' behaviour imposed on entertainers in a Britain that had prudishly obliged Billy Fury to moderate his sub-Presley gyrations. P.J. Proby's splitting trousers were yet to come. Therefore, though the Dave Clark Five indulged in mild clowning and winking at the girls, their chief mode of expression had to be purely musical supplemented by a happy-go-lucky onstage atmosphere and, when they eventually afforded it, sharp, stylish costumes.

By then, the famous Five line-up had found each other. Clark and Huxley (now transferred to bass) had taken on guitarist Lenny Davidson, who'd met Dave while weight-training in a gym in Enfield. With experience in two local bands, the Off-Beats and Impalas, Lenny had developed an economical, staccato style, which in a later age would be described as 'funky'. The group's dark horse, he would display unprecedented vocal abilities during the most trying phase of the group's career, six years later, by gamely singing lead on two of their latter day hits.

Denis West Payton was enlisted from a jazz band, the Mike Jones Combo, managed by Clark, to replace Jim Spencer, who'd quit to become a solicitor. A gifted multi-instrumentalist, Payton contributed most of the woodwinds as well as harmonica and guitar to the group. His big moment in the early days was in *Yakety Yak* in which his King Curtis stylings came into play on one of the few occasions that the Five yielded to lengthy improvisation. Indeed, they were among the few successful 'sixties acts to feature a sax.

More immediately obvious onstage was the remarkable Mike Smith, a classically trained pianist-turned rock'n'roller from Edmonton who, like Clark, was a judo-karate exponent — a reassuring asset in the more unrefined venues. No slouch on vocals either, he had been a reliable standby when Saxon's voice needed a rest. When Stan failed to materialise at an air base engagement in Hertford, Smith took over permanently as front man, becoming as much the public face of the Five as Clark himself, his husky baritone hybrid of McCartney and boxer Henry Cooper being the group's most consistent trademark.

More a commercial merger than a bunch of lads playing together for the hell of it, the Five were blessed in having in their drummer a man with an instinct for the manouevres necessary to give that extra push up the ladder; all the way up, when the time came. This was always present from the times he begged for bookings in the jive hives of Tottenham to his refusals of million dollar offers to tour the States just one more time a quarter of a century later. Controlling every aspect of the enterprise, even in the pre-hit years, he prudently formed a publishing company for the Five's compositions named after his favourite football team (Spurs, of course). Apparently, Dave would suggest the type of number the public would buy at any given moment and the others would put their heads together to see if anything in the catalogue came close to his ideas, most original material coming from the pens of Davidson, Smith and Clark himself.

Without Dave's off-stage machinations the Five's saga would have had far less significance, which is why a later criticism that they ought to be 'The Mike Smith Five' carried little weight. Clark was the manager, composer, set designer, record producer and, above all, the bloke who paid the wages. 'He's the boss,' declared Payton to *Merseybeat* in 1964, 'and he's a good one. He tears strips of you though, if you step out of line — but you can always tell when its coming.'

In Your Heart: *the antique sound quality of the Dave Clark Five's debut B-side was achieved when Ember pressed a demo previously taped in a converted garden shed. Note the incorrect spelling of the group's name.*

With a workable line-up consolidated by his leadership, Clark got things moving in 1961. Their first recordings were modest affairs, mainly demos for other artistes, but in 1962 the Clark-Smith instrumental, *Chaquita* (based on the Champs' *Tequila*) was chosen

as the Five's debut single and released by Ember, a label of no great merit. Clark always leased masters — the original recording of a song — to record companies to maintain quality control on output and ensure that no middlemen shared in royalties.

Moving up-market to the Pye subsidiary, Piccadilly, *First Love* spotlighted Davidson in a Duane Eddy mood. The company had actually pressed the Five's first vocal A-side, *I Knew It All the Time*, when the artists concerned impressed a Columbia talent scout who saw them at their home venue, Tottenham Royal, where they had started as relief band for the Johnny Howard Orchestra.

Columbia — like everyone else — was looking for an answer to Parlophone's Beatles. But though the Five were close to Merseybeat in spirit, they were by nature more polished and presentable than their Lancastrian counterparts. Wearing matching suits, playing to a fixed programme, and leaving all continuity to the singer, they were what a respectable company executive in those naive times expected a good pop group to be. Dealing with an attitude they understood, Columbia allowed Clark the run of their sophisticated Lansdowne studios in London's Holland Park as well as a larger royalty percentage than most other pop artists of the day, many of whom shifted more product than Clark but ended up poorer, owing to a lackadaisical regard for business. Columbia also advised Dave to get a good agent. He responded typically, and the Five became the first straight beat group to sign with the powerful Harold Davidson firm, who also had Sinatra on their books. This ensured that the group appeared on the prestigious American TV slot, the Ed Sullivan Show, more times than any British band before or since.

This most lucrative chapter in the group's history began with the dance craze reworking of the nursery rhyme *The Mulberry Bush*, which, despite their TV showing on THANK YOUR LUCKY STARS, missed the charts, though it sold quite well over the six months before Clark's thrilling production of *Do You Love Me* muscled in to peak at No. 24 in October 1963. The publicity involved the Duke of Edinburgh in some funny business over 'the Blues,' a dance peculiar to the Tottenham Royal club, which involved a step called 'the Duke' — referring to the Consort's gait. In an open letter to Buckingham Palace, Dave apologised for his group's cheek to which Prince Philip cracked back that it was O.K. by him. Gormless as it was, it gained the Five a toehold in the national press which proved useful a few weeks later when they went for the jugular.

Encroaching on public consciousness with its two-beat hook *Glad All Over* occupied the top slot for a fortnight in January 1964. It had been a cliffhanger whether or not its flip, *I Know You*, would grace the A-side instead but market research among Royal regulars provided the answer. However, *I Know You* reappeared on the enigmatically-titled E.P., *The Dave Clark Five*, which cleared the decks for the rowdy *Bits and Pieces* to splinter the charts in April. Extremely primitive, with monochordal verses, this stopped one short of Number One, probably because its stamping plank/snare drum ostinato caused its banning by many dance hall proprietors worried about their sprung floorboards.

Collectively, all Columbia tracks thus far had sounded like a glorious row. After the merest preamble, the entire quintet would hit their instruments at once while Smith, bawling rhyming couplets through an echo chamber, led the unison responses. The drums, well up in the mix, thumped and clattered; the bass pulsated; the guitar spluttered and dranged; the sax grated, and the whining Vox Continental organ held block chords. Never using fade-outs and pausing only for some crude percussive riff (clearly designed as the selling point), the spring of 1964 was the Dave Clark moment, never to return.

They were the first British group to undertake a major US tour in the vanguard of the Beatles. Lacking the scousers' large scale promotion campaign, they were greeted by a mere handful of inquisitive fans when they landed at New York's Idlewild airport in March 1964. However, within a week, with *Glad All Over* high in Billboard's Hot 100, they could no longer venture on the streets unrecognised and unmolested. Rick Huxley was treated for a badly gashed face when the Five were mobbed by 5,000 hysterical teenagers in Washington, D.C. Shortly afterwards, Mike Smith suffered broken ribs in a similar crush.

Though Clark was to become a hard-nosed Americanised businessman, it was only on their return to England that he cautiously turned the band fully professional. Their debut in this capacity was at the pinnacle of British showbusiness — topping the bill on SUNDAY NIGHT AT THE LONDON PALLADIUM — but this accolade was minor compared to their systematic conquest of the USA which, for the rest of their career, they took for every cent they could get. This was reinforced by regular bi-annual treks across the continent to promote their many chart breakthroughs. For a short spell, they became arguably the world's top group as an insatiable demand for Clark merchandise was fully exploited, to the extent of scheduling a gap as

little as six weeks between albums of frankly sub-standard material.

To all true British Five afficianados, SESSION WITH THE DAVE CLARK FIVE was the only real Clark L.P., because succeeding collections were creamed off dozens of tracks released only in the States. To the chagrin of their home following, the only chance of seeing their idols in concert was when they nervously performed two numbers in the 1965 Royal Variety Show. This frustration was amplified when, studying the music papers, you would often notice a Clark record you were never likely to hear in the UK, climbing the American charts.

Although they scrupulously plugged their singles on British TV, this was only market research for the States. Flops at home could be recouped abroad for more negotiable tracks. For example, *Look Before You Leap* petered out after one week in the UK Top 50, but its flip, *Please Tell Me Why*, promoted as the A-side in the US, sailed effortlessly into the Hot 100. Earlier, Clark had pushed another British B-side, *Because*, in the same way, and its Number 3 placing reflected his wisdom. This ballad — a sort of Dave Clark *Yesterday* — was the closest the Five came to creating a 'standard'. It was covered most memorably by the Supremes.

The group's second career peak was in 1965 with their only major feature film, CATCH US IF YOU CAN, and its by-products. Directed by John Boorman, this movie was more downbeat than A HARD DAY'S NIGHT, but its monochrome hues gave it a likeable lyricism. It was a typical tale of wonderful young people running away from the old squares' sordid commercialism (really, Mr. Clark?). Though there was an oblique attempt to push Rick as the group clown, only Dave was permitted any real character development, playing opposite Barbara Ferris — the first choice for the role, Marianne Faithful, having rejected the part as 'too poppy.'

Every silver lining has a cloud, and hopes of a chart comeback in the neglected UK were dampened by a disturbing series of Top 20 misses. They also touched their musical nadir with 1966's appalling *Tabatha Twitchit* with its vulgar recycling of the *Glad All Over* hook.

Turning his back on psychedelia, Clark clutched at

Cool ruler: Dave Clark - drummer, composer, record producer, film director, businessman — and ex-stunt man. Cash for an early Five studio session was procured by his two days of crashing cars for an Adam Faith feature film.

'Together for a long, long time' (left to right) *Mike Smith, Lenny Davidson, Denis Payton, Rick Huxley and Dave Clark.*

the straw of *Everybody Knows*, written by Barry Mason and Les Reed (mentors of Leicestershire crooner, Engelbert Humperdinck, 1967's star turn in the British charts), which the Five took to Number 2. This was also their last sizeable *Billboard* entry as US sales finally began a downward spiral.

After a farewell concert in Canada, Dave retired his Five to the studio, apart from flying visits to the States to guest on the occasional middle-of-the-road spectacular. Much lost British popularity was regained when Dave's Big Five film company produced a critically-praised television portrait of the group, HOLD ON IT's THE DAVE CLARK FIVE! intended as the first of a series that was aborted through lack of sponsorship. They left a latter day vinyl debris characterised by bandwagon jumping, American covers and a few good records. Dave folded the group in 1971 shortly after the Beatles' more sweeping exit.

On the surface, the Five's commercial prosperity was seemingly beneath contempt, supported by the least discerning of the record-buying public. Yet this was to grasp the wrong end of the stick, though the stick still existed. To assume that theirs was a tale of corrupted endeavour is to misinterpret the concept of the Dave Clark Five who, before 1967, shifted over forty million units. With never an outside manager or Svengali, they were probably the most successful self-contained business entity in the whole of British pop. They were non-committal, if not honest, about their bourgeois conservatism as they ruthlessly moved into the Beat Boom, took their cash, and got out again. At the same time, within pop's essentially crass idiom, they were also craftsmen of the highest order. Though they could be subtle and restrained — even experimental — the Dave Clark Five will always be remembered for the stomping smashes of 1964, the number of which can be counted on one hand. But even the group's non-existence did not prevent posthumous chart action when the album TWENTY-FIVE THUMPING GREAT HITS roared to the top of the Christmas lists in 1977 — significantly, the high summer of punk.

Dave Clark became, like the less level-headed Beatles, fabulously — some would say, disgustingly — rich. It was said that if anyone criticised his music, he would justify himself by pulling out a wad of fivers. Maybe any fool could bash drums, but who could become more popular than Jesus and have the sense not to make a song and dance about it?

The Most of Herman's Hermits

It was surprising that during the Beatles' unfruitful Decca audition in 1962, the 'serious' George Harrison took the lion's share of lead vocals, injecting a strong humour into those selections that required it. He continued to supply the slapstick back at the Cavern with his Cheeky Chappie renditions of perennial favourites like *The Sheik of Araby* and Harry Champion's *I'm Henery the Eighth I Am*. This music hall element of the Beatles' early stage act was to have a lasting, beneficial effect upon one of their fans, a certain Peter Blair Denis Bernard Noone, who regularly negotiated the thirty-six miles from Manchester to Liverpool to catch this scouse band that everyone was talking about.

Not that the Manchester beat scene was sterile — by 1963, it was next on every London recording manager's hit list after the cream of Liverpool had been pressed into service. Though lacking Merseybeat's organized gig network, bands could still be scrutinised at venues like the Three Coins in Deansgate or the Twisted Wheel in Brazenose Street off Albert Square. Once there was even a 'Manchester Cavern' near the Market. Parlophone hooked the biggest fish, signing the Hollies, though Columbia did well to spot Freddie Garrity. However, there were to be other opportunities a year later with a second wave of Mancunian talent in which the main protagonists were Herman's Hermits, fronted by that noted Cavern dweller, Peter Noone.

Born in 1947 to a musical family in the suburb of Davyhulme, Noone formed his first group, the Cyclones, before reaching adolescence. He was to transcend the humble wedding and Bar Mitzvah circuit when some older boys from his Stretford Grammar School invited him to join their band as general factotum, mainly on piano and guitar. Operating as The Heartbeats, the personnel included engraver Karl Green on bass, barber Barry Whitwam on drums, and student Derek Leckenby on lead guitar. Noone, who had taken formal drama lessons, found less mundane employment as a television actor. Using the stage name 'Peter Novack,' one of his more celebrated parts was that of Len Fairclough's son in Granada TV's CORONATION STREET at their nearby studios. The Heartbeats sensibly capitalised on Noone's eminence by allowing him to monopolise the lead vocal spotlight.

Peter Novack and the Heartbeats soon became well-known in South Lancashire for their lightweight brand of pop, drawn from current hits, Merseybeat standards and the songbooks of Buddy Holly, the Everly Brothers and other mainly white rock'n'rollers. For all their later fame they never outgrew these musical roots. On several occasions they supported Peter's idols, the Beatles, at the Cavern, eventually topping the bill there when Merseybeat entered its death throes. As Noone's instrumental offices decreased, another guitarist was required. Though not struck with their technical ability, telegraph engineer Keith Hopwood threw in his lot with the Heartbeats, recognising their easy professionalism.

Hopwood's assessment was shared by Mickie Most, who sounded them out at a concert in Bolton. His attention had initially been caught by a publicity photo of the goofy-looking Noone that Most felt betrayed star quality. After vacillating whether or not to sign Peter as a solo artist, he decided that, in keeping with the times, the whole group would prove a better proposition. As no-one would know who was on the records anyway, the Heartbeats' shortcomings could be overcome by replacing them in the studio with a phalanx of sessionmen. Onstage, it wouldn't matter so much as, hopefully, their playing would be buried beneath the sound of screaming girls. Most didn't like the name though. Didn't somebody just mention that Peter looked like that cartoon character, Sherman? Let's call him 'Sherman'. No? All right, what about Herman and the Hermits? Herman's Hermits! Yeah! With Most in the driving seat, the Hermits — formerly the Heartbeats — were to vanish behind their sixteen-year-old selling point. Though neither Noone or his group let themselves be computerised to the degree of American ciphers from Fabian to the fictional Archies, it was their submission to Most's masterplan that guided them with mathematical precision to success.

With the highest calibre of sessionmen and arrangers at his disposal, Most also procured a rich crop of well-crafted songs suited to Noone's limited but fairly tuneful range, mainly from the pens of jobbing British songwriters like Tony Hazzard and Carter-Lewis, as well as from American teams such as Goffin and King, who set the ball rolling with the Hermits' first two singles. Rival artists who were also professional composers such as Ray Davies, Graham Gouldman, and Donovan, also contributed. As the group were not expected to donate to this A-side output, Most's demarcation line between composers and performers was a throwback to the Tin Pan Alley policy of an earlier pre-Beatle era.

American High School pop was also plundered for apt material. From this source came Sam Cooke's *Wonderful World* and *Silhouettes*, a remarkably original beat ballad of mistaken identity which sold a •

million for The Rays in 1957. The latter represented Herman's Hermits at their most attractive; much of its appeal emanated from Noone's clumsy phrasing and Jimmy Page's galvanising guitar section.

Their debut, *I'm Into Something Good*, toppled the Kinks from Number One in September 1964. But Most regarded this as merely a dry run for the USA, where it entered the Cashbox chart at No. 88 to shift a quarter of a million units within ten days — a sluggish performance by later standards. After all, it was for America that Herman's Hermits were designed.

The US music industry had long regarded British pop as merely the furnisher of nine day wonders like Lonnie Donegan or the Tornados. But by the mid-sixties it was virtually unstoppable in the wake of Capitol's promotion of the Beatles. Other record companies likewise yelled 'Klondike!' before fully exploiting the Limey acts on their rosters. However, though there was no serious sign of wavering, the impetus relaxed slightly by late 1964. Even Beatles singles at this time (admittedly only album cuts like *Slow Down*) fell on comparatively stony ground. Though no writing was on the wall yet, there was a definite slow moment in the UK battle for exports.

In this interval after the 1964 spring offensive, America was ripe for reconquest by Noone-Herman and his investors. Resembling a younger John F. Kennedy — a likeness first noticed by Most — Herman could scarcely miss in a maternally-minded society that was later to concede to the adoption of Cabbage Patch Dolls. Promoted in a like fashion, Noone magnified the impudent schoolboy persona he had been developing since CORONATION STREET. Behind the cloying television face, a shrewd operation was at work. What fellow Mancunians, Freddie and the Dreamers, had merely hinted at, Herman's Hermits took to the limit by hammering home their Britishness with the same passion that caused Chubby Checker to twist like a lunatic in 1961. On record, this was achieved by dredging up ancient artefacts from the Golden Days of Empire such as *Two Lovely Black Eyes* from the World War I era, George Formby's *Leaning On a Lampost* from the next War; after that, the old Cavern standby (by another George) *Henery VIII* and, most blatant of all, *Je Suis Anglais*.

The British themselves wouldn't have worn it. Though *Mrs. Brown You've Got a Lovely Daughter* went down well at the 1965 *New Musical Express* Pollwinners Concert, Herman's musical flagwaving was seen by his own kind as a sales gimmick for their daft transatlantic cousins to be decently buried on albums. Tellingly, no Hermits L.P. made much of a

splash in Britain. The singles weren't guaranteed smashes either, especially if released in a heavy week. At Christmas 1965, *Show Me Girl*, for instance, swamped by new 45's from the Kinks, Beatles, and Supremes, barely managed the Top 20. As long as they didn't put out any of that 'Old Tyme' drivel though, they just about walked the line in Britain before slumping in mid-1966. Yet even in this, their darkest hour, I knew a vicar's daughter who still swore by them. Britain hardly mattered to Herman anyhow while 'Hermania' filtered across the USA like bubonic plague. Before he left his teens, Herman was rich enough to buy a thousand vicarages.

Naturally, he was despised by the blossoming underground. When he reciprocated this dislike, he earned the esteem of middle America where his clean, conservative image was seen as a return to sobriety after the depravities of hairy monsters like the Stones and, even ghastlier, those ugly Pretty Things from

Flying visit: Herman and his soft-focus Hermits breeze into Britain from the States to entertain on RSG, 1966.

whom God temporarily spared America. The vehicle of no scandal, Herman was a regular in *16* — a US teenage magazine which never probed deeper that his conception of a 'Dream Girl' and whether he ever dated fans.

Herman's decline in the States around 1967 was not for any tidy reason such as the growth of psychedelic 'album–orientated rock.' Storms from that camp could be weathered — after all, the songwriters he used were good enough for the Yardbirds and Hollies. It was simply that the Americans were beating him at his own game by taking leaves from Most's book. The hardest blow was dealt by a cabal of California businessmen who hired four amenable youths to play an Anglo-American pop group in a nationwide TV series. These boys also sang on records for which the services of top Hollywood songwriters, sessionmen and producers had been negotiated, as had the fullest distribution network and record company backing. Though the project's blueprint was the Hard Day's Night-style Beatles, it was noticed that the group heartthrob, Davy Jones, had a Manchester accent and

If you leave them alone, they'll go away: Peter Blair Denis Bernard Noone contemplates whether to send out a road manager for some lacto-calomine.

had been a supporting actor in Coronation Street. With the advent of the Monkees, Herman became strictly last year's model overnight.

Accepting with the best possible grace that they'd had a good run, Peter and the lads looked homeward. Here, their fortunes took a turn for the better as they racked up a fair number of easy-listening hits until Noone went solo in 1971. This was thanks largely to the new BBC Radio One's middle-of-the-road programming as well as their own renewed omnipresence, which enabled them to recover lost ground. Nevertheless, this re-establishment was only a parochial postscript compared to their howling successes abroad.

Minus Karl Green, the Hermits drifted into a cabaret graveyard before boarding the 1960s revival bandwagon, where they felt brave enough to front

themselves with a makeshift 'Herman', new rhythm guitarist Garth Elliott. The genuine article had been expected to follow the footsteps of Tommy Steele or, more pertinently, Gerry Marsden and enter showbusiness proper, but it wasn't until 1982 as 'Frederick' in a West End production of The Pirates of Penzance that he showed any inclination in that direction. Before that, his public appearances were mainly confined to a US nostalgia tour with other British Invasion veterans in 1975. Temporarily reunited with his Hermits, he finally managed to pack Madison Square Garden.

There was also his new band, the Tremblers, with whom he tried — with a little assistance from his friend, Dave Clark — to re-enter the rock arena on a more contemporary footing far removed from the 'favorite color' nonsense of *16*. In an interview in 1983, punctuated with references to new wave acts like the Pretenders plus the occasional calculated swear word, he seemed to be trying hard to convince those who reviled his previous incarnation that he 'Wasn't Such A Bad Bloke After All'.

In the Hollies Style

Apart from the Beatles (whom they outlived as a unit), the Hollies scored more UK singles chart entries than any other group between 1963 and 1970. Consisting mainly of married men, with a guitarist sporting an old-fashioned Tommy Steele quiff, their image relied on little beyond obligatory stage costumes, jocular bonhomie and short-lived gimmicks like the wearing of shoulder bags. Nevertheless, they were the most distinguished band to emerge from Greater Manchester, fusing as they did fertile imagination with industrious pragmatism.

Seen by most as the group's prime mover, Graham Nash was unobtrusively slipping out of a Mothers of Invention concert at the Albert Hall in 1967 when his heart sank to his Courreges boots as an adolescent voice bawled, 'It's Graham Nash of the Hollies!' through the Kensington twilight. As the awe-struck youth panted up to him, Graham's inbred professionalism smothered a likely seething annoyance as amiably he asked the boy if he'd enjoyed the show and listened politely to some tongue-tied and embrassing response. Instinctively, he'd played 'Mr. Nice Guy' instead of losing a fan by telling me to get stuffed.

His ability to suffer fools gladly owed much to his Manchester showbusiness background. The home of Granada Television, JUNIOR SHOWTIME, and of Sooty's TV shows, the entertainment capital of the North of England inspired in its beat groups a deep commitment to their craft.

In a similar manner to Peter Noone, Glyn Poole, and other Lancastrian showbiz brats, Nash and Harold 'Allan' Clarke first sang together in assembly at their Salford Primary School before graduating to the prestigious Manchester Cabaret Club in their teens. As

Tea and biscuits '64 (left to right) Allan Clarke taps his foot to Tony Hicks' guitar while producer Ron Richards chats to Graham Nash and Bobby Elliott. Eric Haydock is symbolically elsewhere.

The Two Teens in fact, they drew from the works of Lonnie Donegan, Cliff Richard and, especially, the piercing harmonies of the Everly Brothers (as well as crooners' standards like *That's My Desire* thrown in for the Mums and Dads).

Encouraged by their parents, Allan and Graham saved up for a 'Guytone' electric guitar each plus a shared amplifier. After an apocryphal period as The Guytones, they doubled their personnel to become briefly The Fourtones before reverting to the duo format as 'Ricky and Dane' in 1959. Seduced again by the dynamic versatility of larger outfits, 'Ricky' Clarke and 'Dane' Nash formed The Deltas two years later with bass guitarist Eric Haydock and drummer Donald Rathbone. Uncertain lead guitarists, Clarke and Nash hired an auxiliary musician named Victor prior to a booking at the Oasis club near the City centre in December 1962. In keeping with the Christmas season, they were introduced as 'the Hollies'.

As the new year dawned, Victor, plagued by vocational misgivings, agreed to honour all dates until a replacement was found. He was still on stage with the Hollies at a Twisted Wheel bash when 18-year-old apprentice electrician Tony Hicks blew in from the small town of Nelson, thirty miles north, to sound them out. Tony also twanged a tough lead guitar in à Burnley band, The Dolphins. Though he had doubts, he agreed to a trial run with The Hollies on a freelance basis. Regularly engaged for up to seven sets a week at Liverpool's Cavern, the Mancunian quintet were honoured one night by the presence of E.M.I. staff producer Ron Richards, who was up North sniffing round for more Beatle-sized talent. When the Hollies were invited to London for a Parlophone recording test, Hicks made his mind up.

Released on May 17th 1963, the Hollies single *Ain't That Just Like Me* gave no indication of anything unusual. The common property of many other groups — notably the Searchers and Applejacks — this Coasters opus was speeded up and stripped of backing vocals and any intrinsic humour. It *was* quite danceable and, with a brace of TV plugs, left a tide mark at No. 23 after three weeks in the Top 50. Not brilliant, but enough to hold on hoping.

This wasn't hopeful enough for Don Rathbone, however, whose resignation necessitated the recruitment of one of Tony's old Dolphin colleagues, Bobby Elliott, who had already known some chart action with the Fentones backing Mansfield's Shane Fenton (renamed 'Alvin Stardust' a decade later). The Fentones' *The Breeze and I*, for example, had been a minor hit before the Hollies were even formed. Sharing the same agency, Galaxy Entertainments, Fenton himself had assisted in a quasi-managerial capacity before the Hollies acquired the less nebulous services of ex-dance band leader Tommy Sanderson.

At EMI's Abbey Road Studios in London, Ron Richards contemplated the Hollies immediate recording future. At this stage, unlike the Beatles, they had no internal source of likely hit material. What went down well in concert? Well, there were the old chestnuts — *Lawdy Miss Clawdy*, *Lucille*, all those Chuck Berry numbers — no, too well known. *It's Only Make Believe?*, *It's In Her Kiss?* Too recent. What about all that Motown and soul stuff? Hmmm. . . . a bit risky. Save them for an L.P. if they ever make one. Let's stick with the Devil we know. What else can we do by the Coasters? *Little Egypt? Thumbin' a Ride? Three Cool Cats?*

The six-year-old *Searchin'* — a Cavern favourite — did the trick by coasting the Hollies to a more presentable No. 12, Next up was an exuberant cover of Maurice Williams' *Stay* from 1960 which cracked the Top 10, aborting the Dave Clark Five's rival version at the pressing plant. When a treatment of Doris Troy's *Just One Look* almost topped the charts in April 1964, the Hollies sound was established.

This hinged on a severe three-part, close harmony ranging from Tony's baritone to Graham's soaring counter tenor with Allan's edgy drawl usually carrying the melody. Though Clarke was portrayed on an E.P. cover holding a guitar, he no longer strummed one on stage. There was also a rumour that the clanging of Nash's rhythm guitar was only heard psychosomatically as it was purposely never connected to any power point.

Elliott, Haydock and Hicks more than compensated for these real or imagined inadequacies. Exploring beyond a plain six string Gibson, Tony, for instance, embellished Hollies recordings with a banjo, exotic devices, and even a *nine* string creation thrust into his hands one night on tour when his usual instrument malfunctioned. He had the subtlety to integrate these into the main sound without their seeming too obviously gimmicks, directing his talent to the general good even though he could have given many of his flashier contemporaries a run for their money.

Now courted by professional songwriters, the Hollies applied their idiosyncracies to many memorable chartbusters, with Clint Ballard's *I'm Alive* their first Number One in June 1965. Nine months later came the second. Aided by a stomping backing track and with Chip Taylor's asinine words notwithstanding, the vocal counterpoint of *I Can't Let Go* was every bit as breathtaking as any of the Beach Boys' choral intricacies. Listeners could be forgiven for mistaking Nash's sustained top E for a trumpet note. As studio performers, the Hollies have never since worked better though they certainly recorded stronger songs.

I Can't Let Go served to obscure memories of an ill-advised copy of George Harrison's *If I Needed Someone* two months earlier. Dogged by the Beatle's own adverse criticism, they still received a back-handed compliment in the *Music Echo's* argument that they had salvaged one of Rubber Soul's poorer selections. All the same, by wooing the same market as the Beatles, the Hollies had to struggle to push this faux pas into the charts. It probably seemed a good idea at the time.

An American breakthrough was a long time coming — possibly owing to their comparative facelessness, having neither the Beatles' offsetting uniformity or the Stones' freakishness. Late in 1965, *Look Through Any Window*, co-written by Graham Gouldman, tentatively probed the Hot 100. But they had to wait another year for the Yanks to really go ape over them via another Gouldman number, *Bus Stop*, which their fellow Mancunian had first demonstrated to Nash in a theatre

Two Dolphins and a Guytone: Tony Hicks, Allan Clarke and Bobby Elliott enter middle age.

dressing room. After this boy-girl-marriage narration placed them at Number 5 in *Billboard*, the Hollies were always guaranteed a fair hearing in the States. As late as 1983, they cruised into the Hot 100 with a revival of the Supremes' *Stop In the Name of Love*, though *Sandy*, in which Clarke's Harry Corbett twang replaced composer Bruce Springsteen's 'Yogi Bear' vibrato, scraped in a few years before.

Eric Haydock, meanwhile, had not lasted the course. Sacked in absentia for 'musical differences' in the lean 1966 period, he may have been used as a scapegoat before these American advances. Almost resigned to being a strictly British phenomenon like Cliff Richard, the Hollies apparently once watched the charts in case the Four Tops' *Reach Out I'll Be There* missed so they could nip in with a UK cover version.

With his bitter freedom, Eric formed Haydock's Rockhouse, mirroring his 'reactionary' musical tastes. He recorded some singles for Columbia, and enjoyed regional popularity in France, but by 1968 Rockhouse was demolished.

Though ex-Kink Pete Quaife was allegedly among those short-listed, another ex-Dolphin, Bernard Calvert, became the new Holly in time for *Stop Stop Stop*. In step with a growing complexity in which Haydock could, apparently, play no part, Clarke, Hicks and Nash under the collective pseudonym 'L.

Ransford', organised themselves as a songwriting team in summer 1964. Chancing their arms with an A-side, *We're Through*, built round James Brown's tumbling *Think* rhythm, followed *Here I Go Again* into the Top 10 in October 1964. Though cautious E.M.I. ordained a return to outsiders for the next six 45's, from autumn 1966 until Nash's departure three years later, all Hollies tracks emanated from the fictitious Mr. Ransford.

Though the tune of *Stop Stop Stop* had been previewed in an earlier flip, *Come On Back* its lyric revealed a maturer dexterity in its feverish account of unrequited desire for an erotic dancer. Another highlight was Graham's *King Midas In Reverse*, an ambitious production which belied its poor showing at No. 18. Salt was rubbed into this wound when their artistic nullity, *Jennifer Eccles*, dedicated to Mrs. Clarke and Mrs. Nash, tripped daintily into the familiar portals of the Top 10 six months later, the philistine public preferring Jennifer's wolf-whistles to the heady cellos of King Midas.

This attitude pervaded the L.P. charts where more experimental albums like FOR CERTAIN BECAUSE and BUTTERFLY could not match the sales of those packed with antique Twisted Wheel style *Mickey's Monkey* type classics, greatest hits, and tributes to Bob Dylan. Many of their most inspired moments were overlooked. Off the cuff examples are the eloquent time signature changes of *Pay You Back With Interest*; the eerie vocal tremelo in *Lullaby to Tim* (sung by Uncle Graham to Allan's son); *Peculiar Situation's* perverse non-rhyming couplets; the mediaeval overtones in *Crusader* and the big band scoring of *What Went Wrong*. There were many more worthy of mention. Sometimes they verged on self-consciousness but rarely did the Hollies make a hash of it. Significantly, a few other artists, notably the Fourmost and, flatteringly, the Everly Brothers, tried L. Ransford songs. But only the Searchers, with *Have You Ever Loved Somebody* from EVOLUTION, made any real impact.

Since he, Clarke and Hicks had sat in on Rolling Stones after-hours sessions in the company of Gene Pitney and Phil Spector, Graham Nash had come to be regarded as a ring-ding groovy cool cat by London's In Crowd. In 1968, in the gloom of late night watering holes, frustration at public doubts over the Hollies' new 'progressive' policy was aggravated as he exchanged persecution complexes with like-minded musicians such as outgoing Yardbird Paul Samwell-Smith and redundant Jimi Hendrix sideman Mitch Mitchell. In this exalted company, the sickening *Jennifer Eccles* was a hard cross to bear. Graham began talking openly about cutting a solo album.

With the other four Hollies he was at loggerheads over the HOLLIES SING DYLAN project. Though it would probably restore them to the album lists, Nash's self-respect had been eroded quite enough thank you. Living in claustrophobic studios and on gruelling back-to-back tours, the Hollies had once even succumbed to pantomime, for Christ's sake.

The group first learned of one of Nash's contingency plans when someone casually mentioned it to Allan Clarke. On the Hollies' previous trip to America, Graham had joined in a sing-song with a couple of blokes round John Sebastian's house. With them he had discussed further musical intercourse. When ex-Byrd Dave Crosby and Steve Stills from Buffalo Springfield breezed over to England for another carouse, Nash left not only the Hollies but also his wife and family, putting action over debate with his new pals. Crosby, Stills and Nash quickly became the darlings of, like, the Woodstock generation, man — their first hit being Graham's *Marrakesh Express*. Though their hippy-dippy warblings weren't everyone's cup of tea, Graham Nash ended up a damn sight richer than if he'd stayed with the Hollies.

With the passing of L. Ransford — the man who never was — the group rallied by recruiting Terry Silvester originally from the Escorts and then the Swinging Blue Jeans, a transfer important enough to warrant a front page splash in *Record Mirror*. Although obliged to look outside the group for hit singles again, the Hollies proved able to continue delivering the goods, beginning with *Sorry Suzanne*, their first chart strike of 1969, through to their biggest post-Nash seller, Kelly Gordon's *He Ain't Heavy He's My Brother*, despite Allan Clarke's prodigal attempt to fly the nest like his old school chum, Graham. The quality of their own compositions became erratic. On one hand was the mawkish *Too Young To Get Married* which brought an edition of TOP OF THE POPS to a standstill. Conversely, Clarke's pulsating *Long Cool Woman in a Black Dress* was genuinely exhilarating and a deserved Transatlantic smash in 1972.

Unlike less fortunate contemporaries, the Hollies' deeper pedigree, lingering hip sensibility and their pulling of unexpected strokes has kept their heads above the waters of mere nostalgia; however it *was* this quality that sent their *Holliedaze* retrospective medley into the British charts in 1981. Most surprising was the reassembly of the old firm for the required TV promotions when Clarke, Elliott and Hicks amalgamated with a supercilious Nash (all the way from Hawaii) and the forgiving Eric Haydock (from somewhere a great deal less exotic).

Face to Face with the Kinks

Ray Davies' weighty personal misfortunes came to a head at a dismal outdoor festival at London's White City in 1973 where he and his entourage were being subtly intimidated by Edgar Winter's malcontented road crew. Eventually, the Kinks shambled onstage after a lot of hanging about. Introducing *Waterloo Sunset*, Ray told the rain-soaked audience that he'd had enough and the group was finished. Though considered important enough to be reported on a BBC news bulletin, it transpired that the underlying cause of the outburst was that Ray's wife, Rasa, had left him and taken the children. However, after an emotional convalescence, he was persuaded by brother Dave and drummer Mick Avory to reconstitute the band and, from this, their lowest ebb, the tide with majestic slowness turned.

Time was when every single by Ray and his boys automatically rocketed into the Top 10. In those heady mid-1960s days, when far more artistes depended on external writers for material, Ray Davies was courted for any songs he felt were unsuitable for the Kinks. While he never spawned a massive money-spinner like *Yesterday* or even *Out of Time*, there were over 150 versions recorded of Ray Davies songs. Among the more successful were Dave Berry's *This Strange Effect* and *Dandy* by Herman's Hermits, which hit hard in the States. Though not amounting to much in sales terms, Peggy Lee's reading of *I Go To Sleep* was a considerable feather in Davies' cap in showbusiness circles, giving him confidence to submit demos to Elvis (even though the King did not deign to use them). Among valiant failures were *Session Man* by Five's Company, comedian Leapy Lee's *King of the Whole Wide World*, and TV personality Barry Fantoni's *Little Man in a Little Box*, which Ray also produced. He even wrote a number for his fan club secretaries which they recorded as the 'Pixies'.

Even without his button-down Kinks, Davies would still have been recognised as an outstandingly prolific professional songwriter. In fact, the American producer, Sheldon 'Shel' Talmy, with whom the group maintained a working relationship for several years, had been initially more impressed with 20-year-old Ray's composing abilities than with the Kinks as a band. In February 1964, Talmy tried *I've Got That Feeling* with the Orchids, three Liverpudlian schoolgirls whom Decca wished to mould into a British answer to the Crystals.

That same month the Kinks themselves made their recording debut with Pye on the basis of an inferior acetate. The first two sessions that the company agreed to finance were not encouraging; so erratic was the young group's playing on Little Richard's *Long Tall Sally* that the better parts of two takes had to be spliced together. With great misgivings, this Beatles standby became their first single, though, predictably, it made little headway. A Davies original, *You Still Want Me*, from the same session fared worse three months later, shifting all of 127 copies. On all four songs in this brace of flops the Kinks closely approximated Liverpudlia — *I Took My Baby Home*, for example, owed much to the Merseybeats' rendition of Benny Spellman's *Fortune Teller*.

In the misjudged interest of opportunism, the Kinks had shelved their own musical roots. For, like most London rhythm and blues groups, they were stimulated by more 'ethnic' influences than the northern bands. They enjoyed modern black American acts like the Miracles and Martha and the Vandellas (whose *Dancing in the Street* was crucified on KINDA KINKS), but the Davies boys' preferences lay in the blues-tinged country of Hank Williams and primal rock'n'rollers from the southern USA. More obvious was a love of gutbucket blues from an earlier period — as far back as the 1930s — which found the brothers at European concerts by veterans such as Leadbelly and Big Bill Broonzy. This shared interest drew Ray to join his younger sibling's amateur group, formed during a school holiday in 1960.

Roping in bass guitarist Pete Quaife (who, like Ray, was a commercial art student) and transient drummers including Mick Willett of Tommy Bruce's Bruisers, the Muswell Hill lads started at the top when they backed singer Robert Wace. Wace, with contacts in high places, engineered bookings at debutantes' balls and other society gatherings at a going rate in excess of £40 plus the champagne dregs. Evidence of Ray's impressions of these events later emerged in songs like *House in the Country* and its companion piece, *Most Exclusive Residence For Sale*. During this time, they also adopted the quasi-Dickensian stage outfits that were to be their visual trademark.

After one particularly embarrassing date in 1962 Wace retreated to the less public role of group manager. For a while the group's name depended on whatever member had negotiated the gig, e.g. 'the Pete Quaife Four.' After an unsettled sojourn as either 'the Ravens' or the 'Ramrods', they became the Kinks early in 1963 when an ex-Boy Scout skiffler and temporary Rolling Stone, Mick Avory, joined as permanent drummer. Having lost their upper crust connections, they worked the less salubrious beat clubs that began

to litter most English cities in Merseybeat's wake before their unhappy first recording date. By mid-1964, despite a Ready Steady Go appearance, they were the group least likely. With Pye's patience snapping, everything hung on that third single.

You Really Got Me was apparently inspired by an improbable hybrid of Rolf Harris' *Sun Arise* and a jerky rhythmic undercurrent in a sequence by saxophonist Gerry Mulligan's band in a film of a Montreux Jazz Festival — but the Kinks' drunken homage to Richard Berry's *Louie Louie*, recorded later, would seem a better pointer to the truth. Though Ray's association with the Orchids had been unfruitful, Shel Talmy still thought this latest effort worthy of his attention. After a few inadequate rehearsals, he and Ray approved a take which featured the piano of sessionman Brian Pugh and Dave's defaced practice amplifier, which gave the number that intangible crunching rowdiness which later ages would cite as primal heavy metal. With saturation plugging and another *RSG* spot, *You Really Got Me* powered to joint Number One by late summer. Against all odds, the Kinks had arrived.

To maximise cash flow, they were obliged to smack out an album. Bolstered by the hit itself and an old B-side, the rushed session yielded a few stage favourites such as Bo Diddley's *Cadillac*, obligatory Chuck Berry outings and, from the acetate that had originally secured the deal, Slim Harpo's *Got Love If You Want It*. More important were Ray's originals which included *Stop Your Sobbing* and a collaboration with new manager Larry Page, the instrumental *Revenge*, which session guitarist Jimmy Page was to re-record with added lyrics. With Press Officer Brian Somerville's sleeve notes, the collection was hastened to the shops where its primitive drive assured it a long run in the L.P. list.

Meanwhile, it was the singles charts that mattered. Apart from one mild miscalculation (*Everybody's Gonna Be Happy*), this presented no problems for the Kinks as hit followed hit for three fat years. They even made considerable inroads in the States. Although they stuck mainly to the spasmodic *You Really Got Me* riff format, they weren't afraid of commercial risks such as a piece Ray composed after a trip to Bombay. With a plaintive, whining vocal and droning guitars, *See My Friend* took the listener to the banks of a sultry Oriental river. Davies' anticipation of the injection of Indian sounds into pop was well-founded, as was the

deliberate guitar feedback preluding *I Need You* in May 1965.

This raw music style was reflected by their disorderly behaviour on the road. Dave's unscheduled tumble into an orchestra pit during the group's guest spot on a Dave Clark Five tour led to an onstage brawl in Cardiff with Avory — his Crouch End flatmate — which resulted in hospital treatment and rumours of the Kinks' disbandment. Tensions of familiarity between the two brothers were also apparent in the footlights' glare. The more public of these disagreements became purely academic as fan riots began truncating every Kinks appearance causing mass cancellations by anxious promoters. They were barred from Denmark after an exceptionally violent uproar during a Tivoli Gardens show in 1965. The group were further disadvantaged by a lengthy Musicians' Union ban from North American for 'unprofessional conduct.'

Regarding his songwriting as a more viable

Kink Kovers and Kouplings: Pub singer Clinton Ford's version of Dandy *sold fractionally more than that of the Rockin' Vickers.* You Do Something for Me, *flip of* You Still Want Me *is the rarest of all officially-released Kinks tracks.*

proposition than being a touring Kink, Ray Davies suddenly dropped everything to forge a new, intrinsically English pop music. The first manifestation of this music, the single *A Well-Respected Man*, was previewed on TV on *RSG* in October 1965. Luckily, this type of music caught on to make the Kinks Pye's biggest sellers, outflanking even Max Bygraves and Lonnie Donegan. A literate watchful lyricism was married to idiosyncratic reconstructions of outmoded musical forms, sometimes dating back to Victorian traditions. It would not be presumptuous to say that the scenarios and characters created in Face to Face, Something Else, and subsequent L.P.'s may be seen as updated parlour poetry. In his pop star tumult, Ray was attracted, amused — even envious — of the culture that produced monologues, tea dances and similarly stylised entertainments — even if its patrons' lives were far harsher than those of their 1960s descendants.

Though Davies usually cast himself as an observer, this new phase revealed much about his own mentality. Belying his extroverted stage antics, a later, gloomy TV interview in 1984 disclosed how little he had had to do with the general pop aristocracy's social life. Lifting the Kinks from the mainstream of rock, he demonstrated the same teenage perversity whereby he wantonly dressed smartly to distance himself from beatnik friends at Hornsey Art College. On a lighter note, his continued support of Arsenal football team and the accumulation of all Kinks press cuttings betrayed a massive sentimental streak.

His laconic, reedy singing was better suited to this second phase of his songwriting career, as were his facial resemblance to Freddie Mills, his Jack Benny gait and the general air of baffled wistfulness that came to be his public image. His natural skill as an actor first came into its own at this time when he took the title role of The Long Distance Piano Palyer — a sort of English provincial They Shoot Horses Don't They — in BBC TV's *Wednesday Play* series.

Dave's extra-mural activities were less ambitious and not entirely of his own volition. He was thrust briefly into prominence in 1967 when his two lead vocal contributions to Something Else were issued as a solo single in the UK with the urgent but elegiac *Death of a Clown* on the A-side. Its Top 5 placing was heartening enough to allow Dave three more shots in his own right; there was even talk of an album but, with only *Suzannah's Still Alive* making any further chart impact, this intriguing tangent to the Kinks' story was terminated, though Dave's Leadbelly rasp was still to front the band occasionally on record and in concert.

Pregnant with ideas, he finally released his solo album in 1981.

Mick Avory was content rattling the traps but it wasn't all smiles with Pete Quaife. Ray only became aware of this when a photo of Pete with his new group, Maple Oak, was seen on the centre spread of the New Musical Express in 1966. After one flop single for Decca — ironically, *Son of a Gun*, attributed to Ray — Pete rejoined. In his absence his commitments had been filled by John Dalton of Mark Four (later the Creation), who was the obvious replacement when Quaife left forever in 1969 to pursue commercial art again and buy a Copenhagen record shop.

His disloyalty was an omen of organisational problems with Pye. From the record industry's catchpenny perspective, the company was justified in foisting a spate of casually programmed budget-priced compilations of old Kinks material onto the market. It was felt that as the group were in disgrace in America, their days were numbered at home owing to pop's essential transience — an indication being *Wonderboy*, the first serious miss. Viewing the Kinks as purely a singles act, Pye overlooked objections that a repackaging strategy, though financially enterprising, would adversely effect the band's new full-priced albums.

The Kinks' stage act had undergone revision to cater for an older audience. Though they had a knockabout, boozy spontaneity, their concert performances in the later 1960s showed a musical regression. In the studio they had frequently augmented the basic quartet with extra guitarists, keyboards and less common rock instruments like journalist Bob Dawburn's trombone on *Dead End Street*, as well as sound effects such as thunder (*Rainy Day in June*) and church bells (*Big Black Smoke*). Wishing to adhere closer to their recorded sound, the group hired auxiliary musicians for touring.

One latter-day Kink, pianist Andy Pyle, quit on the grounds that he'd had his fill of being 'part of Ray Davies', a backhanded compliment to a man who ceased trying to stay ahead of his rivals, daring instead to stubbornly follow a path so unfashionable that lesser talents overtook him in terms of mass acceptance. That the Kinks survived the 1970s while most of the rest went under was testament enough of Ray's tenacity.

In fact, they rematerialised in 1983, like ghosts from the recent past, to plug *Come Dancing*, a new single that had somehow contrived to chart. During a decade's absence from the Top 50, their presence had still been felt — albeit by proxy — via vinyl respects paid by the likes of David Bowie, the Rezillos, and, of course, the Pretenders. With eyes on the main chance, the Kinks prudently worked another of these tributes, *David Watts* (a 1980 hit as revived by the Jam), into their concert set when, almost for old times sake, they topped the bill at the prestigious Reading Festival in 1982.

Over the Atlantic, where paradise had been regained when *Lola* minced high into the Hot 100 in 1970, they became bigger than ever when a marked increase in album sales in the 1980s had ended years in the middle league of the adult orientated rock hierarchy. While British Invasion contemporaries like Herman's Hermits had re-entered the States on the nostalgia ticket, the Kinks — like the Stones — sustained interest with their latest output. Aided by hard-bought experience, something of a Kinks Komeback had been pulled off.

Well-respected men: Screaming Lord Sutch and the Savages are joined onstage by Ray Davies.

45

A Midnight Ramble with the Stones

The Rolling Stones were a rhythm and blues sextet formed in London circa 1962. Their gimmick was long hair. The one who didn't have long hair wasn't allowed onstage with the other five. They had their first hit in 1963. They kept on having hits. Their singer had big lips and danced about. He was the most popular with the girls. The newspapers often printed stories about the Rolling Stones being rude. A big fuss was made when three of them went to prison for taking drugs but were let off. The one who took the most drugs died. All the same the group continued to entertain people with much the same sort of music they'd always played.

Elaborations and regurgitations of the above information may be found in numerous Stones

Bravo, Rolling Stones! Included here are three Stones-associated records by other artists and an extract from a cartoon series about a circus family managed by a man named Turner.

biographies. The most 'balanced' view is that of Philip Norman, but if it's salaciousness you're after, there's an account by 'Spanish' Tony Sanchez, their narcotics dealer. More soothing still are back copies of the Sunday newspaper filthies in which The Wicked Life of Brian Jones ('strangely old at 25') is a hardy perennial. Bill Wyman and Mick Jagger have also written, or are writing, autobiographies.

I know a Kentish landscape gardener whose Bible used to be the very first Stones memoir, *Our Own Story*. His cousin had apparently 'been out' with one of them but this relationship must have been purely platonic; after a Boy Scout meeting in 1964, the patrol second of Beavers assured me that the Stone in question was to undergo a sex change operation so that he/she could marry one of the others. Two years later, another Scout spent nearly three hours pacing up and down outside a record shop deliberating whether to spend three weeks paper round savings on AFTERMATH. At a wedding reception, his uncle, donning a woman's wig, had done a flawless imitation of 'Mike Jaggers' as *Satisfaction* shook the Dansette. A bloke at school had attended the New Musical Express Pollwinners Concert where Jagger's shoe sailed into the crowd with one particularly energetic Tiller Girl goose step. This boy had been assaulted during a school lunch hour by some 'manly' types who hacked off his nape length locks in safe assurance of leniency from a deputy headmaster who in 1966 still regarded a Presley quiff as a sure sign of effeminacy.

The accumulation of these incidents and disclosures added to my own adolescent confusion. In macho Baden-Powell circles, brutalised by grammar school, it was still cool to like Stones *music* but what couldn't be admitted was finding their androgeny guiltily transfixing. A simple image such as the cover of their debut E.P. — a pop Sarajevo assassination — could trigger a ten year running battle with Authority over hair. With much the same attitude as a World War I trench private soldier resigned to the stray bullet at 'Wipers,' I would practice being Jagger before the bedroom mirror, to the detriment of physics homework and on the understanding that within the hour I could be eating my teenage heart out in front of that same mirror after an enforced visit to the barber.

It had, therefore, to be an imperceptible reverse-psychology process. Like *1984* and Winston Smith yelling abuse at Goldstein, you'd tell your mother that the Stones were morons and join in the sniggers when Max Bygraves centred his jokes on a blow-up of Jagger with a Yul Brynner pate on Sunday Night at the London Palladium, despising in secret comedians like Bygraves and Ted Rogers who, knowing the prejudices of their audience, would only have to twang 'Ah wanna be your lover baby, ah wanna be your man' to get a laugh.

Long hair was a red rag to local 'cowboys' as well as teachers and parents. In Aldershot Magistrates Court in 1965, a labourer accused of assaulting a complete stranger offered the plea 'well, he had long hair, didn't he' as a defence. Even when it became acceptable for studs to be hirsute, you could still get worked over out of jealousy by those whose coiffure was governed by work conditions, such as members of the Armed Forces. Nevertheless, it made your day if, convinced of his wit, some budding Oscar Wilde bawled 'get yer 'air cut' from a passing car while his grinning mates twisted round in the back seat to gauge the effect of this witticism on you. You weren't insulted — you were proud. At last you'd pulled wool over Authority's eyes long enough for it to show. By inviting persecution, you felt you were sharing something with the Stones.

Some went further than trying to simply look like a Stone. At seventeen I rampaged through *Sympathy for the Devil* to my own acoustic guitar accompaniment in church when the youth club was permitted by some 'swinging vicar' to take over Evensong one Sunday. With the restraint of clutching an instrument removed, my interpretation of Jagger's stage craft was among the factors, that caused my underhanded but understandable dismissal from a folk-rock group named Turnpike in 1973.

Only in retrospect did I learn how wide of the mark my conception of the Stones' hard, flashy lifestyle was. In a conversation with former member Dick Taylor in April 1984, I was half expecting him to be bitter and twisted about missing the millions. Instead he was attractive in his phlegmatic candour, reflecting that if he'd stayed on, he, like Brian Jones, might have ended up face down in a swimming pool.

Of course, the Stones were always pretty cheap. Fancy crediting the chanting of hysterical girls as *We Want the Stones* — an opus composed by Nanker-Phelge. As if Sinatra would ever cover that. Look at the places they played — a tour of the Channel Islands or sharing a Texas stage with performing seals. They even turned the Albert Hall into a bear garden. They were never above pennypinching or even a good old-fashioned publicity stunt. Much depended on the mood of the hour. In 1962, Brian Jones as leader gazumped the promoter of Richmond's L'Auberge into paying them £2 10s over the £10 originally agreed. Seven years later, a whim precipitated the unpleasantness at Altamont.

Portrait of the author as Mick Jagger: Clayson leads Turnpike through John Barleycorn *at Long Sutton Village Hall, 1971.*

Yet it was their grubbing, arbitrary opportunism that brought them closer to home than the decorated Beatles. Lacking the studio freedom bequeathed by E.M.I., the Stones didn't so much compromise as deviously warp Decca's stringent traditions, as in their sly booking of off-peak studio hours to be unfettered by the sanctions of snoring recording managers. On other occasions, they threw in the towel, as in the matter of the BEGGAR'S BANQUET graffiti sleeve. These style wars were reflected in their fans' struggles against more parochial and domestic squares.

The Stones had detractors among their own rebel kind too. In 1978, many quarters of the music press waxed sycophantically about the glories of punk, damning the Stones with faint praise without acknowledging their precedents of outrage. A decade earlier, flautist Ian Anderson of Jethro Tull, likewise biting the hand that fed him, had slammed the Stones' musicianship with pointed reference to Brian Jones.

Much of the criticism was well founded but, essentially, it didn't matter. Journalists have to make a living even if it involves toadying to someone called

'Johnny Rotten'. Who the hell are Jethro Tull anyway? True, the Stones were as culpable as anyone else of bandwagon-jumping (witness the trendy sitar on *Paint It Black* or the basic Sergeant Pepper concept of the martyred SATANIC MAJESTIES). As for their playing, I was appalled at their careless tonality on the television showing of *Stones in the Park*, but the point was that I hadn't been aware that anything was wrong when the notes were first hung in the air.

At Hyde Park in 1969, I joined in the booing of the Battered Ornaments, who had the onerous task of preceding the Stones onstage. With musicians of the calibre of Chris Spedding and George Kahn, the Ornaments' avant-garde jazz, like the better-received King Crimson's earlier set, demonstrated a more commanding instrumental precision than anything the bill-toppers could produce. While the Strolling Ones kept everyone waiting in the heat, some half-wit near the guest enclosure begged Edgar Broughton to get up on the boards to lead the half-million spectators through his celebrated exorcism, *Out Demons Out*. 'We don't mind if the Stones do one less number', the supplicant airily generalised, indicating the sweating multitudes behind him. He wasn't very popular. Any other group's most rabble-rousing showstopper could not be allowed to subtract a split-second from even the lousiest Stones presentation.

After Mick's oration for the drowned Brian and the freeing of his butterflies, the group lurched into their only public performance of Johnny Winter's *I'm Hers and I'm Yours*, kicking off a two hour set. As the other Stones, augmented by Ginger Johnston's African Drummers, jammed the fateful *Sympathy for the Devil* finale, Jagger was already motoring across the Serpentine, bound for Ned Kelly's Australia and more lurid headlines concerning a girl and drugs.

I can't recall anything special about individual numbers; only the claustrophobic, midnight atmosphere that pervaded any given moment of this open air summer's afternoon. The only remembered flash of levity was when someone shouted 'oi Mick. . . .do *Mona*'. 'Yeah, we'll try 'n' get to that,' replied Jagger knowing that even with rock'n'roll revival in the air, they'd never get to *Mona* in a donkey's age. The buggers at the back couldn't see, but who cared about them? One determined soul clung to the top of a lamp post for the duration. At the end, everybody near me was up, shoving, kicking and doing the Crawdaddy *en bloc* to the interminable row pouring from the P.A. Limping to the Tube afterwards, I noticed two contradictory ideologies — a bootlegger checking his tape and some enviromentalists clearing up litter — for which they were rewarded with virtue and a copy each of *Honky Tonk Women*.

In spring 1982, the Metropolitan Line trains were on strike and the Stones were on at Wembley Stadium. I hadn't thought of going until offered two tickets cheap by a mother of three whose husband's back was playing him up. Diving on the London train straight from work, I arrived at Paddington Station in the driving rain. Rather than waste money on a traffic-jammed bus fare, I decided to leg the seven miles to Wembley at Scout's Pace, *i.e.*, quick march for 20 paces then double 20 *ad nauseum*. Well, Jagger was a keep fit fanatic these days, wasn't he?

He was a lot fitter than I was when I reeled up to the turnstile two hours later. All seats were taken but I'd missed the dub reggae and the J. Geils Band, thank God. Eventually I stood among the common herd on the pitch, while Princess Margaret and her children luxuriated in a special compound elsewhere.

Dead on time the main event piled onstage. There was Ian Stewart, the one who'd looked too normal, finally allowed out — and there was old Bill, promoted to number three — *il était un rockstar en règle*. He'd probably been the brains behind the delving into the past of old rockers other than themselves — *Chantilly Lace*, *Twenty Flight Rock*, etc. — which were slipped in to balance the recent smashes like *Start Me Up* and the ambles down Memory Lane. Though the dark clouds and thickening twilight were more suggestive of the witching hour than Hyde Park had been, the mood was lighter, friendlier. Spanning twenty years and all aspects of their chosen musical form, the Rolling Stones had come to terms with their past and present situation. They had become archetypal units of their own, especially since occurrences like SATANIC MAJESTIES and Altamont had taken them out of their depth, obliging them to concentrate on the possible. The audience had seen it all before but so what? The girls gasped, rather than screamed, when Mick took his shirt off. The music was still only one step from chaos but the sound was crystal clear and the Stones still rode 'em on down. During the fixed *Satisfaction* encore, I wickedly wondered what would have happened had the set ended with politely brief applause instead of the howling approval, foot stomping and girls taking off their bras.

Afterwards, I found the fellow to whom I'd sent the other ticket — the same Scout who'd finally bought AFTERMATH, whose uncle was the Jagger mimic. Though he'd since become a frozen food executive, any pretentions of respectability temporarily evaporated through breathing the air round the Stones.

Stones alone: attention is directed at Keith Richards' continued obsession with Chuck Berry and a rare flexi-disc of Jagger's spliced-up medley of excerpts from Exile on Main Street.

Unable to immediately get out of the car park or find a pub, we shadow-boxed round the streets of Wembley incanting *I'm Smokin' Joe Frazier* over and over again and asking passers-by if we'd missed the Stones concert. Driving back we indulged in a cowardly game of slowing down to chant an adaptation of a nappy advert at gangs of skinheads. Luckily we never stalled. Nearer the motorway we stopped the car to take artless photographs of street furniture.

Home by 3.15 a.m. I was back to reality. In seeing the Stones again, I'd come up for air. Though I've since resumed getting older, I'd reaffirmed my self-image that night. In the bathroom mirror at dawn, I saw not a mortgaged thirty-year old with a pregnant wife, but an eighteen year old boy, long haired, as beautiful as a girl and mad as a hatter.

Waltz for the Who

For all their pillhead nightbird aura, the Who's background was, like the Yardbirds', mundanely suburban. Roger Daltrey, John Entwistle, Douglas Sandon and Peter Townshend were in the same year at Acton Grammar School in West London. When they left, John — a trainee tax officer — and Pete joined a traditional jazz outfit on trumpet and banjo, respectively. Later, they adopted more familiar instruments in Pete Wilson's Confederates, who copied the Shadows. With Wilson's help, art student Townshend recorded his first composition, *It Was You*, in a Northfields studio.

Meanwhile, Roger had married and found employment as a sheet metal worker, the occupational hazards of both interfering with his efforts to teach himself to play guitar. Learning that John possessed an electric bass, Roger cajoled him into a band he was forming with Doug Sandon on drums. This was to have more vocals in it than the Confederates — sort of like Johnny Kidd or that new lot from Liverpool. Adding Townshend on rhythm guitar, they became first the Scorpions, Ealing's answer to the Beatles, and then the Detours, seeking work in the social clubs of outer London.

On the same circuit they ran into the Beachcombers from Wembley, who went in for Californian-style pop numbers like Jan and Dean's *Bucket T* and the Regents' *Barbara Ann*. They'd actually made a couple of records but their energetic drummer, former Sea Cadet bugler Keith Moon, considered this to be the fullest extent of the Beachcombers' ambitions. Thinking that the Detours' prospects were more attractive (especially as Sandon had given notice), Keith, with dyed hair and matching ginger suit, presented himself at a Detours booking in Greenford. Before the evening was out, Moon was in.

Daltrey shelved his guitar to concentrate on most of the lead vocals and the group changed its name to 'the Who' in 1964. They gained two managers. Helmut Gordon handled the cash, and Pretty Things publicist Peter Meadon found them work closer to the heart of London and, boasting that they were the first *authentic* Mod group, negotiated a one-off singles deal with Fontana. Having phased out their Middlesex wedding reception repertoire, the Who gave Meadon's sales pitch a veneer of truth by updating existing London R'n'B styles to appeal to prototype Mods. This involved a generous injection of Motown and James Brown to complement the Bo Diddley-Howlin' Wolf urban blues mainstays. They also agreed to fulfil the Fontana contract as The High Numbers. Referring to the most self-assured, assertive dancers at Mod discos, *I'm the Face* was essentially *Got Love If You Want It* grafted to Meadon's Modspeak lyrics. Despite some Radio Luxembourg plays and a feature in *Fabulous*, this lumbering disc fared badly. Unperturbed, the High Numbers grew as a live attraction with their flashy interpretations of the *Shout — Mickey's Monkey — Heatwave* genre plus obscurer items like Garnet Mimms' *Anytime You Want Me*.

Via a mutual friend, Meadon invited entrepreneur Kit Lambert, then filming a pop documentary, to a High Numbers recital in a dingy Wealdsdon pub. Within a short while Gordon and Meadon were ousted as the group's mentors by Lambert and his partner, Chris Stamp. Born to a musical family, like Townshend, and as flamboyant as the extrovert Moon, Lambert and his new acquisitions had much in common.

The new regime's first act was to revert to the band's earlier name. For residencies at the prestigious Marquee and Scene Clubs, advertisements promising 'maximum R'n'B' featured the now famous Townshend windmill guitar pose (on permanent loan from Rolling Stone Keith Richards). But the hawking of a Who demo of *Smokestack Lightning* round the record companies drew a blank. Eventually it came to the intrigued notice of Shel Talmy, who coaxed Decca, against their better judgement, to grant the group a small initial pressing on their Brunswick subsidiary.

It was decided that modelling the group on the Kinks, Talmy's main production concern, was the safest bet for the Who's debut 45. Townshend's *I Can't Explain*, based on the salient points of the Muswell Hillbillies' recent smashes, graced the A-side of *Bald-Headed Woman*, a medley of two Talmy numbers dashed off for the Kinks' first album. Despite the Who's objections, Kinks sessionmen were present on both tracks.

Against the minimalist policy of Decca's press office, the group's visual impact on TV, aided by pirate radio plugs, precipitated a yo-yo progression into the upper reaches of the charts. One of their strongest assets was the wild-eyed Keith's thrashing performance which, though gratuitously busy, still maintained a precise backbeat; much of this was learned from the Pretty Things' Viv Prince who deputised when Moon was indisposed. More exciting was the Who's practice of

Shout and Shimmy: John Entwistle, Roger Daltrey and Pete Townshend front the Who during Reading Jazz and Blues Festival, 1965.

closing their act by smashing up their equipment amid smoke bombs, flashing lights and feedback lament, usually when journalist or camera crews were about. This was recreated aurally on the next two singles, the devastating *Anyway Anyhow Anywhere* and the Mod anthem, *My Generation*. Though the doctrines of auto-destructive artist Gustav Metzger were bandied around, this development's most plausible origin was Pete's capitalising on accidental damage to his guitar sustained on the Marquee stage. A by-product of these excesses was to draw audience attention away from the Who's indifferent vocal harmonies (overcome on record by using a professional singing trio).

Stamp and Lambert garnered further publicity by exaggerating the group's Mod sartorial extravagance and, more seriously, by booking them to play venues like Margate's Dreamland and other seaside Mod strongholds on Bank Holiday weekends when there were likely to be newsworthy clashes with Rockers.

The Who's passive role in the propagation of this youthful violence became internalised as rumours reached fans about friction in the ranks. Roger hated Keith. Pete thought the other three were old women. Two of them were leaving to start something with two equally discontented Yardbirds. Pete and Roger were amalgamating with drummer Gibson Kemp and his bass player, Klaus Voorman. Roger was to be supplanted by either Boz Burrell of the Tea Time 4 or Kenny Pickett from Pete's fave raves, the Creation. The Shakedown Sound's Jess Roden took lead vocal on a Who recording. Pete stifled John, John was jealous of Pete. No-one bit back harder on his anger than Roger. And so the bickering went on. Yet the Who's personnel remained unchanged for 14 years until ex-Small Face Kenny Jones replaced the hard-living Moon, who expired in 1978.

Daltrey became less domineering with Townshend's increasing confidence as a songwriter during sessions for the first L.P. Even though an exploratory promotional copy was reviewed in Beat Instrumental in July 1965, on the album that reached the shops, most of the American soul covers had been put aside in favour of Pete's originals such as *Much Too Much* and a revamped *Out In the Street* as well as an instrumental collaboration with session pianist, Nicky Hopkins. There may have been suspicions that the covers didn't do justice to the original classics but a mood persisted that the group's maturing style was no longer suited to the restrictions (and stingy royalty rate) imposed by Decca.

With the next single, *Substitute* in the Top 10 in March 1966, the Who switched to Polydor. During this clean sweep, they also ditched Talmy but not before their last intended Brunswick release, *Circles* (alias *Instant Party*), had been the subject of a complicated legal matter. The Graham Bond Organisation as 'the Who Orchestra' were hired to provide the B-side, *Waltz for a Pig* which wound up on the back of the original version of *Substitute*.

Using Entwistle's French horn on the ill-fated *Circles*, instrumental experiments continued modestly with the employment of acoustic guitars (*Substitute*), weird percussion effects (*Disguises*) and more of John's mastery of the brass family. After a BBC radio Light Programme — later to become Radio 2 — airing of *I'm a Boy*, disc jockey 'Cheerful' Charlie Chester complimented the Who on their *marvellous* driving beat.

In the States, it wasn't so easy despite network TV appearances, full page *Billboard* advertising and a long tour supporting Herman's Hermits. Gradually, however, came hopeful signs as a couple of their singles became regional chartbusters and the more fanatical of their American following began donating expensive guitars for Pete to ritually destroy. With a lot of hard work and concession, they finally obtained a sizeable hit with *Happy Jack* around the time of their startling performance, in flower-power get-up, at the Monterey Festival in 1967. One annoying compromise was over censorship of *Substitute* by their USA record label on the nebulous grounds of racial prejudice — the offending line 'I look all white but my dad was black' being recorded as 'I try walking forward but my feet walk back' (almost a direct quote from *Circles/Instant Party*).

Apart from his triumphs with the group, Townshend as a composer *per se* was not as prosperous as Lennon-McCartney, Jagger-Richard or even Ray Davies, though the Merseys came close to a hit with his *So Sad About Us*. Like the Kink Komposer, Pete (and the Pretty Things) began work in the questionable 'rock opera' medium, as well as spawning a substantial number of cover versions by minor acts such as Fleur de Lys and the Untamed (whom Shel Talmy briefly groomed to supercede his departed Who). The Barron Knights' *Lazy Fat People* and Oscar's *Join My Gang* were among significant Townshend songs unrecorded by the Who. Later he had more luck as a producer, notably for Arthur Brown, Thunderclap Newman (built round an art school idol, pianist Andy Newman) and, to a lesser degree, Aylesbury performance artist John Otway.

Towards the end of the 1960s when the Who were the darlings of the University circuit, the media latched onto Pete as a quotable 'articulate' pop spokesman,

Mad Goose: *Prior to his joining the High Numbers, Keith Moon's previous group, the Beachcombers, recorded on Columbia — primarily providing accompaniment for London vocalist Pat Wayne.*

though many found him tiresome and patronising in his efforts to come across as a regular guy like any other boring 'good bloke' from Pudsey to Plymouth. Admiration for Townshend and his blokeism bordered on worship from New Wavers, the Jam being his most conspicuous devotees. Among vinyl acknowledgements of this was a frenzied *Substitute* by Pete's drinking partners at the Speakeasy club, the Sex Pistols.

Pete had always been a great fan himself from his membership of the Creation fan club to his proud familiarity with poet Stephen Spender in a later capacity as a publishing executive at Faber and Faber. Recommending emulation of the Stones as a recipe for any new group's success, Townshend, Moon, and Daltrey hurriedly knocked out a single of *The Last Time*

and *Under My Thumb* as the Who's contribution to Jagger and Richards' legal costs during their celebrated drugs trials. Less like a publicity stunt was his private musical eulogy to the late Brian Jones (*A Normal Day*) in 1969. With no qualms about admitting their preferences, the Who encored with Free's *All Right Now* a year later.

A superb bass guitarist John Entwistle, was, compared to his old school chum, very much an also-ran composer in the eyes of the world. Nevertheless a small minority — including myself — found his macabre, cynical songs the most agreeable aspect of the Who's output. Though John himself preferred Pete's paean to self-gratification *Pictures of Lily*, the discerning Jimi Hendrix's favourite Who number was Entwistle's *Boris the Spider*. Other areas covered might not have been everyone's bag, but a man who wrote pop ditties concerning alcoholism, miserliness, voyeurism, insurance swindles and other improbable topics was not to be easily dismissed. His taciturn stage presence belied a love of performing,

In the city: the Who record an 'In Concert' programme for BBC Radio One at London's Paris Theatre, 1971.

later expressed in his leadership of at least two Who splinter groups as well as his turbulent bellowing of *Twist and Shout* on a Channel Four television rock show in 1983.

Keith Moon's onstage exhibitions pervaded nearly every aspect of his short life. After deductions for damages he inflicted in hotels, theatres, etc., Moon's fee for his last UK tour with the band was a paltry £40. In a lucid moment, he confessed that his role as group newsmaker was only for publicity. Nonetheless, that he sustained his maniac persona throughout his career suggests a deeper motivation. Though his antics necessitated extreme sanctions from the group, such as expulsion from recording sessions, his assets were considered greater than his liabilities. His buffoonery (like parading around London clubs in Nazi attire) would often deteriorate into a nonsensical frenzy and, eventually, there would be the bizarre, unpredictable behaviour that made headlines. That this was exacerbated by fame and wealth was demonstrated in the fiasco of his only solo album, cluttered with 'guest appearances' by other layabouts of the Hollywood Raj (surf guitarist Dick Dale, an old hero of the former Beachcomber, being an exception). Many who knew him were bemused but not entirely surprised at his passing.

Sensible Daltrey was Moon's antithesis, although he could be relied upon to attend to the most onerous public offices on the group's behalf such as his courageous self-immersion into a bath of cold baked beans for the cover of SELL OUT. Though he co-wrote *Anyway Anyhow Anywhere*, he was the Who's least prolific composer. But his later extra-mural activities thrived the best by showbusiness standards. These included hit records in his own right, starring roles in large budget feature films and, as an accolade to his increased versatility as a singer, a move into light opera — not bad for a former workshop apprentice.

Were the Who ever real Mods? If they were, they surely belonged to the greasiest end of the spectrum. After Mod faded circa 1966, they felt it was safe to insert old favourites like *Summertime Blues* and *Shakin' All Over* back into the set. It was also cool for Pete to say he liked esoteric exponents of rock'n'roll like Link Wray and Creedence Clearwater Revival. By 1973, this was further compounded by his and Moon's contributions to THAT'LL BE THE DAY, a film set in the late 1950s. That same year, Entwistle's band Rigor Mortis paid its respects to the form over a complete L.P., with renditions of *Lucille*, *Hound Dog* and the self composed *Gimme That Rock'n'roll*.

Even if this apparent *volte-face* had taken place in 1965, it's likely that the Who would have survived, owing to the toothless nature of Mod. (Witness the sudden isolation by his peers of the central character in the Who's own Mod retrospective film, QUADROPHENIA.) Largely resulting from a so-called Mod revival in the 1980s, the Who enjoyed a brief chart run after a long absence. Though their Brighton Dome show was packed with nouveau Mods (looking spottier and punier than the original article) Pete and Roger's derisive catcalling of the 'we are the Mods' doggerel went unchallenged. Fifteen years earlier the general response would have been similar though true hardcore Mods like Jimmy Cooper — staring humourless creatures anyway — would have felt betrayed.

The worst kinds of Mods were akin to updated teds or embryonic skinheads. *En bloc* they would barrack and catcall loudly throughout movies, except for the sexy bits where they'd go all quiet. The mildest reproof could turn them even uglier; 'just because we're in a picture house don't mean I can't knock your teeth so far back down your throat, you'll have to stick a toothbrush up your. . . .' etc. Optimum danger occurred when they failed to 'get off with a bird' at a dance or a party. Slit-eyed with some stimulant or other, they would seek more brutal sensual pleasure. If you so much as glanced at them, the action could be *you*, whether you were a Rocker, another Mod or just an average Joe.

Beyond the pale of London, the 1950s didn't really end until 1966. All the excesses the London Mods allegedly indulged in belonged to speculation while sharing a communal cheap cigarette behind school bicycle sheds. Swallowing amphetamines like black bombers or puffing a joint was a big deal. Mod clothes weren't much more than gang uniforms in which no pretence was made towards keeping up with Carnaby Street front-runners. By the time the gear hit a local high street, it was probably 'out' anyway. You *could* be outwardly 'in' as long as you had Chelsea boots, cord jacket, denim shirt, wide kipper tie and Billy Bunter striped hipsters — even if you wore them to every school hop until you outgrew them. Some followed Roger Daltrey's enterprise in customising clothes to Mod standards on mother's sewing machine.

Being superficially Mod was a soft option because your parents were less likely to moan about your turnout. You could even own a scooter as long as you didn't get into fights with boys in leather windbreakers or *smoke* these 'Purple Hearts' that you read about in the papers. However (unlike acne made less virulent with lacto-calomine), no backcombing, pulling or applications of Dippety-Do could disguise the short hair imposed by parental deprivation, heavy atmospheres and bribery. Only in the music press and on the TV would the clouds part to allow glimpses of transient gods like the Who at play. Meanwhile, you made the best of a bad job, sprucing up for another small death in the village hall dancing to the local heroes.

The Yardbirds Got Art If You Want It, Babe

Talking about the Yardbirds, most stress the contributions made by three of their five lead guitarists. Sensational as they were, interest in Jeff Beck, Eric Clapton and Jimmy Page has tended to displace the innovations of the group as a whole. More discreetly influential were its more permanent members — Jim McCarty, Chris Dreja, Keith Relf and Paul Samwell-Smith. Though they lacked the cohesive image cultivated by many of their peers, the Yardbirds, in their breathtaking performances and imaginative musical realisations, transcended content to leave a lasting impression on pop. In an otherwise rather waspish autobiography in 1982, even a former manager, Simon Napier-Bell, admitted 'there were four rock bands in the world that really counted. . . .and the Yardbirds was one of them.'

As a straight blues band they were often spellbinding in their pioneering of extended improvisation, or 'rave up'. These were kept firmly under control, whether an exquisite dirge like Eddie Boyd's *Five Long Years* or a speedy demolition of Chuck Berry's *Too Much Monkey Business*. As a pop group they entered areas far removed from their blues core. Probably the earliest pop explorers of Indian sounds, they also integrated Gregorian chant and other eruditions into their records in a manner that would appear to outsiders to be rather slap-dash. As McCarty elucidated to me in 1983, 'We'd start with a basic rhythm and bass pattern and then. . . .sort of build it up.' *Shapes of Things*, recorded at the Chess studios, was apparently assembled from a riff doodled by Relf, with Samwell-Smith scribing most of the lyrics. Its successor, *Over Under Sideways Down* (a title suggested by Napier-Bell) was intended as a kick in the direction of Bill Haley of all people though it mutated into what Paul described as 'happy Russian rock'n'roll'. While he organised the backing track, Relf was elsewhere collating the words — which had started as a discussion of sexual positions, before emerging as a more general observation of 1960s hedonism.

Certain items belonged to individual Yardbirds. Among these were Keith's *Farewell* and *Only the Black Rose*, while Paul presented the elegiac *Turn Into Earth*, written with his future wife, Rosie, to the others as a *fait accompli*. The lighter *Hot House of Omagarashid* was the brainchild of Dreja.

Unlike the Beatles, the Yardbirds' time and facilities in the studio were always limited — though any lifting of these restrictions may have detracted from the

Five Yardbirds (left to right) Jim McCarty, Jeff Beck (seated), Chris Dreja, Paul Samwell-Smith and Keith Relf.

proceedings' spontaneity and endearing imperfections, such as the muffled 'amen' unscripted on the fade of *Still I'm Sad*. Certainly no cover version, from David Bowie's *Shapes of Things* to *I Can't Make Your Way* by Paul and Barry Ryan ever surpassed the Yardbirds' original.

The group was hatched in the indistinguishable London suburbs centred round Teddington Lock. In 1960, sandwiched between two other Hanworth Road schools, stood Hampton Grammar where a sixth form group trod warily amidst official disapproval — all pop musicians took drugs and had sex, didn't they? In truth, their masculine charms notwithstanding, the only stimulants available to 'Sean and the Country Gentlemen' were in local pubs, where they played as a change from providing interval music at school dances. They were particularly proud of their renditions of *Shakin' All Over* and *Apache*, in which guitarist B.D. Smith duplicated Hank Marvin's Stratocaster twanging on his Gretsch Country Gentleman.

Smith's entrance into the civil service was a typical career option for a grammar school boy from London's middle class conurbations as, was the casting aside of adolescent follies like pop groups. However, before attaining man's estate, he and the other Gentlemen had taped a demo of *With Love*, a number written by Brian Samwell-Smith, elder brother of rhythm guitarist Paul. E.M.I. recording manager John Schroeder was sufficiently interested by the copy he was sent to book the lads for an Abbey Road recording session. Nothing concrete came of this, so *With Love,* trite though it probably was, became a priceless Yardbirds-associated artefact.

No longer either a Gentleman or a schoolboy by 1961, Paul, as a week-end beatnik, loafed around with the Kingston Art School crowd who frequented L'Auberge Cafe or, after opening time, nearby pub The Crown. With deceptive casualness, he encountered a scruffy painting student in frayed jeans named Keith Relf, a former Leatherhead Grammar School pupil who had merged into the Art School's counter culture. With another would-be Dharma Bum, Roger Pierce, he had started to learn blues guitar and harmonica, dreaming of riding the rails and living rough like Kerouac's Dean Moriarty. But the nearest Keith came to this was when he was employed by Paul's father as an electrical engineer; Paul and he would hammer fixing plugs into flint walls whilst hollering blues laments and planning a group to be called 'The Metropolis Blues Quartet.'

The Quartet came to rehash ethnic blues mainly at the Station Hotel, a bohemian haunt in Richmond. In this semi-acoustic genesis, Relf on vocals and harmonica was backed by guitarists Samwell-Smith and Laurence Gains. A drummer called Brian was replaced by an ex-Country Gentleman, Jim McCarty. Gains was to be supplanted by Anthony 'Top' Topham and Chris Dreja from another art college in Surbiton. During these re-shuffles occurred an incident at a Kingston Jazz Cellar booking where a smartly dressed drinker confronted Paul with the words, 'I tell you what, do me a favour — don't play any more solos'. Taking this blunt request to heart Paul borrowed a home-made bass guitar from Keith. Unaware that Relf had been lent the instrument himself, Paul customised it by removing the frets. When Relf and the owner's wrath had abated he then applied himself to approximating the technique of Ricky Fenson (Richard Brown), bass player of the Cyril Davies All-Stars.

Davies himself, as founder of a Harrow blues club, was approached by Paul and Keith in their campaign for more bookings for their group, now operating as the Yardbirds. Another port of call was Georgio Gomelsky's Crawdaddy in Richmond Sports Ground club house, off Orleans Road and where, in spring 1963, they were asked to deputise for the Rolling Stones. McCarty: 'When we started out, we followed Stones-type material but we decided not to do any numbers they did. We used to watch them quite a lot.' No less a bluesman than John Mayall opined in *Bam Balam* that the Yardbirds were 'appalling', but as Stones substitutes, their treatment of the works of Slim Harpo, Jimmy Reed *et al.* soon overcame initial resentment.

With Gomelsky as their manager, the group began earning enough to go professional. Relf, for example, gave notice at the Isleworth antiques firm where he used his artistic skills to 'distress' furniture. At the same time lead guitarist Topham was ousted owing to his extreme youth and 'musical differences'. Into his shoes stepped Paul's Jazz Cellar critic who, it transpired, knew Keith. As well as invigorating the Yardbirds with his over-amplified fretboard eloquence, Eric Clapton also acquainted them with more modern American R'n'B such as the Isley Brothers' *Respectable* and the Vibrations' *My Girl Sloopy* — which, with *Paff....Bum*, I cannot help but feel became the worst track the group ever recorded.

As the Stones had taken blues to the hit parade, the Yardbirds were well placed to do likewise (even if detractors like trad jazz trumpeter, Kenny Ball apparently regarded it as 'rock'n'roll with a mouthorgan'). On the strength of a demo cut in Morden, a recording contract was secured with Columbia who released the shortest of many takes of Billy Boy Arnold's *I Wish You Would* as a debut single. However, aided by publicity photos taken outside Twickenham Girls Grammar School, it was the next 45, *Good Morning Little Schoolgirl* that elicited a modest chart entry in October 1964, and they were named 3rd Brightest Hope in a Melody Maker poll. It is likely that this disc would have progressed further had not the asthmatic Keith been laid low for several weeks with a collapsed lung. Burly, saturnine and Irish, Mike O'Neill of the Authentics (antithesis of frail, allergic, emotional Relf) was, nonetheless, an adequate understudy for the

May 1966: as well as tinkling harpsichord for the Yardbirds, Brian Auger was with Steampacket before forming his more successful Trinity with Julie Driscoll in 1967.

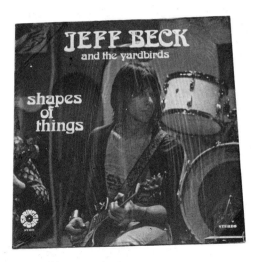

'Jeff didn't get a credit on Shapes of Things *when he really should have done because, although he just played lead guitar, it was the way he developed it when the song was being formed . . . .' — ex-Yardbird, 1984. This song was later revived by Nazareth and David Bowie as well as Beck himself. Among lesser known tributes are recordings of* I Can't Make Your Way *by Tony Blackburn and the Ryan Twins, Paul and Barry.*

engagements Georgio was unable to cancel pending Keith's recovery.

With Keith's return came his father, Bill, whose attitude towards his only son's antics had undergone review. When the Yardbirds needed transport Mr. Relf, far from a previous curt disinterest, not only provided a van but also agreed to act as road manager. It was his bespectacled figure who held the audience boom microphone like a Watusi spear when the Yardbirds recorded their first L.P. live at the Marquee Club in winter 1964.

Traversing the country on one night stands or supporting stars like Billy J. Kramer on tour, they felt the vague unease of a minority cult act poised on the threshold of national eminence. Later, in 1983, Samwell-Smith reflected to me 'had we continued to play just blues, we would, in the end, have broken through (but) at the time we were desperate for a hit because you can't tour America without one. You suddenly get on television — everything opens up for you. It's no good saying 'we're a great blues band' when there's three thousand people in England who've ever heard of you. We'd have to have had kept playing the Crawdaddy and Station Hotel otherwise'.

It was with Paul that Eric was most at loggerheads over musical policy. This came to a head when Graham Gouldman's sparse demo of *For Your Love* arrived on Gomelsky's desk. Doubtful of its suitability as a third single, he abdicated his producer's chair to Samwell-Smith. The record began and ended with what one reviewer called the 'sexy sound' of Brian Auger's harpsichord with two other sessionmen on bongos and bowed double bass, while the group piled in for the jarring *eleven* bar tempo change in the middle. By the time *For Your Love* swept to Number 2 in the UK charts, Clapton was in John Mayall's employ, where he could play blues as much as he liked.

Though he declined the offer himself, Jimmy Page recommended an alternative replacement in Jeff Beck, a Wimbledon art student. No Clapton duplicate, Beck's guitar playing displayed eclecticism and unpredictability in compatible amounts. Drawing on the countrified rockabilly of Paul Burlison of the Johnny Burnette Trio, and Gene Vincent's Blue Cap Cliff Gallup, as well as the T-Bone Walkers of this world, he was ideal. The Yardbirds entered their two year golden age as the hits kept on coming — *Heart Full of Soul*, *Evil-hearted You*, *Still I'm Sad* (apart from Relf's derivative *I Ain't Done Wrong*, and two instrumentals, plus the first group original) *Shapes of Things*, and *Over Under, Sideways Down*.

McCarty told me that after one Marquee concert, two 'sharky types' wanted to sign Keith as a solo singer but it was only as a tangent to the Yardbirds that Relf released singles in his own right, rather as Dave Davies did with the Kinks. As producer of *Mr. Zero*, Paul conjectured, 'the general pressures were that way — I was keen to do some producing and Keith wanted to do something in his own right as opposed to being lead singer with the Yardbirds'. Though he wasn't as enthusiastic about this Bob Lind number as Samwell-Smith, Relf's edited *Mr. Zero* filtered to the charts' lower reaches. Unhappily, despite a TV plug on READY STEADY GO, the follow-up, *Shapes In My Mind*, was unable to match even this unassuming Top 50 showing. A promotional copy of this disc wrongly titled *Make Me Break This Spell* (from a lyric in the first verse) fetched a large amount in a German auction in 1978. A more deliberate deceit was present on its B-side, harmonica instrumental *Blue Sands*, which though attributed to Keith — excellent harmonica player though he was — was actually by the Outsiders, hired in the interests of economy by Simon Napier-Bell who by 1966 had taken over from Gomelsky.

More than any other famous 1960s group, the Yardbirds are remembered for what they did not do.

Golden Eggs: the rarest Yardbird-related singles here are Samwell-Smith's work with the Washington DC's and Relf and McCarty's Together — which was preceded by the more obscure Reign which also involved Robin le Mesurier, son of the distinguished late British TV actor.

Keith did not cut a third single as 'Keith Dangerfield'. Jim McCarty is not the gentleman of the same name who was in Mitch Ryder's Detroit Wheels and then Ted Nugent's Amboy Dukes, though a book inspired by Lennon's slim volumes featuring Jim's prose and Chris's cartoons was in the works, curtailed by the Yardbirds' punishing schedule. And the Yardbirds never issued any discs under the name 'Philamore Lincoln.'

These myths notwithstanding, the most ubiquitous Yardbird in the studio was Paul Samwell-Smith who, weary of years on the road, left the band in June 1966. With a Hammersmith Christmas season with the Beatles and a five day block booking at a Hollywood stadium the only exceptions, the Yardbirds had been forever on the move. Even 'days off' were filled with interviews and photo sessions. The final straw came at an Oxford University May Ball when Paul and Jeff were obliged to share lead vocals as Keith had contrived to

appear onstage roaring drunk, behaving in a manner akin to that of Johnny Rotten ten years later. In his delirium, Relf had injured himself in the dressing room. McCarty: 'Mama Cass and the Hollies were doing all this karate stuff and they got him to do it on a chair — I think he broke his fingers'.

They were able to continue in a recognisable form for another year but the group never really got over Paul's departure. A limited but adventurous bass player, his principal abilities lay in his co-production of all the big hits. According to McCarty's fatuous sleeve notes to the eponymous L.P. that came to be known as ROGER THE ENGINEER, Samwell-Smith had 'all the qualities of Burt Bacharach, Phil Spector and Richard Wattis (noted comedy actor) all rolled into one'.

Though Jimmy Page was persuaded to take Paul's place, he reverted to a more customary role as co-lead guitarist with Beck as soon as Dreja became proficient enough on bass. Apart from a cameo role in Antonioni's BLOW UP film, the only recording credited to his line-up was the psychedelic single *Happenings Ten Years Time Ago*, which some consider an aural nightmare, while others share author Tim Hibbert's view that it was 'the greatest 45 over released.' It sold

Twenty Long Years: McCarty rattles the traps at Angie's in Wokingham with Ruthless Blues, June 1983.

well in the States but its comparative failure at home precipitated the Yardbirds' most despairing strategy when, at Page's suggestion, they enlisted the services of Mickie Most, well-known manufacturer of chart sounds. Though there was an increasing demand for albums by 1967, McCarty, while agreeing that Most was 'a protagonist in our down fall', remarked 'if you didn't have a hit single, you were a fading band'.

The Yardbirds were, indeed, a fading band. Forbidding much elaboration, Most's productions included the tolerable *Little Games*, a sly USA — only *Ha! Ha! Said the Clown* and the hated *Goodnight Sweet Josephine*, all by external composers thus reflecting a creative impasse. Only excerpts from the LITTLE GAMES L.P. and *Think About It* — a B-side — showed fleeting sparks of the old fire as, during their penultimate and most harrowing US tour, the live set deteriorated (as evidenced by the doctored LIVE YARDBIRDS album from the final American trek). Though the NEW MUSICAL EXPRESS incorrectly reported that following Beck's sacking, the band would henceforth be known as 'Keith Relf and the Yardbirds', Relf was still disgruntled at the attention lead guitarists were getting — especially as he fought to be heard amidst overwhelming volume. At this stage, all that mattered was raking in as much loot as possible while honouring existing contracts. Apart from a few half-hearted rehearsals by Dreja, Page and Terry Reid, the Yardbirds effectively folded after a showdown at Luton Technical College in 1968.

A group called 'the Yardbirds' took the Marquee stage on July 22nd 1983 during the club's anniversary celebrations. Dreja, McCarty and Samwell-Smith, with help from guitarist John Knightsbridge of Ruthless Blues and Nine Below Zero's Mark Felton on harmonica, backed John Fidler from Medicine Head for whom Keith Relf had been benevolent overseer, producing Medicine Head's chart debut in 1971. Fidler's presence was a poignant touch, as Keith had been killed by electrocution in 1978 while practicing guitar through a faulty amplifier. Though he was a good musician and lyricist, it was his instantly recognisable singing style that was his legacy to pop. Because of his general ill-health, he lacked the lung power of an Ian Gillan or Robert Plant but he had a wide expressive range, from the aching desolation of *Turn Into Earth* to sneering contempt on *Rack My Mind*. His influence certainly pervades the highly individual voices of Alice Cooper, David Bowie and their acolytes but, as Keith himself came to realise, he better functioned as part of a group rather than as a solo entity.

After another concert in Surbiton, the 1983 Yardbirds recorded an L.P. under the guise of A Box of Frogs which, with guest appearances by Jeff Beck and Rory Gallagher, hopped to No. 45 in the USA charts to a fair critical consideration. In the change of name, Paul, Chris and Jim had been sensible, blighted as they were by a more glorious Yardbird past — a near impossible yardstick for any band.

OUT OF TIME

How the Old Guard Coped

When British records made the UK charts in the early 1960s, it was usually with solo stars like Marty Wilde, Tommy Bruce and Frank Ifield. If their backing groups appeared at all, it was in identical stage outfits, skulking in grey mediocrity beyond the main spotlight. Occasionally, vocal groups would put up a fight but these were mainly duos like the Allisons or Caravelles, swamped in orchestration or their producers' ideas. Sure, there were the Shadows, Tornados and Johnny Kidd's Pirates, but some figured that groups of guitarists were on the way out. Take that lot from up North, the 'Beetles' — they'd arrived much too late. They'd be better off finding another hair-sprayed, Italian-suited Johnny Gentle or even another degenerate like that Tony Sheridan; we know these things, Mr. Epstein.

British pop before the deluge: amid the American copies, dance crazes and showbiz schmaltz were all too rare gems such as Newley's epoch-making IDLE ON PARADE E.P.

The Viscounts and More 'Ace' Vocal Groups

As the Beatles and victims of the same passion thumbed noses at the wrong-headed London music industry in 1963, most of the old guard couldn't get a hit to save their lives, even when they paid cursory heed to current trends. An illustration of this is the matter of the Viscounts, a trio of entertainers in the Mudlarks-King Brothers tradition. Unlikely to be caught titillating Reeperbahn fancies with their rehearsed patter, *salvo pudore* comedy and blank perfect harmonies, they were smart chaps you'd wonder about if they 'dated' your sister. As groups were unfashionable, the Viscounts records were regarded as adjuncts to their earnings in variety, though they managed two moderate entries into the chart around 1961. Generally they went in for American covers, cash-ins (e.g. *Mama's Doin' the Twist*) and 'rocked-up' showbiz detritus like *Money Is the Root of All Evil*. Quite. When the Beatles came around, up popped the Viscounts on prime time TV emasculating a mildly choreographed *I Saw Her Standing There* while the Palladium's 'Beat the Clock' orchestra sight-read in the pits. They raised a few screams by association but by 1964, the Viscounts couldn't get arrested, together with 'Britain's *ace* vocal group', the Brook Brothers and their hastily-assembled 'Rhythm and Blues Quartet', as well as the Original Checkmates, the Kestrels and all the rest of them. The Dowlands from Bournemouth went out in a blaze of glory, taking *All My Loving* to No. 36 in 1964 (though David still performs around Poole). But the best remembered of the whole bunch were the Springfields, who specialised in commercial folk. Though the group split up as the storm broke, their soot-eyed girl singer, Dusty, achieved spectacular success in mainstream pop shortly afterwards.

The Viscounts knock 'em dead on THANK YOUR LUCKY STARS. Gordon Mills (centre) had more luck later as manager of Tom Jones and Engelbert Humperdinck.

63

Side by Side with Karl Denver

The weirdest sound of the genre was that of the Karl Denver Trio. With Jack Good's patronage, they hit the charts with *Marcheta* in 1961, and kept things mildly buzzing for several years before the cats decided Denver was no longer cool. Karl's tortuous, gargling vocal and insane hick-yodelling were wrapped round *Mexicali Rose*, *Indian Love Call* and other country-pop favourities, but his biggest smash was a treatment of

Wimoweh, which at Number 4 in 1962 beat the retrospectively better-known Tokens version by 12 places. The Beatles guested frequently on the Trio's BBC radio series, SIDE BY SIDE The favour was returned when the Trio supported the scouse quartet on producer Good's American extravaganza, SHINDIG. In fact, Karl and his boys were regular freak exhibits on many pop package tours until they sank into the secure ooze of cabaret and a roaring trade at open air festivals in Africa.

Side by side: Karl Denver (right) passes an idle hour in the gym with wrestler 'Dirty' Dominic Pye.

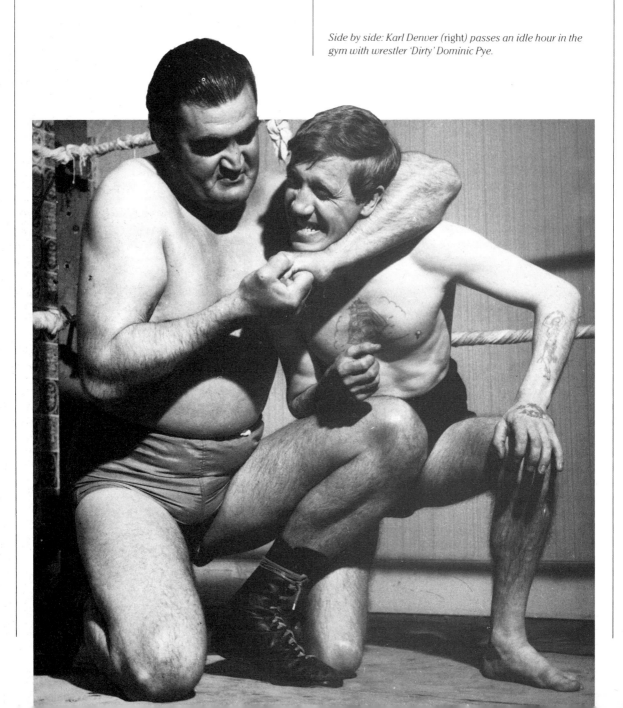

On the Move with Adam and the Roulettes

Adam Faith had seen the group boom coming and, zooming in sharpish, had made the switch smoothly from lightweight ballads with pizzicato strings to ersatz Merseybeat. First he'd hired himself a new writer and arranger in Chris Andrews who, as 'Chris Rovell,' had sung in the Hamburg clubs, knew the field and could, therefore, provide his client with made-to-measure nouveau rockers. The change of colour from red to

Adam Faith ponders his next move.

The Roulettes (left to right) Peter Thorp, Russ Ballard, Bob Henrit and John Rogan. As well as working with Adam Faith and Unit Four Plus Two, they scored a couple of minor hits before Ballard and Henrit left to join Argent in 1969.

black of the Parlophone labels of Adam's records aptly signified the new policy. 'Adam Faith with the Roulettes' it said now, and it was with this visible guitars-and-drums quartet that Adam returned — which was one in the eye for those bands who'd made it just because they had the right accent and hairstyle. Adam had had *his* hair brushed forward since he started carving the UK charts up four years earlier. Now it was October 1963 and he was back where he belonged, having shaken the curse whereby his previous three singles had had barely a sniff at the Top 20. On TOP OF THE POPS again, he was set up for another four years; driven by walloping drums, clangorous guitars and unison male backing vocals almost as loud as his own wobbly, androgenous singing, *The First Time* had the desired effect of reaching the Top 5. Its follow up, *We Are In Love*, did nearly as well. There were some pretty tough B-sides too. With the Yanks seemingly 'having kittens' over anything from the green and pleasant land, Adam had a sole American smash with *It's All Right*, UK flip of *I Love Being In Love With You* which, only making No. 33 in May 1964, was the final vestige of Faith's Big Beat period.

Enough of the old Adam had remained to satisfy the faithful — you only had to listen to him enunciate the word 'blue' in *We Are In Love*. But, obliged to appear straight after the Rolling Stones on an NEW MUSICAL EXPRESS Poll Winners show, he cast aside the piddle-de-pat *Stringbeat* niceties of his ante-Merseybeat past; ready to murder his own grandmother, he built on Jagger's foreplay and proceeded to shave 'em dry the Roulettes bucked and shimmied around him. Was this the same young man who, as principal boy Dick Whittington, had led a children's chorus through *Lonely Pup In a Christmas 'Shup'* as 1960 rolled into 1961?

With the poll concert screams ringing in his ears, Adam was still level-headed enough to understand his essential pop star frailty. Cashiering the Roulettes, he took a restless two year farewell from the charts beginning with a cover of Lou Johnson's weepie *Message to Martha* at No. 12, with Bob Lind's song, *Cheryl's Going Home* waving him out of sight in 1966. By this time, he was already ensconced in repertory company touring the provinces in obscurity. Learning his new craft the hard way, he developed into the actor it had crossed him mind to become when as, Terry Nelhams, he worked as a Rank Screen messenger boy in 1955. Nevertheless, having kept his finger in various pop music pies, his *I Survived* became a minor hit in 1974 though successful manager Adam had done more than merely survived by then.

The Crazy World of Joe Brown

Joe Brown's skiffle group, the Spacemen, were originally employed as accompanists on OH BOY. Good used Joe's effervescent charm and hair ('like a frightened dish mop') first as a solo guitarist before letting him graduate to vocals and star billing over the rest of the lads, renamed 'the Bruvvers'. From their first release, an arrangement of *The Darktown Strutters' Ball*, Joe Brown and the Bruvvers hovered near the Top 30 for two years before sweeping in with *A Picture of You*, co-written by Bruvver Peter Oakham, which effectively conveyed the impression of some backdated seaside fairground in the holiday season — Blackpool, Margate or, most appropriately, Southend. You could almost smell the cheap perfume and jellied eels.

Because he rather overplayed his hand as a gorblimey Plaistow cockney — such as in his part as East End layabout, Alfred Higgins, in the film WHAT A CRAZY WORLD with the late Harry H. Corbett — hits came only sporadically after the rise of Merseybeat and, like the Viscounts, cash flowed mainly from sources where attractive personality was more important than hit parade status. Joe and the Bruvvers' stage act included numbers from musicals like OKLAHOMA and BYE BYE BIRDIE as well as getting religion with a setting of *All Things Bright and Beautiful*. Another highlight was a rivetting *Hava Nagila* climaxing with Brown plucking behind his head.

Yet, despite this kitsch, he remained a respected musician in the business. With a talent deeper than showmanship, he had played Scotty Moore to Billy Fury's Elvis on the 10-inch L.P. THE SOUND OF FURY in 1959. Later, he and the group were much in demand backing touring American legends such as Gene Vincent and Johnny Cash. When the well of hits truly ran dry in 1963, there was still session work.

In 1982, Joe's guitar was heard on his Berkshire neighbour George Harrison's GONE TROPPO album. Ironically, one of Joe's rare chart entries since 1963 had been a version of *With a Little Help From My Friends*. There had been a time when the Beatles had been second billed to Joe's boys at the New Brighton Tower. During the two day build-up to this, the fascinating London aliens had been mobbed signing autographs at N.E.M.S. Record Store as well as packing the Cavern over two lunchtime sessions. For their part, the less famous Beatles plugged the Tower show by incorporating *A Picture of You* into their act for bookings a week prior to this event. A year later they virtually had a licence to print money, while Joe and his group were in Arthur Haynes Show obsolescence.

Johnny Kidd and the Pirates' Odyssey

No voyage round the backwaters of British Beat would be complete without sighting Johnny Kidd and the Pirates. Though their period of optimum impact took place at the turn of the decade, they belonged to both 1950s rock and the era beyond the 1962 watershed, managing to stay afloat until Kidd's death in a road accident near Preston, Lancashire, in October 1966. There is no reason to suppose that, had they been able to continue, the group would ever have disbanded. Like his idol Gene Vincent, Kidd always had plenty of work assured with or without record success. At the very least, this was down to a melodramatic stage act enhanced with Captain Pugwash costumes, galleon backdrop, cutlass, eye patch and Long John Silver taped overture. The enduring influence of this presentation was most keenly felt when Adam and the Ants borrowed most of its aspects during their British chart domination in the early 1980s. With a similarly sparse crew of guitar, bass and drums, Kidd would rock'n'roll 'em over with a sweaty intensity rarely experienced in British pop before 1962. He was also one of the few home-grown rockers who didn't go smooth at a time when the UK charts were riddled with brilliantined Bobbies and regular Rickies from across the Atlantic.

On the recording front, Kidd's trove of hits included *Please Don't Touch* (revived in 1982 by Motorhead and Girls School) and the climactic *Shakin' All Over* at Number 3 in mid-1960. Both equalled anything from the annals of American classic rock, leaving other honourable British attempts like Cliff's *Move It* and *Jet Black Machine* by Hounslow's Vince Taylor way behind. However, after *Linda Lu* in April 1961, Johnny and his men were becalmed outside the charts for nearly two years.

At the start of the new age, the Pirates consisted of bass player John Spence, guitarist Mick Green, and drummer Frank Farley. With his burly frame and dazzling combined lead/rhythm technique, Green was ideal first mate as the group subtly adjusted hard rock with a massive shot of rhythm and blues. The new cargo of numbers — *I Can Tell*, *Shop Around*, *Stupidity*, *Dr. Feelgood* etc — were also featured by the Big Three, Beatles, King Size Taylor, Rory Storm and other looming Liverpudlians. Fifteen years later, many of these cropped up again in the repertoire of noted pub-rock outfit Dr. Feelgood, whose guitarist Wilko Johnson was outspoken in his admiration and debt to Kidd's Pirates.

Lord of the flies: Johnny Kidd (Frederick Heath) relaxes on his desert island paradise with three dusky maidens.

Not entirely co-incidental, Johnny's change to R'n'B was beneficial in the short term. With booking fees falling off slightly, any old port in a storm will do. The initial pay-off arrived in the form of the jaunty *I'll never get over you* which shipped to Number 4 in September 1963. Their chart absence and personnel reshuffles gave the group much of the aura of a fresh sensation to those whose interest in pop began with *Please Please Me*. Merseybeat's vaguely nautical connotations certainly lent themselves to Kidd's image — on THANK YOUR LUCKY STARS, during the 'somewhere, somehow' bridge, Johnny, with arms folded (Alan Badel as vaudeville buccaneer) gazed off centre, searching an imagined horizon for a girl with an angel face. He'd started looking for her in a Lancashire port on the Irish Sea.

The follow-up, *Hungry for Love*, ran aground at an humble No. 20, much sales potential being drained by

Dropping the pilot: The Pirates in June 1966 were (left to right) Frank Farley (drums), Mick Green (guitar) and Johnny Spence (bass). Reforming in 1977, they became popular on the British pub–college circuit.

the Searchers' rival version. There was also mutiny among the deck hands. Interviewed before a BBC Radio One 'In Concert' special in which the reformed Pirates starred with the Argonauts and I in 1977, Green, Farley and Spence intimated that Kidd had listened to arbitrary management suggestions that the quartet should moderate its style towards easy-listening country-and-western to suit cabaret now that the hits had dried up. The idea of a third coming was brushed aside as electric organ was introduced on a 1964 treatment of *Your Cheatin' Heart*. Green may have regarded its use as an implied slight on his ability, as was an increased reliance on double-tracked lead

vocals and even a female backing chorus on a couple of occasions.

By 1966, Johnny was still zigzagging the country with yet another crew of Pirates, this time, a group formerly known as the Regents who had literally turned up on his doorstep to ask for the job. After a last resort remake of *Shakin' All Over* failed to find a passage into the charts, Kidd was reduced to support spots and one nighters. Psyching himself up after the soundcheck in cockroach dressing rooms, Johnny may have reflected that his true vocation had always been to cut up rough with the 100% rock elixir that a loyal following would pay to see regardless of passing fashion. Gone was most of that country corn; the ship was back on course. Despite the unsavoury surroundings, Johnny Kidd was feeling positive. For all anyone knew, a chance to hit the big time again was lurking just round the next bend.

Constantly: Cliff and the Shadows

Unlike Kidd and Adam Faith who revised their tactics to disconnect themselves from the ancient regime, Cliff Richard and the Shadows didn't even bother to compete. Why should they? Though younger on average than the Beatles, they had been a pop institution since 1959 — kings of the Palladium rather than the Cavern. Their story has been told many times before in a legion of biographies and treatises, some by Richard himself, but the definitive work is probably Mike Read's *Story of the Shadows* (Elm Tree, 1983). This being so, I'll keep my bit short.

The Beatles may have hogged the headlines but, behind the scenes, Cliff, Hank Marvin, Bruce Welch and the other Shadows were already known quantities all over the free world bar the States. Predictably, though the Shadows were invited to Paul McCartney's riotous coming of age party, many of the new breed of pop heroes and, by implication, their fans loved to hate the old order. Nevertheless, smiling indulgently, the Shadows kept punching out the same brand of guitar airs iced with dance steps that had always caught on while Cliff shovelled out a greater proportion of potboiling ballads like *Constantly* and *Visions* until the danger had passed. Sadly, his infrequent rockers of this time developed an unprecedented sterility as if he felt obliged to humour his old following despite an inward shudder, reliving the excesses of a flaming youth rendered old as the hills by Merseybeat.

Revelling in their uncoolness, the Shadows and their sometime vocalist plunged deeper into high class

War Lords: undefeated by major personnel reshuffles at its onset, the Beat Boom Shadows were Brian 'Hank' Marvin, the late John Rostill, Brian Bennett and Bruce Welch.

pantomime, evangelical Christianity and Songs for Europe. Like his darling Elvis, Cliff's films — with the Shadows in cameo roles — degenerated into quasi-musicals of cheery unreality. Where in the world would you find a gang of shiftless garage mechanics prepared to customise a bus free of charge so that a bunch of jumped-up little smarmers could hightail it to Greece as Cliff did in SUMMER HOLIDAY with Melvyn Hayes, Una Stubbs and other wonderful young people?

Set against this slag heap of squaredom, there was still much to praise. For a start, the Shadows had recovered from the loss of Tony Meehan and the charismatic Jet Harris by enlisting drummer Brian Bennett (formerly with Neville Taylor and the Cutters) and, after ex-Marty Wilde Wildcat Brian Locking's

The Young One: Cliff beatles his Elvis hair, circa 1966.

Jehovah's Witness activities led to his resignation in November 1963, John Rostill, bass guitarist from the Zoot Money band (after entreaties to session man John Paul Jones had fallen on stony ground).

Apart from the hitless Sounds Incorporated, the Shadows were the only popular UK instrumental group of the mid-1960s — unchanging masters and sole competitors in the market. In the shade of the Big Beat, they continued producing material at least as good as anything prior to 1963. The lush *Atlantis*, for example, knocked the overrated *Wonderful Land* into a cocked hat. *The War Lord* and Hank's own *Geronimo* were as menacing as *Frightened City* or *F.B.I.*, while *Rhythm and Greens*, 'a raving great send-up of the R. and B. scene', showed a band with a sense of humour. The most profitable vocal concession to the Beat Boom was *Don't Make My Baby Blue*, again by Hank, at Number 10 in September 1965.

This was the biggest seller since 1964. But their lowest chart entry, *The Dreams I Dream* at No. 42, was the writing on the wall in 1967. The next year they were down to closing the opening half of a Palladium variety show with fifteen minutes of early hits and pointless comedy.

A decade earlier they had reflected Cliff's glory as the Roulettes were to reflect Adam's, but by the middle of the 1960s the Shadows had thrown down a line to Richard by composing as well as providing accompaniment on several of his big hits. Among these were *On the Beach*, with Cliff's lyrics and a leitmotif from *Twist and Shout*, and *I Could Easily Fall* from the ALADDIN pantomime of 1964. Their songs were also recorded by the Swinging Blue Jeans and Frank Ifield but it was always Cliff who had first refusal.

Cliff had shown that it wasn't all Eurovision and Wishee-Washee when he cut a Jagger-Richard number, *Blue Turns to Grey*, in 1966, but it wasn't really until the mid-1970s that he was truly out of his artistic coma. With the Beatles out of the way, he revamped his musical aspirations and, with the help of new technology and younger minds than producer Norrie Paramor's, finally broke into the USA charts after a twenty year wait, entering the 1980s more famous than ever.

At the same time the Shadows, having revised their musical values too, were delighted to find that there was still a place in the public heart for instrumentals. Yet, though they enjoyed chart honours with new material like *Don't Cry For Me Argentina*, in their 1980s revivals of *Telstar* and *Riders In the Sky* they were rifling the catalogues of long gone acts who fell by the wayside even before the Beatles messed everything up.

The Tornados and the Rest

In the early days, if Joe Meek liked your group, you stood a fair chance of Making It. Ranking with Brian Epstein as one of the age's tragic figures, there are many — I, for one — who would rate Meek, as a record producer, far higher than Phil Spector for inventiveness and originality in his easy juxtaposition of outer space aetheria and funfair vulgarity. From his North London studio in Holloway in 1962 came the other-worldly *Telstar* by Meek's house band, the Tornados. The quintessential British instrumental, it unbelievably topped the US chart, where no Limey group — not even the Shadows — had made much headway. As such, *Telstar* played Eric the Red to the British Invasion of the American continent in 1964. It also anticipated many of the electronic ventures of a subsequent and less innocent pop generation.

Formerly Billy Fury's backing group, the Tornados were the only serious challengers to the Shadows' suzerainty. However, they were only to last as long as their console Svengali — and were finished as chart contenders by the end of 1963. Among the reasons were Merseybeat's levelling blow and the exit of bass guitarist Heinz Burt, around whose blond Aryan visual appeal Meek had built the group from top flight session men, as well as shanghaiing the entire crew of Colin Hicks' Cabin Boys. Also, new ideas were getting thin on the ground; *Life on Venus*, for instance, almost-but-not-quite repeated the *Telstar* melody while *Early Bird* and *Stingray*, issued in 1965, too harked back to Roger Jackson's switchback organ sound. After a desultory go at bluebeat, *Pop Art Goes Mozart* tried a Mod approach *pis aller* but shortly after the follow-up, *Is That a Ship I Hear*, occurred both the penniless Meek's suicide and the interrelated disbandment of the Tornados.

The history of the minor British instrumental groups is, apart from a few individual players, outside the scope of this present work yet their collective influence had far-reaching effects. Most of them owed much to the Shadows — a Tornados Vox Continental involved too much capital outlay and a Johnny Paris sax lacked the logical learning process of a guitar fretboard. Though the Volcanos with *Polaris*, fitted the Tornados mould, it was more common in some out-of-the-way

Sounds Incorporated (left to right) Alan Holmes, Griff West, Barry Cameron (who doubled on keyboards), Tony Newman (later in the Jeff Beck Group), John St. John and Wesley Hunter. (over page)

Globetrotters: the Tornados take the stage in 1963 as (left to right) Roger La Verne (Roger Jackson), ex-Pirate Brian Gregg, Clem Cattini, George Bellamy and Alan Caddy.

The Beat Group even reared its machine head in national politics when it transpired that Labour leader (and Gene Vincent Fan Club Member) Neil Kinnock had once strummed guitar in South Wales combo, the Rebels — renamed Los Banderos.

town hall dance around 1962 to witness a quartet happily presenting a set consisting exclusively of deadpan Shadows imitations, even down to the bum notes Hank played in *Man of Mystery*. The fellow with the Stratocaster might be sporting Marvin horn-rims while the peroxided bass player was a Jet Harris doppleganger who transfixed the girls with his 'brooding intensity'.

Though some local pretty boy might be hauled onstage to be Cliff, Adam or Billy for a while, he was not regarded as an integral part of the group. The concept that the group rather than the star could be a credible means of expression owed much to the groundwork of these grassroots craftsmen struggling with dodgy equipment and transport, amateur dramatic acoustics and jeering audiences. Another attraction was the implied cameraderie of a Group, reminiscent of the lately repealed National Service minus the barracks discipline. Also, you didn't have to be Charles Atlas to join a Group — look at four-eyed Godhead Hank, stunted Jet or tubby Tornados drummer, Clem Cattini. It was the Group's workmanlike blokeism rather than any macho conviction that was admired; gruff onstage taciturnity frequently translated to the uninitiated as 'professionalism'. No less an authority than Jimmy Page once remarked (in *Trouser Press*) that 'some of those Shadows things sounded like they were eating fish and chips while they were playing'.

The instrumental group's death rattle was heard as Kent's Sounds Incorporated and the can-canning Peter Jay and the Jaywalkers from Clacton were hired to warm up audiences for the Beatles on several nationwide tours. Demonstrating the permanence of the swing towards vocal groups, apart from those mentioned elsewhere, the number of English instrumental groups who made the charts during the five years from 1962 can be counted on the fingers of one offensive gesture. The last of these was the Second City Sound who reached No. 22 in 1966 with a treatment of Tchaikovsky's First Piano Concerto. Less execrably po-faced was *Saturday Night at the Duck Pond* by Bristol's Cougars which managed Number 33 three years earlier. On this robust adaptation of Tchaikovsky's Swan Lake theme, the tortured Russian composer was credited on the record label under the pseudonym 'Keith Owen'.

FIVE
LONG
YEARS

They Weren't Only In It For the Money

Many 1960s groups were motivated by a single-minded, neo-evangelical zeal to further the cause of one favoured musical form irrespective of financial reward or personal popularity. Perhaps the most altruistic were the Joystrings, a 'beat' group organised by Captain Joy Webb of the Salvation Army's South London Training College at Denmark Hill.

Overlooking Ecclesiastes VI.5 and using the Devil's Music to Spread the Word, a prolific number of Joystrings' discs flowed from the pressing plant of Regal-Zonophone, including two chart entries in 1964.

Other outfits went on more secular crusades, as did Liverpool's Chants, who specialised in 'doo-wop'; the Silkie from Hull with upbeat modern folk; the Executives and Roy's Boys, who persisted with Shadows-style instrumentals, and Shakin' Stevens and the Sunsets, who began churning out Teddy Boy rock'n'roll on the eve of psychedelia. In the latter case, tenacity was eventually rewarded; but it would have been enough for these dedicated combos merely to have had somewhere to play.

With Corps funds providing an Hofner President guitar and violin bass plus a Vox organ and amplification, the Joystrings' prayers were answered when It's an Open Secret (that I Love My Saviour So) *and* A Starry Night *both ascended the UK Top Fifty in 1964.*

River's Invitation — From the Ealing Delta

By far the most vital of these minority interests, the blues, grew as a bohemian cult partly provoked by scorn for the Top 10 toot-tooting of 'traditional jazz'. Yet it was trad trombonist Chris Barber who was a major catalyst in the development of the British blues movement. In the teeth of monetary losses (such as that sustained on a Muddy Waters concert at St. Pancras Town Hall), Barber underwrote national tours by other leading American bluesmen throughout the 1950s. Other jazzmen like Humphrey Littleton and Ken Colyer may have arranged a few more bookings for blues artists but Barber actually sank cash into the form's conservation, believing — with skiffle scribe, Brian Bird — that blues was the main content of jazz. At his prompting, the National Jazz League acquired its own London Club in Oxford Street, the Marquee, which was to become a key shop window of the blues brigade before venturing into more generalised pop music. For all his efforts, Chris was unjustly castigated as an opportunist when, after riding the craze that turned trad into pop, he championed the Stones as they took R'n'B into the charts. Yet it is doubtful whether Jagger *et al* and other musicians would have considered making a living from their specialist tastes without Barber's groundwork.

It had been two sacked Barber sidemen, Cyril Davies and Alexis Korner, who, at the suggestion of his manager, Phil Robertson, formed the legendary Blues Incorporated in 1961. Having antagonised trad fundamentalists throughout the 1950s with their blues predelictions, guitarist Korner and harmonica-player Davies were out in the cold again for daring to use electric instruments in emulation of Sister Rosetta Tharpe and Muddy Waters.

A home for Blues Incorporated and acolytes was found in a downstairs room between a jeweller's and the ABC teashop on Ealing Broadway. Opening on May 17th 1962, the new club was patronised immediately by blues zealots from the West London suburbs and beyond. On that first evening, there was something for everybody, ranging from Scrapper Blackwell's *How*

In 1961, a surefire way of getting up a jazzman's nose was to remark: 'Yeah, I dig jazz. I like Acker Bilk . . . . George Chisholm . . . . Kenny Ball . . . .' To crass Joe Soap, 'jazz' meant Stranger on the Shore, Siamese Children, *uniform fancy waistcoats, plinking banjos and bandleaders who thought that a hoarse monotone was all you needed to sing like Louis Armstrong.*

A substantial part of Blues Incorporated's audience were students and weekend ravers whose 'pads' were strewn with some of the items pictured here. There were a lot of beards and nuclear disarmament badges among the future Stones, Pretty Things and Yardbirds in the throng.

The noblest British bluesman: the late and sadly missed Alexis Korner always used his influence to find work for deserving young blues groups. In February 1980, he turned up at Cherry's Wine Bar, Reading to sit in with Roger Barnes' Motley Crew (later Jive Alive).

Long How Long, a skiffle favourite originating in the 1930s, to the more modern *Ain't Nobody's Business* by Jimmy Witherspoon, a frequent visitor to Albion's shores throughout the 1960s. At later meetings, clientele would learn of other blues venues such as the Crawdaddy, Eel Pie Island, or the Tuesday night residency at the Marquee (now moved to Wardour Street) conferred on Blues Incorporated by promoter Harold Pendleton.

Overtaken in commercial terms by those it encouraged, Blues Incorporated's loose musical policy allowed a rapid turnover of personnel thus prohibiting the clear visual identification required as ignition point for chart success. There would have been marketing problems anyway with the middle age, baldness and obesity of certain members precluding teenage acceptance. Who would scream over baggy-trousered Cyril sweating over his mouth-harp or moustachioed Alexis, seemingly old enough to be anyone's Dad?

Fortunately, this did not figure in the band's calculations. Blues Incorporated was buoyed by amateur enthusiasts, semi-pro at most, as earnestly devoted to blues as other cliques were to water sports, numismatics or animal welfare. Who gave a damn about the general public? When Decca offered Blues Inc. a contract in late 1962, it was a breakthrough for the movement rather than the group.

As a hangover from trad, it was primarily an instrumental unit, instigating a respect for musical ability that came to a head in the guitar hero worship later in the decade. Though the smoky growl of Alexis and the harsher tones of blond giant Long John Baldry, were semi-permanent fixtures, a constant flux of vocalists were drawn from the audience. Among those who felt the urge to sing were Herbie Goins and Ronnie Jones, two black US servicemen, as well as ex-Larry Parnes cipher, Duffy Power. Anyone could have a go. Less experienced hollerers in the queue were Paul Jones, Steve Marriott, and a nervous economics student called Mike Jagger who had to screw himself up with a few beers to snarl *Around and Around*. Another future Stone, Charlie Watts, beat the skins for a few months while a 20-year-old slide guitarist calling himself 'Elmo Lewis' blew in from Cheltenham with a transfixing *Dust My Blues*. Also passing through the ranks prior to the group's disbandment in 1964, were subsequent members of the Artwoods, Gary Farr's T-Bones, Cream, the Nice, Pentangle, Led Zeppelin — you name 'em. For some, however, the honeymoon was over quickly. Ex-Stone Dick Taylor summed up succinctly to author John Pidgeon in 1976, 'we thought Alexis Korner's band was fantastic the first week and quite good the second but by the third week, we thought it was really a bit off'. Nevertheless, Korner and Davies, for all their self-imposed stylistic limitations, were the noblest British bluesmen of them all.

Saturday Night Function — Country Blues

It was in 1983 that a former Yardbird enlightened me about the financial aspirations of the early London blues bands: 'If you were a good band — as good as Cyril Davies — you'd get £120 a night depending on the gate. I was working for my father as an electrical engineer and I could see that one night at Eel Pie Island per week would give us £20 a week in our pocket each which was what I was earning for a full five days work as an electrician....it was something I liked doing as well'. They were the lucky ones. In the sticks, success was ruled out by geographical isolation as in the typical case of Reading's Blues Committee who, with no agent or even a private telephone,

Cyril Davies preaches the blues in deepest Berkshire. Following Cyril's death in 1964, Baldry formed Steampacket and then Bluesology (with Elton John) before achieving schmaltzy solo success with a 1967 UK Number One Let the Heartaches Begin.

Refusing to compromise the blues with any Jaggeresque capering, Manfred Mann lookalike Mike Cooper stands still and dour while the rest of Blues Committee perform defiantly seated — Chicago rent party style.

considered themselves fortunate to scrape up a support spot at the Marquee, let alone topping the bill anywhere.

Like the Yardbirds and Animals, they got chances to back visiting blues potentates such as Sonny Boy Williamson, Fred McDowell and Jimmy Reed (who, according to Committee singer, Mike 'Drivin' Wheel' Cooper, was 'drunk for breakfast'). With little time to rehearse, star and pick-up band would entertain at the local hop with simple, mutually familiar standards of the *Boom Boom — I Got My Mojo Working* variety during which the audience, usually dignified by the presence of university undergraduates, would blame musical errors on the group rather than the jet-lagged viellard fronting them. He was the genuine article, wasn't he? What did the town oiks accompanying him know about blues? Actually, in their own right, the oiks could probably give a more technically-accurate account of their idols' repertoire, but as they weren't black Americans, who could possibly love them?

Some, like the Yardbirds, adjusted themselves along more commercial lines or else, like the Blues Committee, fell by the wayside. A few individuals remained true to their blue star. Mike Cooper, for example, became, like Duster Bennett, a cult celebrity during the second wave of British blues in the later 1960s. (Hitting a trough of poverty in 1984, he slapped a pile of his albums on the counter of Reading's Unemployment Benefit Office to emphasise his right to sign on as a blues musician.)

Macclesfield John Mayall

There but for fortune went John Mayall, whose blues came down from Cheshire. Unlike Cooper, Mayall, almost despite himself, had become a contradiction in terms — a blues millionaire. Though his will to succeed was more apparent, he still shared with Cooper, Korner, Davies etc., an unconcern about hit records and a lifelong dedication to his chosen vocation. Beyond this commitment, his disciplined organisational approach commanded respect — terrified admiration in some instances. By the time he dismissed his purposely unstable Bluesbreakers in 1968, he had become a British Beat institution, working most nights for good money, selling albums steadily if unremarkably, and continuing to attack his music from new angles — with a big band, solo, without a drummer, as a jazz fusion, duetting with white Chicago blues grandee Paul Butterfield....

The number of musicians who could claim a Mayall session to their credit runs into three figures, whether bass guitarist John McVie who endured on and off for six years, Eric Clapton and his eighteen months, or Peter 'Ginger' Baker, drummer for two days. Among outfits the Bluesbreakers spawned were Fleetwood Mac and Colosseum while the Stones, Free and McGuinness-Flint all turned to Uncle John when vacancies arose. However, though all good men and true, not every Mayall man became a megastar. For every Peter Green there was a Jeff Kribbett; for each Jack Bruce, a Keith Tillman; for every Aynsley Dunbar, a Pete Wood (who?).

It was surprising that Mayall himself went the distance considering the hard road he travelled from his Macclesfield birth in 1933. Attending Manchester School of Art, the blues so captured his imagination that by the time he left to work for an advertising agency in 1949, he had painstakingly taught himself boogie-woogie and related styles on the piano. Chucking in the agency job, he was a window dresser when he made his debut in a trio at the city's Bodega Jazz Club in 1950.

This took place a year before Arkansas blues crooner Big Bill Broonzy's London concert marked the British blues movement's sluggish conception 'down South.' Meanwhile, the War Office, concerned about the stalemate that the British Army, supporting the Americans, had reached against the North Koreans, sent for John Mayall.

As a clerk in the Royal Engineers, Private Mayall's contacts with US soldiers and the American Forces Network on the radio broadened further his understanding of blues, jazz, swing and general Americana. On a visit to Japan, he bought a guitar. After demobilisation, a full-time college course in graphics gave him time to find his feet musically. In

John Mayall's commendable sense of historical perspective was evidenced in his copious sleeve notes which once even included musical keys of tracks recorded.

days when advertisements for amplifiers 'with a 10 watt punch' appeared in *Melody Maker*, John struggled with record player amps and no bass player as well, as D.I.Y.-ing some of his own instruments (such as a *nine* string guitar customised from his Japanese purchase).

From this improvised chaos surfaced Mayall's first proper group, the Powerhouse Four of 1961. After jamming with Blues Incorporated at the Bodega a year later, Mayall was invited by Alexis Korner to bring his quartet (renamed Blues Syndicate) to London. They'd get £20 a night between them. Korner would fit them in at either his short-lived Blues City in Tottenham Court Road or Klook's Kleek in West Hampstead (where Mayall was to cut his first L.P., JOHN MAYALL SINGS JOHN MAYALL in 1964).

As he had added harmonica to his keyboard, guitar and vocal abilities, Mayall's London opening was preceded by publicity comparing him to multi-instrumental jazzman, Roland Kirk. Doing his best to live up to it, 'London's New Raving R'n'B Sensation' was so encouraged by audience response that he decided to move to the capital. Any Mancunian sidemen unwilling to do likewise were replaced. Alexis knew people, and there were the small ads in *Jazz News* or *Melody Maker*.

Labouring in graphics design, Mayall played clubs in the evenings. A typical weekend would take him to Manchester's Twisted Wheel on Saturday, with Sunday evensong at The Place in Stoke-on-Trent. In February 1963, John Mayall's group now re-named Bluesbreakers, cautiously went pro.

Though hinged on a Chicago sound, they tackled a wide spectrum of blues forms from the badlands of rock and soul to the rural exorcisms of Robert Johnson. In between lay works by Otis Rush, Elmore James, both Sonny Boy Williamsons, J.B. Lenoir (a special favourite), Freddie King . . . . all filtered through Mayall's lithe, full-throated lament.

However, by 1966, Mayall's own autobiographical songs were monopolising needle time on L.P.'s. Most were at least the equal of the non-originals. A couple were actually quite catchy. *Telephone Blues* — one that wasn't — 'deserves to be a hit' said *Melody Maker* in 1965. That same year, a Mayall composition even entered the singles charts when Georgie Fame took *Something* to No. 23.

Despite John's self-conscious, jocular continuity in concert, among reviewers' epithets describing his music were 'joyless', 'grim satisfaction', 'savage' and 'no spark of humour'. Yes, he did get a bit turgid but continuous pressure of tour schedules may have contributed to this. Yet he was a funny man in other ways. If working in the vicinity, he might repair to the tree house he had constructed in his parents' Bramshall garden where, it was said, he would psyche himself up by yelling and cavorting like Tarzan or by perusing his collection of erotica before setting out for the sound check. In studio and dressing room, he'd tape record conversations and similar aural debris for editing as musique verité on record — the best example being on Keith Hartley's HALFBREED L.P., which starts with an extract from the telephone call in which the drummer was given the elbow by the autocratic Mayall.

Occasionally, he would consult his musicians before hiring and firing their colleagues but intrinsically, John Mayall was a firm adherent to the leadership principle and enforcer of his own order. As the suspensions of John McVie testified, he wouldn't tolerate boozers — and God help you if you were caught with drugs. He was tight with cash too. Eric Clapton's blistering, bluesy axework greatly assisted Mayall's passage into the album lists, but the ex-Yardbird was only paid a standard Musicians' Union fee for his pains.

In the van, Mayall would repose in a bed in the rear while the rest languished cramped on the front seats with amplifiers on their laps. Well, he'd done his bit in the Army, hadn't he? At least they wouldn't ever have to square bash in Aldershot. Anyway, who signed the contracts? Who hassled with Decca, haggled with promoters, handled the Press and all that? Who mapped out musical direction? Right! You got it in one. Muggins Mayall, that's who! Poor old devil, he needed his rest. Look at the crow's feet round his eyes. He must be nearly as old as Alexis Korner.

Once, at Jack Bruce's insistence, Mayall held a rehearsal, but usually he didn't bother. Arriving for a show in Helsinki in 1969 with only a bass player, he hastily persuaded guitarist Keith Relf and drummer Jim McCarty from Renaissance (and, coincidentally, former Yardbirds) to make up numbers in every sense of the phrase. Often, even as the customers filed into the hall, Mayall would be backstage outlining a new number to his Bluesbreakers amidst the support band's monotonous blues jam, snide remarks, primadonna tantrums and the usual dressing room squabbles. At showtime, knowing only the key and a vague chord structure, Mayall and his merry men would premiere the song. Yet from this mixture of autocracy, eccentricity, parsimony and chance operation, they invariably brought the house down. For John Mayall, it was a 'Hard Road' all right — all the way to the top.

IF YOU GOTTA MAKE A FOOL OF SOMEBODY

Comic Relief

The first business of any pop group is to be liked. Though many believed that they needed no self-abasing humour to make themselves more palatable to the public, a lot of 1960s groups sugared their concert sets and recorded output with varying degrees of conscious comedy. Indeed, there were a number of bands whose raison d'etre was critically centred on getting laughs but it was noticeable that most of these relied in the first instance on straightforward R'n'B or ballads as A-sides, even if a comical stage act assisted in their promotion.

Ready, Freddie Go!

The heavyweight chumps of 1960s pop comedy were Freddie and the Dreamers. Like the Hollies and Herman's Hermits, their roots lay in Manchester's popular entertainment tradition. In 1956, sixteen year old Freddie Garrity won a razor as first prize in a Sale talent contest with an Al Jolson impersonation. Sucked into skiffle's vortex, Freddie, on a cheap guitar, with his brother Derek, a tea chest bassist, constituted half of the Red Sox, runners-up in the North-West Skiffle Competition of 1958. Subsequent bookings in Greater Manchester's labour halls and cinema intermission spots kept them busy but, attempting to monopolise his charms, Freddie's predatory girl friend prevailed upon him to leave the group (though allowing him to sing in the less demanding John Norman Four). His equipment was sold to guitarist Roy Crewsdon who eight weeks later invited Garrity to join him in the Kingfishers, much to the chagrin of the lady from whose embraces Freddie extricated himself for the grander passions of rock'n'roll.

Founded on Garrity's extraordinary onstage vitality, the Dreamers came into being in 1959. With bass guitarist Peter Birrell and drummer Bernard Dwyer were guitarists Crewsdon, who doubled on harmonica, and Derek Quinn, from Allan Clarke and Graham Nash's Fourtones. From the common bedrock of *Kansas City, Money* and other numbers everybody did sprang their trademark comedy routines. Among their antics were trouser-dropping, random sketches, can-can kicks, slapstick, amateur acrobatics and an element of lip-trembling, doe-eyed pathos that some found endearing. Any loose ends were firmly tied in the hothouse emergency of a club residency in Hamburg where Garrity's 'just a minute!' catch phrase originated.

For aspiring pop stars, they were a weird bunch. Apart from podgy bruiser Pete Birrell, there was Dwyer's passing resemblance to television's oily Coronation Street lothario, Mike Baldwin; Crewsdon's perpetual sunglasses doing little to soften his dour shiftiness; and Quinn, the best looker of the lot, blighted with premature baldness. Finally, there was spindly, four-eyed Freddie — the chap who got sand kicked in his face by beach bullies. A hybrid of Frank Spencer and Buddy Holly, he was once described as 'the sort of pop star you wouldn't mind your girl friend liking'.

Waiting in the wings of showbusiness, Freddie had kept the wolf from the door as a mechanic, a brush salesman and, ultimately, a milkman. Legend has it that, delivering pints one morning, he learnt from a radio announcement that the BBC's Manchester studios were holding auditions for local talent that very afternoon. Taking fate by the hand, Garrity immediately rounded up the Dreamers and thrashed the rattling milk float to the television centre. There, the group were rewarded with a smattering of TV appearances which led to a Columbia recording contract in May 1963.

A Merseybeat stage favourite, *If You Gotta Make a Fool of Somebody*, that the Beatles had included in their Cavern set, was an obvious choice for the first venture to the Top 50 interior. Freddie himself preferred the James Ray original of 1961, but this singalong R'n'B opus was well-suited to his Gerry-Marsden-with-a-hernia voice and the tempo of the Dreamers' act. Ten years later, Ron Wood and Keith Richard weren't above reviving it, while Rod Stewart affectionately high-stepped it Freddie-style at a London show at the Kilburn Gaumont State. However, all Freddie needed was a THANK YOUR LUCKY STARS TV spot on May 21st 1963 for his clowning to sleepwalk the record to Number 3 by mid-summer, beating off a rival version by Buddy Britton and the Regents.

On its way down, it collided with the follow-up, *I'm Telling You Now*, which went one better, aided by a strong flip, *What Have I Done to You* (penned by former Raindrop Johnny Worth, who had earlier done wonders for Adam Faith). The A-side resulted from a collaboration between Garrity and another professional songwriter Mitch Murray, who had been responsible for Gerry and the Pacemakers' first two Number Ones. Murray alone came up with Freddie's third smash, *You Were Made for Me*, which, over Christmas, also shot to Number 2. The Beatles apart, Freddie Garrity, for just one incredible moment, ruled British pop.

*Ready Freddie Go (*left to right*) Roy Crewsdon, Mike Quinn, 'Frantic' Freddie Garrity, Bernie Dwyer and Pete Birrell yuk it up for their admirers in 1964.*

With the New Year, the Yuletide Lord of Misrule could not stay the onslaughts of newcomers like Dave Clark, the Stones and the Animals. Over the next twelve months, Freddie and his funsters declined to also-rans in UK chart stakes, hovering 'twixt 12 and 20. A major problem was that their releases, though still catchy, sounded similar in style and content to the man in the street; they were all medium-paced Merseybeat exercises. It was possible to predict, for instance, exactly when the half-verse guitar break would occur. Significantly, their most successful disc during this fidgety retreat was a treatment of the Four Tunes' *I Understand* — a slow, sentimental ballad. Quoting

Auld Lang Syne in counterpoint, it temporarily restored the band to the Top 10 as Britain slept off 1964's Christmas dinner. That it was presented without a trace of humour demonstrated the limits of the group's knockabout japing (though, lest we forget, Freddie introduced the Pogo on a crowded READY STEADY GO dance floor some twelve years before it was popularised by the late Mr. Vicious). As the countdown to 1965 crept closer, Garrity and his Dreamers in funny hats mimed an earlier hit on the programme. Inspired perhaps by the self-immolation of Charlie Parker, Freddie stopped pretending to sing, electing instead to stuff paper streamers into his mouth.

A more appropriate setting for this idiocy was in pantomime, where the group had made its debut in 1963 at Chester as jesters in the Royalty Theatre's production of CINDERELLA. After *Thou Shalt Not Steal* terminated their UK chart run two years later, the quintet further refined this, their natural element, by recording a larger proportion of overtly humourous material such as Ronnie Hilton's *Windmill in Old Amsterdam*, an entire album devoted to light Disney film songs, and Graham Gouldman's *Susan's Tuba*, which sold two million in France in 1969. When the band wound up circa 1970, it seemed fitting that, with Pete Birrell, Freddie should land on his feet in children's television — chiefly as general factotum of Independent Television's LITTLE BIG TIME.

Not surprisingly, the Dreamers and Freddie had accepted more film work than many of their less visual contemporaries. Apart from a cameo role in JUST FOR YOU (a 'parade of top pop singers' also starring the Applejacks and A Band of Angels among others), they performed *Sally Anne* and the Hollywood Argyles' *Short Shorts* (with inevitable downfall of same) in WHAT A CRAZY WORLD with Joe Brown and Marty Wilde. More thespian talents were displayed in EVERYDAY'S A HOLIDAY (retitled SEASIDE SWINGERS in the USA) in which, as holiday camp chefs, Freddie and his mates shone with *What's Cooking*, a six-minute kitchen sink mini-opera anticipating the Who's *A Quick One* by three years. In 1965, a short, *Cuckoo Patrol*, was banned in some American states for allegedly belittling the Boy Scout movement.

As his hit parade fortunes subsided at home, the New World belatedly went as nuts over Freddie (as it would over Benny Hill's saucy inanities fifteen years later). In the few months of 1965 that were his before a new messiah held sway, Garrity was king of North America. The twenty month old *I'm Telling You Now* sliced to Number One in the Hot 100 as a wire through cheese. Twist paladin Chubby Checker cashed in quick with *Do the Freddie* which the lad himself also took to the USA Top 20. The former Red Sock's grinning mug was omnipresent on TV while box office returns for his concerts were astronomical. However, with the spread of another Mancunian pestilence, 'Hermania', Freddie and the Dreamers became as old hat as they had long been in fair Albion.

As his name was announced by Alan Freeman on a 1982 edition of the Channel Four television nostalgia programme, UNFORGETTABLE, Freddie cleared his throat as the faithful Pete counted in the young recruits for whom the Big Beat was only a dim recollection. Looking pretty much the same as he did in 1963, 'Frantic' Freddie turned on the catherine wheel eyes and bounded onstage to jack-knife and leap through *I'm Telling You Now* — not forgetting to insert his little 'just a minute!' somewhere along the line.

Barron-Knights Hold Court

The birthplace of eighteenth century radical politician John Wilkes, the market town of Leighton Buzzard also cradled the Barron-Knights who, with the exception of latecomers like the Scaffold and the Bonzo Dog Doo-Dah Band, were the only beat group to score big hits with records specifically designed to be funny, all medleys comprising take-offs, with new lyrics, of current favourites. Notably less successful were any deviations from this model, such as a straight version of Sinatra's *It Was a Very Good Year* and the banal flower power spoof *Here Come the Bees*. It was very much a case of giving a dog a funny name, because the Knights were actually a band who could always deliver a diverting evening's entertainment far beyond the dictates of passing trends.

Originally a trio, guitarist Pete 'P'nut' Langford, bass player Barron Anthony (Antony Osmond) and singer Toni Avern were joined by drummer David Bellinger from another Bedfordshire group, the Wanted Five. In 1961, with Avern better employed in a managerial capacity, an additional guitarist Jud Hopkins (replaced by Butch Baker) and vocalist Duke d'Mond (Richard Palmer) were added. The latter's name was originally emphasised in the billing as he was fundamentally front man to a backing group until a more democratic policy evolved. Possibly d'Mond was sensitive about his non-instrumental role, as in subequent publicity snaps he often contrived to clutch a harmonica or minor percussion instrument to counteract this impression.

Within two years, the Knights became a hard-working professional outfit with bookings as far afield as Basildon and Swindon as well as a Hamburg season. A key venue on this southern England circuit was the nearer California Ballroom, Dunstable, where they frequently appeared with the Dave Clark Five — cordial encounters which had an incidental bearing on the Knights' future career. To a repertoire of popular hits such as Gene Chandler's *Duke of Earl*, the Dixie Cups' *What a Guy*, and Mel Tormé's *Comin' Home Baby*, was introduced an increasing element of comedy less crass than that of Freddie and the Dreamers though, as in the case of the Manchester mob, jealous hard cases were less likely to regard a group making monkeys of themselves as rivals for female favours. This was also why other bands were happy to employ them as support acts; the Beatles did so at their Finsbury Park Astoria Special with the Fourmost in 1963. Nevertheless, a testimonial for the Knights' polished stage act came from one noted

Rick Huxley of the Dave Clark Five deputised as a Barron-Knight during a two-month hospitalisation of Barron Anthony in 1971. His passing resemblance to Anthony allowed any technical breaches of contract to pass unnoticed.

Pop! Go The Barron-Knights: there is strong suspicion that much of the 'live' banter on the debut L.P. of (left to right) Langford, Anthony, Ballinger, d'Mond and Baker was beefed up with canned audience reaction, courtesy of Lansdowne studios.

dance hall lout who, after seeing them in Aylesbury, was inspired to 'get a worthwhile guitar and really work at it'. Eventually, Bill Wyman became bass guitarist in an even more famous group.

Coincidentally, it was the Rolling Stones' future co-manager, London agent Eric Easton, who helped procure the Knights' record contract with Columbia. However, the first two Columbia releases, Langford's *Jo-Ann* in 1963 and a revival of H.B. Barnum's *Peanut Butter* in January 1964; both failed to click. The clincher arrived in July when the marathon *Call Up the Groups* — based on The Four Preps *Big Draft* — marched to Number 3 after a sensational READY STEADY GO preview. Among those aurally caricatured were Wyman's Stones, the Searchers and, played by petite P'nut, Freddie Garrity. In the States, the Bachelors' bit was replaced by a send-up of the better-known Animals.

The Knights had three more palpable hits, *Pop Go the Workers*, *Merry Gentle Pops* and *Under New Management*, all returning to but not quite capturing

their earlier vision. Less major were the prim *Come to the Dance*, at No. 42 in the afterglow of the first smash, and *An Olympic Record* which ran to No. 35 in 1968. The remainder of their singles went adrift in the vinyl oceans though a brace of E.P.'s sold well.

The most precise representation of the band's modus operandi was encapsulated on their debut L.P. The Man of the Moment was Pete Langford who, as well as singing lead on a verbal warping of the standard *Heart* (re-titled *Skin*) from US comedian Allan Sherman, provided all four group originals. These varied from the country flavoured *Come Back* to the chiming beat-ballad *Don't Call Me* which would have been a good A-side for anyone but those roly-poly 'Baron-Nits'. The L.P.'s closer, the folky *Where Are You Going* featured a remarkable guitar break by Baker via Hank Marvin. Butch also home-spun a Woody Guthrie monologue with much acoustic fretboard twiddling that would have made him the toast of any folk club. The ubiquitous Mitch Murray got his oar in with his leguminous *Beetroot Song* which, owing much to Harry Champion, would have wowed 'em in the States had it been sung by Herman Noone instead of Duke d'Mond.

Despite valiant attempts, the Knights could not free themselves from the categorical chains imposed by those who bought their ephemeral medleys and enjoyed the concert skylarks and patter. Audience expectation was such that had they ever cut the cackle for more than five minutes, things would have turned nasty. It was hardly unexpected that every one of their latter day recordings yukked it up as they built up considerable goodwill in supper club cabaret, where good comedy always commanded substantial fees. In 1977, they returned to the charts with *Live in Trouble* followed by *A Taste of Aggro* a year later. Further proof of the power of persistence came when a gold album, NIGHT GALLERY, and a TV series accumulated more loot for them than all their 1960s smashes put together. With the business still centred in Leighton Buzzard, Anthony, Baker, Bellinger, Langford and d'Mond entered the 1980s laughing all the way to the bank.

Rockin' Berries in Town

Not laughing quite so loud were the Rockin' Berries. (In June 1984, they played a Bingo Hall in Reading where the Knights wouldn't be seen dead!) Mind you, the Berries hadn't got lucky with a weighty CBS Records deal; their last hit *The Water is Over My Head* flowed out of the Top 50 after a mere fortnight in 1966. Though shades of comedy had always been present in their act, it wasn't intended as the Berries' bread and butter. In their day, the group produced some of the most credible disc offerings of all 1960s bands who ended up in variety.

As the name implied, they were steeped in classic rock of the Berry-Vincent-Lewis-Presley genre. Formed in Birmingham in 1971, the Berries — vocalist Clive Lea, guitarists Chuck Botfield and Geoff Turton, drummer Terence Bond and Roy Austin on bass — spent much of the next two years in Germany, augmented with a pair of saxophonists. Metamorphosing from boys to men, the band dropped the horns on their return to native soil to chance their musical arms with Decca. With the firm's publicity division in somnolence, the first two singles, one a version of James Ray's *Itty Bitty Pieces*, were goners.

Disillusioned, the Berries waited almost a year before trying again with *I Didn't Mean To Hurt Her* which began a more rewarding relationship with Piccadilly Records. Grazing the charts, this attractive outing was nipped in the bud at No. 43 when the follow-up, the more commercial *He's In Town* was rushed out to combat the Tokens' threatening original on R.C.A.

Touring the UK supporting P.J. Proby, the Berries had met Hollywood producer Kim 'B. Bumble' Fowley, who suggested this throbbing sob-story as a surefire hit for some enterprising fellows. This judgement proved correct; it elicited screams in the Berries' next round-Britain trek of the year with Manfred Mann. Shrouded in chanting harmony, Turton's falsetto rather than Lea's grittier baritone carried *He's In Town* to Number 3 by the close of 1964.

The band intended to follow it with *Funny How Love Can Be*, written for them by the Ivy League but, inexplicably, Piccadilly vetoed this idea in favour of a safe revival of Jack Scott's *What in the World's Come Over You* from 1960. All right, so this got to Number 23 but the Berries must have eaten their hearts out as the League's rejected song orbited into the Top 10. Nevertheless, paradise was regained in June 1965 when a superior cover of USA combo the Reflections' *Poor Man's Son*, with low Lea and high Turton sharing

vocal honours, made Number 5. This piece was also distinguished by an unusual skipping guitar section enchancing the backing vocals, which sometimes broke into suitable toiling grunts.

Though their debut L.P., IN TOWN, cruised the backstreets of the album lists, the end was nigh as far as the charts were concerned; two more minor entries and that was it. Fortunately, contingency plans had been laid, a panto season in Great Yarmouth being a reliable indicator of future direction. In keeping with the demure nature of their hits, opportunities could

*Wah wah woo: Rockin' Berries (*left to right*) Clive Lea, Chuck Botfield, Terry Bond, Roy Austin and Geoff Turton in mid-leap.*

have been seized to ditch the comedy. Instead, on television READY STEADY GO, the Mod audience were treated to the Berries' 'hilarious' farce of Elvis' latest hit, *Ain't That Lovin' You Baby* sung by Lea in drag as he made eyes at Turton. Their 'Rockin' nomclature didn't help either.

A move towards family entertainment was more evident on their albums, where arrangements of songs by Burl Ives, Benny Hill, George Formby and Charles Penrose (the Laughing Policeman) nestled uneasily against works by Burt Bacharach, the Lettermen and Johnny Ray, with rare uptempo concessions to trendiness — like the Dixie Cups' *Iko Iko* — tossed in for good measure. Well. . . . all this rock business wasn't going to last forever, was it? At one point, the

'Rockin'' adjective *was* plucked from the group's name. In this new field, a zenith was rapidly reached when, in 1967, the 'Berries' entertained at the Royal Command Performance.

With Turton in the hotel business (after a lucrative solo windfall in the American charts in 1969 under a pseudonym), and Lea's impressions enlivening the frolics of the Black Abbotts comedy team, Chuck Botfield was the only original Berry left at the 1984 Reading bingo club booking. In a 1983 conversation with journalist Fred Dellar, Chuck seemed a little bitter and twisted about the way things had turned out. Nonetheless, he maintained that with the right song, the Rockin' Berries could reap another vinyl harvest. Look at the Searchers. Look at the Kinks.

Fourth and Fourmost

Look at the Fourmost? Like the Berries, their recording career began earnestly enough before they started playing it for laughs though they had more than their fair share of tragedy; guitarist Mike Millward's leukemia condemned him to an early grave in 1966, four years after he joined the band when Joey Bower had (for much the same reason as Freddie Garrity left the Red Sox) declined Brian Epstein's offer of management. Bower, drummer Dave Redman and singing bass guitarist Billy Hatton had all been involved when guitarist Brian O'Hara proposed the formation of a group in 1958. Raised in the depressed Dingle suburb of Liverpool, the four youths had been impressed by the example of seventeen year old Hatton's Miles Street neighbour and ex-singing partner Ronnie Wycherley, who, in October of that year, had wormed his way onto the bill of a Larry Parnes ROCK EXTRAVAGANZA over the water in Birkenhead, and to lasting fame as 'Billy Fury'.

Though admiring this extreme strategy, O'Hara's playboys, sensibly seeing music as an exciting hobby, set the ceiling of their ambitions in local clubs, as 'the Blue Jays' — until they heard of a Scottish group of the same name. Minus pigmentation, 'the *Four* Jays' parochial reputation culminated in a respectable placing in Merseybeat's poll of 1962 for their competent but rather polite executions of American favourites like *The Girl Can't Help It*, *Respectable* and many Coasters numbers. On the way, drummer Redman had been supplanted by former architect Dave Lovelady, who had previously backed King Size Taylor.

Though he had guided the Beatles, the Big Three and other scouse acts to national stardom, Epstein's overtures to the Four Jays fell initially on deaf ears, until the majority warmed to the notion of going professional. Nevertheless, they were intelligent lads (28 General Certificate of Education examination passes between them according to publicity handouts) and, as such, appreciated the transient character of pop. With O'Hara as principal advocate, they prepared providently for a career as all-round entertainers, symbolising this policy revision by a name change to the 'Fourmosts' and then, at Brian's prompting, to the more symmetrical 'Fourmost'.

Being Liverpudlians, comedy — rather than tap dancing or knife throwing — seemed the obvious path to take. Starting in the Cavern with slick parodies of established acts like Cliff, the Vernons Girls, the Goons and old Ronnie Wycherley, this was to lead to an eight month run at the London Palladium with Cilla Black by May 1964. According to the Times correspondent, 'for sheer charm, they stole the show'. Highlights of their spot included a *September in the Rain* riddled with impersonations, *Happy Talk* (anticipating Captain Sensible by many years) and *With These Hands* in which Hatton's arms grew longer and longer.

A periodic attendant at the London Palladium Argyll Street season was another notable humourist, John Lennon who, with Paul McCartney, gave the group its first two hits. After all, the Fourmost belonged to Liverpool and Liverpool looked after them. The sprightly *Hello Little Girl* previously offered to Gerry Marsden, was taken into the Top 10 in winter 1963. Not quite as profitable in the New Year was *I'm In Love* which got stuck at Number 17 (an alternative option to this had been *It Won't Be Long*). Apart from guesting on many of their shows, later Beatle favours, particularly from McCartney, were bestowed, with Fourmost covers of *Here There and Everywhere*, *Maxwell's Silver Hammer* (overlooking *Something*) and Paul's attempt as producer to breathe life into a Fourmost treatment of *Rosetta* which lost a chart bout with Fame and Price in 1971.

In 1964, the group turned from their Beatle benefactors to composer Russell Alquist whose *A Little Lovin'* became, at Number 6, their biggest smash. As the Mersey bubble burst, the group were unfortunate in drawing attention to their origins by their portrayal of the *losers* in a battle of the bands contest in the film *Ferry Across the Mersey*. With its Panzer march tempo, *How Can I Tell Her* lost its nerve at Number 33 though a note-for-note copy of the Four Tops' *Baby I Need Your Loving* struggled to Number 24. Their Top 50 swansong, Leiber and Stoller's *Girls Girls Girls*, was an attempt at unashamed comedy via Hatton's affected lead vocal cross between Donald Duck and Frank Muir. As the New Vaudeville Band opened the floodgates on a brief craze for old tyme whimsy with *Winchester Cathedral*, the Fourmost had a go by digging up George Formby's *Aunt Maggie's Remedy*, but essentially their chart days were numbered as were, in more absolute terms, Mike Millward's and Brian Epstein's. The Fourmost, having exhausted their negligible teen appeal, teetered on the edge of the beckoning cabaret circuit. By the 1980s, each original member had left, gone to garage and decorating businesses every one.

The Fourmost prepare to mime A Little Loving *for Pathe News (*left to right) *film editor Doug Warth, Billy Hatton, Brian O' Hara, David Lovelady, cameraman Les Isaacs and Mike Millward (obit.)*

91

Sutch is Life

Finally, this discourse would not be complete without mentioning Screaming Lord Sutch and the Savages — the most famous English pop group who never had a hit. The plebian David Sutch was a Harrow plumber's mate in 1960 when he convinced a local instrumental group that, though it had been intended he should manage them, he could better serve as lead singer.

Screaming Lord Sutch believing an April Fool joke that one of his records has actually made the charts.

Within eighteen months of their first booking at a working men's club, they cut their debut single *Til the Following Night* (a vampire epic) under the supervision of Joe Meek.

Backed with an echo-chambered dash through *Good Golly Miss Molly*, this set the format for Sutch's recordings, which were to be evenly divided between straight rock'n'roll/R'n'B ravers and horror spoofs like *Dracula's Daughter*, Sutch's own composition *All Black and Hairy*, *She's Fallen in Love With the Monster Man* (revived by the Revillos in 1981) and, receiving most media attention, *Jack the Ripper*, popular on video juke boxes. *I'm a Hog For You Baby* from the Coasters was coupled with *Monster in Black Tights*, a revised *Venus in Blue Jeans*.

However, the record sales and dull singing voice of this fabled aristocrat were secondary to The Stage Act, which leaned heavily on that of black rock 'n' horror star from Ohio, Screamin' Jay Hawkins, with a nod towards the garish carryings-on of Wee Willie Harris. Described as 'something between a Viking Chief and the Wild Man of Borneo', Sutch's props included leopard skins, bull horns, coffins, monster feet and, later on, Roman chariots, togas and laurel wreaths. Moreover, his Lordship's hair was long enough to warrant splashes in Britain's more trivial newspaper tabloids well before the advent of the Stones. Hanging around with Jim Morrison at Toronto's Rock'n'Roll Revival Festival in 1969, he was galled at the slicker 'outrage' of Alice Cooper's electric chair and gallows, though the 'hellfire' of Arthur Brown and King Kurt's gross slapstick were his more direct descendants.

Like John Mayall's Bluesbreakers and Blues Incorporated, membership of the Savages was a baptism of fire for many subsequently well-known musicians including Ritchie Blackmore, Nicky Hopkins, Matthew Fisher and pianist Paul Deah (who, as 'Paul Nicholas', starred with Adam Faith and David Essex in the 1974 feature film, STARDUST). In the studio, Sutch was at times joined by 'heavy friends' Jeff Beck, Jimmy Page and Keith Moon, among other ex-Savages, who tried to rescue two Sutch L.P.'s on Atlantic in the 1970s.

His tenacity is worthy of admiration. Peddling the same old rubbish, his hitless years were punctuated by predictable but career-sustaining publicity stunts. He ran a pirate radio station. He stood for Parliament. He got engaged. He cavorted with unclothed females outside 10 Downing Street. He boarded every topical bandwagon going to become yet another British eccentric institution — a sort of rock'n'roll Mrs. Shilling.

THE ONES
IN THE
MIDDLE

The Strange Effect of Dave Berry and the Cruisers

In 1984, Dave Berry was still in the running. He'd even rated in the New Wave explosion eight years earlier when the Sex Pistols did one of his B-sides, *Don't Gimme No Lip Child* with 'all that pushin' and shovin'' Their bass player, Glen Matlock was a big Berry man, shown when his post-Pistol group, the Spectres, retrod *This Strange Effect*. Dave was also special guest of later Malcolm McLaren clients, Adam and the Ants, at the Strand Lyceum, where he brushed aside a hostile audience like matchsticks.

For most bigoted punks, the Berry stage act was as new and disquieting an experience as it had been for those who first saw it on TOP OF THE POPS in 1964. An almost unclassifiable showman, it was not enough for him to merely stand up and sing a song. A solitary searchlight would home in on fingers curling round a flat surrounded by darkness. It might take a full five minutes for Berry, once likened to a gay vampire, clothed in black, to emerge completely. As evidenced in David Bailey's Sunday Times photograph in 1982, he would then glower furtively from behind an upturned leather collar. Among other ploys brought into play were abstract hand ballets and, over an entire instrumental break, the slide of a hand mike over his shoulder to the small of his back. Inspired vaguely by Gene Vincent's crippled melodrama, the performance would have been sinister without the subtle merriment in his Oriental eyes. Below the Beatle haircut his face resembled a coquettish Chuck Connors. The perpetrator of possibly the most original stage concept of the group era, third rate traces of Berry were later observed in such diverse performers as Jim Morrison, Julie Driscoll, Alvin Stardust and Faye Fife. He even made an impression on Bob Dylan, who in a sequence in the 1965 cinema verité, DON'T LOOK BACK, is seen working out the chords to *Little Things*.

Born David Holgate Grundy in Beighton near Sheffield in 1941, he attended Woodhouse secondary school where, though other lads had football, train-spotting, and like pastimes, he would be digesting all the latest trivia from the music papers. An electric welder at eighteen, Grundy began his musical career as half of an Everly Brothers-type duo. In 1961, he assumed his stage surname when invited to front the Cruisers, who had risen from the ashes of another local combo, the Chuck Fowler R'n'B Band.

In parochial venues such as the Esquire and Mojo Clubs, Berry and the Cruisers flogged a predominantly Chicago blues repertoire, from Muddy Waters to Dave's idol, Chuck Berry. Other influences were John Lee Hooker, Billy Boy Arnold and Champion Jack Dupree (who, incidentally, took up permanent residence in nearby Halifax, Yorkshire, in 1962). The relaxed laconic singing styles of Slim Harpo and Ford 'Snooks' Eaglin also left their mark, while one of Dave's few compositions, *You're Gonna Need Somebody*, was derived from a piece by Mississippi blues legend Robert Johnson. Occasional forays into rock'n'roll included Vincent's *Get It* ('welldowelldowop — hephephep').

The Break came when Mickie Most, then a freelance talent scout, knocked out with their performance in a Doncaster club, supervised a demo taping for submission to Decca recording manager Mike Smith, who liked Dave and the group but found Most's plans for them unworkable. Smith himself occupied the producer's chair when the Cruisers and Berry signed to the label shortly afterwards. As it had taken E.M.I.'s accursed Beatles fourteen hours to cut their debut *L.P.*, Smith was aghast at the eight it took the anxious Yorkshire boys to record a cover version of *Memphis Tennessee*, with a session drummer replacing Cruiser Pete Thornton into the bargain. In future, he told them, they'd be replaced — with the obvious exception of the singer — with hired musicians quicker off the mark. The Cruisers could then learn the music off the record for live work. Apart from hurt pride, it wouldn't matter. No-one would be any the wiser. O.K. lads?

The time-saving Smith had no grumbles about the Number 19 position of *Memphis*, thirteen places behind the original by Dave's namesake, Chuck. However, when the follow-up, a gristly work-out of Arthur Crudup's *My Baby Left Me* seized up at Number 37, a change of tactics was in order. By then, the team most preferred for Berry sessions was: guitarists Big Jim Sullivan and Jimmy Page (doubling on harmonica), John Paul Jones on bass, drummer Bobbie Graham and backing vocalists the Breakaways whose Vikki Brown (wife of Joe) duetted with Dave on *Sweet and Lovely*, flip of his third release, Burt Bacharach weepie *Baby It's You* which, despite having also been covered by the Beatles, made a more hopeful Number 24.

The next two singles, *The Crying Game* and its twin, *One Heart Between Two*, heartbreak ballads by ex-teacher Geoff Stephens, were tailor-made for Dave's cartoon spookiness. The first took him into the Top 5 in September 1964 while the second battled to Number 41 three months later, but they were so similar in arrangement that it could have gone either way. Both featured fragile zither glissandos and tearful guitar legatos on which Sullivan, pulling rank on young Page, employed a volume pedal to create an unprecedented electric cello effect that the Beatles were to copy on *Yes It Is* the following year. Over this, the Rother Valley bluesman had found another voice. With all traces of Snooks Eaglin *et al.* gone, Berry's mournful baritone anticipated Bryan Ferry's more affected crooning by eight years. (Ironically, after one booking in 1978, a starstruck young lady asked Dave, in all sincerity, why he had left Roxy Music.)

By 1965, a trio led by former Sheffield city hall employee (and owner of a twin-necked Gibson), Frank White, had supplanted the original Cruisers, bar one. Still a sometime Cruiser in the 1980s, rhythm guitarist Alan Taylor had been a student at Chelsea Art College when Dave, fresh from school, used to visit him at his Earl's Court flat. During these London weekends, Grundy acquired a layman's knowledge of surrealism and related art movements that may have forged antecedents. What was certainly unusual among 1960s groups was supplementing the Cruisers' road crew with a lighting engineer. His job was to synchronise the peculiarities of each auditorium's son-et-lumiere system to Dave's stage antics, which were as predetermined as any Broadway musical. In fact, a sidetrack to Berry's career at this juncture was a major role (the Cliff Richard part) in a production of EXPRESSO BONGO for a Westgate-on-Sea theatre season. Surprisingly, Berry was given no more opportunities to develop this thespian side of his curious abilities.

Meanwhile, back in the charts, a cover of Bobby Goldsboro's *Little Things* had restored Dave to the UK Top 10 but, apart from a disinclined 1966 recording of the sentimental *Mama*, this was the last bite of that particular cherry. The withdrawal from Top 50 favour was by no means smooth. A gift from an admirer, Ray Davies (whose Kinks had premiered it on SATURDAY CLUB), *This Strange Effect*, while duplicating *My Baby Left Me*'s indifferent showing in Britain, was Holland's biggest selling disc ever. This country also brought personal joy to Berry, who met in Amsterdam his future wife, Marti, with whom he settled in the market town of Chesterfield on the edge of the Peak district in 1968.

Other honourable failures included another Goldsboro opus, *If You Wait for Love*, a Bee Gees number, *Forever*, and the most sympathetic treatment of Pete Dello's ballad *Do I Figure in Your Life*, which was as inexplicable a miss for Berry as it had been for

Dave Berry plugs Picture Me Gone *on RSG in November 1966.*

THURSDAY, NOVEMBER 15 — 8 p.m.

Swinging Sixties Show

Starring: DAVE BERRY & THE CRUISERS
RICKY VALANCE & THE VALENTINES
("Tell Laura I Love Her")
Compere: RON MARTIN
— A Superb Evening of Music & Comedy —

TICKETS: £5.50 & £5.00
— Prizes for Best 60's Costume!! —
LICENSED BAR * DANCING *FOOD AVAILABLE
Priority Booking Mon. Oct. 1. Public Booking Mon. Oct. 8

In 1984, Dave Berry recorded a radical rearrangement of the Miracles' Tracks of my Tears during a break from his cabaret schedule which included Blazers in Windsor and Camberley Civic Hall.

Dello's own band, Honeybus, in 1967. By 'Sod's Law', an inferior version by another Sheffield pop star, Joe Cocker, later elicited most interest. (Cocker's backing group contained two ex-Cruisers — one of whom joined the author's Argonauts, briefly, in 1978.)

Fuelling a growing disenchantment with Decca had been a session in which Dave found himself intoning new but equally schmaltzy words over the backing track to *Mama*. Fortunately, the cheapskate result, *Daddy*, was rejected during the company's customary Tuesday morning board meeting. Another odd decision was the issue of two Berry albums within eight weeks of each other, to the detriment of both. Rather than stay on with the old firm, Dave defected to CBS in 1970.

The lowest point of his career occurred five years later when easy-listening twosome Peters and Lee, thinking Berry was safely out of the way, had the nerve to revive *The Crying Game* — unsuccessfully I might add. By that time, Frank White and his boys were back at their Friday night residency at the Pheasant in Sheffield 5 while, with Alan and transient Cruisers, Dave derived a living from the submerged world of cabaret and nostalgia engagements where current chart standing had no meaning. Like the Searchers, Nashville Teens, and others, he had been driven to update some of his ancient smashes, the last attempt to date being in 1980 when, directed by Marmalade vocalist Sandy Newman and recording engineer Nick Horne, he shamelessly recut *The Crying Game* at Woodcray Studio, Wokingham.

In 1985, his distinguished past is still his bread-and-butter, but an abiding interest in new musical developments and the hiring of youthful backing Cruisers dismissed notions that Berry was content with any safe supper club plod. Against all odds, it is feasible that Dave Berry in his forties could once again slither back into national prominence.

Spencer Davis Goes Gear

After the London locusts had picked Liverpool and Manchester clean, that mighty Cerebus, *TV Times*, predicted that from Birmingham would arise the new Titans of Teen. However, though England's Second City housed over 200 groups in 1964, only a handful enjoyed lasting success. A latecomer amongst them was the Spencer Davis Group who were, theoretically, the least probable contenders.

Unlike the Black Country's harder selling bands led by showmen of the stature of Mike Sheridan and Carl Wayne, the Davis combo excluded current hits from a specialist repertoire unfamiliar to most of their audience. Nevertheless, the initial reaction of an early admirer, Wolverhampton vocalist Neville 'Noddy' Holder, later of Slade, is worth quoting at length: '. . . . and then this spotty kid on the organ screamed "I love the way she walks" and launched into that old John Lee Hooker number *Dimples* . . . . gosh, my mouth fell open and I felt a chill down my spine. That was the night I discovered rhythm and blues for the first time'.

The spotty kid was fifteen year old Steve Winwood who, three years earlier in 1960, had been pianist and featured singer in his elder brother Mervyn's mainstream jazz eight-piece. Sharing the brothers' taste for the differing sophistications of Roland Kirk and Count Basie, Redcar drummer Peter York was a later member, though by 1963 the band were becoming more and more attracted to the earthier sounds of the blues.

A more eclectic enthusiast was a Birmingham University German graduate called Spencer Davis, who began his showbusiness career in a Swansea Scout Gang Show at the age of sixteen. An able 12-string guitarist, he regularly occupied a short solo spot in a trad jazz band at the Golden Lion in West Bromwich, which is where he became friendly with York and the Winwoods. When the jazz residency finished, Davis was asked to stay on as main attraction. Not confident about sustaining interest for a whole evening, he approached Pete, Mervyn ('Muff') and Steve for a semi-professional musical merger.

Unassuming and economically equipped, they began as 'the Rhythm and Blues Quartet' before settling ultimately for 'the Spencer Davis Group' in April 1963 (the punchy juxtaposition of an unusual forename with a common surname having subliminal magnetism as in 'Lorne Green', 'Reinhardt Skinner' or 'Powers Boothe'). Despite the distinction granted to Davis, the Group's major assets were the younger Winwood's multi-instrumental talents and instinctive feel for American negro vocal stylings, which quickly acquired a more personal timbre. As their reputation grew, it became customary for their billing to be extended with the phrase 'featuring Steve Winwood'; the Group affirmed this prominence in song titles like *Stevie's Blues, Goodbye Stevie* and the more obscure *Stevie's Groove*.

Throughout their four year existence, the quartet rarely ventured outside R'n'B which in their terms ranged from rock'n'roll to the country blues, via soul and gospel. Though similarly motivated acts such as the Stones and Small Faces used the same frame of reference, the Spencer Davis Group displayed a tighter, more polished attack behind Steve's controlled agonising or the blander tones of Spencer himself. As well as cutting worthier versions of American numbers simultaneously covered by lesser artists, they also dared to record material less assured rivals would shun, such as *When a Man Loves a Woman*, issued within three months of black soul star Percy Sledge's original, as well as anticipating the late 1960s Blues Boom with a rendition of *Dust My Broom* from Elmore James. But the consolidation, rather than development, of these abilities caused the loss of direction that exacerbated their demise in 1967.

Following a necessary advancement to London's club circuit in mid-1963, an atmospheric Thursday night performance at the Flamingo so impressed Decca recording manager and blues fanatic Mike Vernon that the Group were invited to tape a five-track demo under his supervision. Though Decca rejected this session, the band came home to roost soon after when producer Chris Blackwell signed them to Fontana under a lease deal with his fledgling Island company.

At this point, the Group went professional after a letter of resignation from York was unaccepted. His trepidation about his old-fashioned but competent mode of drumming was unfounded, as it added much to the band's individuality. With Pete toiling over his kit, the debut A-side choice was the same song that had awed young Holder — *Dimples*.

Nevertheless, they were obliged to wait until their next release for even the most minor Top 50 excursion. However, the driving intensity of *I Can't Stand It* (originally by portly gospel duo, the Soul Sisters) was outdistanced by *Every Little Bit Hurts*, a contrasting downbeat ballad which crept to a less modest No. 41. This showing was aided by the Group's miming in the B-feature film POP GEAR, as well as a more dramatic live television outing on READY STEADY GO (Steve's pimply face shrouded in shadow).

Spencer Davis's German studies were put to good use in the Fatherland with his lead vocal on the group's medley single of Walter Kollo's Der War in Schöneberg *and the traditional* Mädel ruck-ruck-ruck. *On the set of the feature film* THE GHOST GOES GEAR *are (*left to right*) Spencer, Steve Winwood, actress Carol White — filling in for Pete York — and Muff Winwood.*

Though the uptempo *Strong Love* served as a chart holding operation, the band came into its own more obliquely when their first L.P.'s healthy placing in the album lists demonstrated that mediocre singles sales were merely a surface manifestation of a deeper groundswell of support beyond the fickle adolescent majority. But, the Sixth Form market apart, the Spencer Davis Group, unlike John Mayall or Alexis Korner, still aspired towards the hit parade. After much deliberation, their next two 45's, *Keep On Running* and *Somebody Help Me*, both satisfied this desire with a vengeance by racing to Number One in the first half of 1966. The band was presented to the screaming teenage patrons of 1965's Christmas edition of THANK YOUR LUCKY STARS, and during their tour supporting the Stones. The plain four-to-the-bar rhythm of *Keep On Running*, enhanced by gimmicky blackboard-scraping fuzz box, was soon wafting from hip London boutiques as well as factories in Redditch. Radio Caroline even worked its seven beat ostinato into a station call sign. Weathering the foreseen accusations of 'selling out', the Group continued to notch up huge hits for the next two years.

Responsible for much of this was the fresh approach

of new American producer Jimmy Miller and, inaugurally, West Indian composer Jackie Edwards. Both of these men, speedily identifying Steve Winwood as the main chance, became the Boy Wonder's songwriting collaborators. Miller later persuaded Steve to sing incognito with his studio band, the Anglos.

The Winwoods had politely declined a request to rearrange some hymns in a modern idiom by their local vicar, but other more appropriate extra-mural activities included Spencer and Steve's production of *Elbow Baby* by London trio the Habits, as well as 'the Powerhouse', a band recorded after-hours at the Marquee consisting of Pete and Steve with Paul Jones, Jack Bruce and Eric Clapton, plus road manager Ben Palmer on piano.

Back on the mother ship, the operation was still running smoothly. Though Jackie and Steve's *When I Come Home* hadn't been quite the smash expected, the Group jumped back into the Top 5 in November 1966 with *Gimme Some Lovin'* in which heavy percussion, monotonal bass and growling organ heightened the tension of Steve's amorous demands. That the Rhythm and Blues Quartet had turned into pop stars was further instanced as they entertained the brats on BBC TV's CRACKERJACK and lip-synched another hit while floating on a raft in the film comedy, THE GHOST GOES GEAR.

On the Continent, they were even more popular, especially in the vital German market, and by 1967, the USA was calling them. Before Miller and Winwood's *I'm a Man* barged up the Hot 100, many American radio listeners were unsure of the Group's skin pigmentation, so precise were Steve's intonations. European youth were likewise confused when *I Can't Stand It* crackled from Radio Luxembourg nearly three years earlier; but over the Atlantic, where the subject of race was of stronger sensitivity, there were airplay problems until the Group's Caucasian ancestry was confirmed by a TV appearance. The veneration they commanded in the States was such that Monkee Micky Dolenz regarded an impending meeting with Davis as akin to an audience with the Pope, exclaiming to *Melody Maker*, 'Spencer Davis wants to see me!?'

Though inevitable eventually, it was unfortunate for Spencer that Steve chose this time to hand in his notice. As the Group's star turn — singer, lead guitarist, keyboard player and composer — he felt that his growth as a musician would be stifled unless he started playing with friends of his own age. Beginning with the formation of Traffic, subsequent events were to prove this judgement to be correct.

A second blow fell with brother Mervyn's departure

*Steve Winwood's Traffic included two members of this Worcester band The Hellians, Jim Capaldi (*first left*) and Dave Mason (*middle*).*

to Island's executive body. Nevertheless, Davis and York rallied by recruiting guitarist Philip Sawyer from the Cheynes, whom they'd first noticed playing at the Bag o' Nails club, and session bass player, Charles McCracken. Their trump card was Dulwich organist and singer Eddie Hardin from A Wild Uncertainty who approximated pretty closely to the Winwood precedent. The songwriting team of Davis, Sawyer and Hardin generated two small hits in the fanciful *Time Seller*, with surging cellos, and the lesser *Mr. Second Class*. With a stronger orientation towards pure pop, it seemed that old Spence would keep his head above water after all.

1967 ended with an ersatz Davis-Winwoods-York reunion in the soundtrack of Hunter Davies' HERE WE GO ROUND THE MULBERRY BUSH film, which alternated tracks by the new Davis group and Traffic, as well as a Steve Winwood composition *Waltz for Caroline* (alias *Waltz for Lumumba*) by the original four who used to stun 'em at the Golden Lion in 1963.

The Legend of Dave Dee, Dozy, Beaky, Mick and Tich

From the agricultural cathedral city of Salisbury came Dave Dee and the Bostons. Chosen from local rockers in 1958 by singer and ex-country dance band accordionist, David 'Dave Dee' Harman, the Bostons (after the haircut) were guitarists John 'Beaky' Dymond and Ian 'Tich' Amey, with bass guitarist Trevor 'Dozy' Davies and a succession of drummers, until Mick Wilson joined permanently as the decade turned. (While a semi-professional musician, Harman as a police cadet was on station duty nearby on that fateful April night in 1960 when Gene Vincent and Eddie Cochran met their tragic car crash at Chippenham. Dave was responsible for Cochran's belongings, including his guitar, until their shipment back to the States.)

The Bostons' stamping ground was mainly the Swindon-Southampton-Salisbury triangle, with a repertoire of current smashes and classic rock. They also rehearsed their own songs, usually by Dave, Beaky and Dozy, many of which found their way onto the B-sides of their 1960s smashes. One that didn't was a Harman composition circa 1960 that, by chance, sounded almost identical to *Da Da Da*, a 1981 hit by Trio, a German group produced by Klaus Voorman (who twenty years earlier had been cultivating the friendship of the Beatles during their residency at the Kaiserkeller).

Not all Hamburg's Grosse Freiheit's imported pop talent was Liverpudlian. *Merseybeat*, in fact, reported in November 1962 that the Star Club was concerned about customer complaints that if you'd heard one Scouse group, you'd heard 'em all. From further afield came the likes of Bristol's Johnny Carr and the Cadillacs, the Graduates from distant South Africa and, via France, Vince Taylor and his Playboys. In Hampshire, Wiltshire and Somerset (home of Acker Bilk) the trad jazz stranglehold on many venues also caused Dave and his Bostons to migrate to Hamburg in 1962.

It was a season at the Top Ten club that made them, transforming a clumsy West Country group into a peerless live act and potential chart proposition. In an atmosphere of frenetic gaiety, the Wiltshire boys' informal clowning evolved into stylized semi-vaudeville routines, and it quickly became apparent how much visiting English-speaking servicemen enjoyed Dave Harman's rich store of dirty jokes. More important, they became celebrated exponents of the pounding *mak schau* beat which, especially when emphasised by Dave's tambourine,

Tich and Dave Dee during a rehearsal on RSG, 1966.

was regarded as a try at an Anglicised Tamla sound. As Dee, himself, reflected from a Magnet Records office in 1982, 'when you've been through your entire repertoire twice in one evening, you have to start improvising'.

On their return to England and a more promising date schedule, they were a hard act to follow, as became painfully clear to the then-chartriding Honeycombs who were blown off at a Swindon booking in 1964 by their ludicrously-named support band (on a night's leave from a Butlin's residency). Because of past disappointments, Dave Dee, Dozy, Beaky, Mick and Tich were bemused when Ken Howard and Alan Blaikley, Honeycombs' managers, offered to take them on too.

Erstwhile BBC employees Blaikley and Howard's combined business and song-writing acumen proved ideal for the pop field. Securing a Fontana record contact for Dave and the lads, they were to steer them to spectacular success, writing all thirteen of their best-selling singles. In 1966, the team gained more UK chart entries than anyone else including the precious Beatles.

Yet, despite startling TV appearances on READY STEADY GO, the first two 45's missed. *No Time*, issued in January 1965, was a curious waltz featuring whistling and Teutonic overtones, while *All I Want*, though a ballad, was nearer to what they were to become. All the same, the third attempt had to make or break it.

You Make It Move, helped by a strong B-side in *I*

Can't Stop (first recorded by the Honeycombs for the US market) made the Top 50 for seven weeks though only reaching a modest No. 26. However, 1966's first effort, *Hold Tight*, with its football chant rhythm and trendy fuzz guitar, squeezed in at a giddy Number 4, precipitating three fat years for the quintet and their mentors which may be neatly split into two periods. The first consisted of singles cut by the group alone in which Howard and Blaikley's raw songs were often drastically rearranged via instrumental experiments like Dave's frequent rhythm guitar, Tich's balalaika on *Okay* and Beaky's latin percussion on *Save Me*. From another trial-and-error rehearsal came the accelerating tempo of *Bend It*.

The extravagant ideas of their producer and ex-Hollywood actor, Steve 'Battle of the Bulge' Rowland, became most prominent after *Touch Me Touch Me* fought shy of the Top 10. It became necessary to try a different approach by supplementing the basic personnel with girlie choruses, brass bands, sound effects and string sections. This changed, say, *Zabadak* from nursery rhyme drivel to a lush desert island sound painting anticipating Lennon's *Sun King* by four years. Strategically released straight after 1967s hot flower power summer, it swept effortlessly into the Top 3.

Most consider *Zabadak* and its two chart successors to be the organisation's most inspired phase, though much of it was executed in a very

*The Windsor Whip Woman, 1984 (*left to right*) Tich, a member of the audience, John 'Mick' Hatchman, Dave Dee and Dozy.*

slap-dash manner. Apart from backing vocals and whip noises (an empty beer bottle zoomed down a fretboard while two bits of plywood were smacked together), *The Legend of Xanadu* was recorded live in the last half hour of an otherwise chaotic afternoon session with a novice engineer.

Promoted with costume drama rather than the old comic capers, the buccaneer spectre of Johnny Kidd, for example, pervaded the publicity angle of *The Wreck of the 'Antoinette'*. The earthy patter had also been moderated in deference to screaming, unhearing female audiences of 1966 as well as criticism from *New Musical Express* moralists. Later artistes such as Roxy Music, Adam Ant, Ten Pole Tudor and even, by his own admission, Jon Anderson (of Accrington's Warriors and later Yes) borrowed from Dave Dee spectaculars from this period.

Geared for the singles market, the group's three L.P.'s tended to be regarded as collections of individual tracks rather than complete entities, padded as they are with A- and B-sides in no logical order. Spotlighting the diverse talents of group members other than Dave Dee, Dymond sings lead on *Nose for Trouble*, for instance, while Amey tries *Mama Mama*. To avoid the regurgitation of Reeperbahn favourites, they relied principally on professional songwriting teams as well as, to a diminishing extent, their own compositions such as the schoolboy howler, *Master Llewellyn*. Though some of these songs were rattled off at the end of the day, there were remarkable moments like the psychedelics of *The Sun Goes Down* and Tich's Hendrix touch on *Shame*. Little sacrificing of

musical effect for comedy was employed, though D.J. Dave Cash introduced the group on their eponymous debut album in inimitable style.

Outside Britain, fortune smiled in almost all territories. Everywhere that is, except the most vital — the USA, where only *Bend It*, *Zabadak* and *Run Colorado* worked up even moderate sales. They'd simply arrived about a year too late for the British Invasion, in which people like Herman and Freddie had shone. Indeed, by 1969, ideas were running out anyway as in the case of *Don Juan*, a desperate recycle of the *Xanadu* blueprint, which got its face slapped at No. 23.

It was not unexpected when Dave Dee officially inaugurated his solo career that same year. As a self-confessed 'frustrated actor', he'd had a TV spot as Caliban in THE TEMPEST as well as entering the living world of literature with an advice column in *Fabulous*. While he followed an easy-listening route, the rest of the crew as 'DBMT' probed a new 'progressive music' audience. Before petering out after one minor chart entry each, both factions encountered the same basic difficulty — nobody was ready to disconnect either of them from their previous incarnation thus requiring DBMT *and* Dave Dee to start again from scratch.

In 1974, they regrouped to resume their recording career on a more modest scale with the ballad *She's My Lady*, issued on Antik, where Dave had channelled his skills into record management. By the 1980s a fuller reformation was well under way, minus Mick who, by then, was proprietor of a driving school back in Salisbury. Replacing him with another local lad, John Hatchman, Dave Dee, Dozy, Beaky and Tich, more favourite uncles than admired elder brothers these days, have brought back much of the comedy though, as they prove time after time in the night spots of the world, they are still able to rock as hard as the best of them. For their propagation of both harmless amusement and Dick Dauntless epics, they will always be remembered (like their blood brothers, the Troggs) as the Unthinking Man's Pop Group, and there is no shame in that title.

The Ballad of Georgie Fame and the Blue Flames

Clive Powell was born in the small Lancashire town of Leigh, which was to be lost in the encroaching industrial connurbation of Greater Manchester. His father was a cotton manufacturer's employee, distinguished by his ability on the piano accordion. Eager to formalise his seven year old son's interest in music, Mr. Powell arranged for Clive to take piano lessons but it became clear that the boy found this regime tiresome. When the dark cloud of daily practice no longer loomed, little Clive confirmed early promise by progressing on the instrument at his own pace, having acquired the rudiments of harmony. As well as singing in the Church choir until his voice broke, Clive, by no means a bookish child, absorbed a hidden curriculum in his mastery of the harmonica and his ingenuity in making castanets from scraps of old slate.

At Secondary Modern in 1954, a friend of his elder sister showed him the basics of boogie-woogie piano. After a few uncomfortable hours sweating over its finger-twisting left hand, Clive became as well-known for his 'jazzy' musical skill as the school bully and football captain were in their chosen areas.

Favouring the ambulatory shuffle of Fats Domino, who he had heard sporadically on BBC Radio's Light Programme, Clive named his first group 'The Dominoes'. At sixteen, he took a giant step towards a musical career when the band won a Butlin's talent contest at Pwllheli in South Wales. One of the judges was drummer Rory Blackwell, founder of one of the first UK rock'n'roll groups. Before the holiday week was out, Powell had joined Blackwell's London-based combo as pianist and featured singer. Out of earshot from Merseybeat's distant thunder, London seemed a better bet for Clive than a supposed wasted life in the social clubs and buffalo lodges up North. He was not to return home to Leigh in a professional capacity until 1966.

Initially, Powell lived in a flat with Laurie Jay and other toga-clad members of Nero and the Gladiators. With funds supplemented by odd jobs such as modelling, the rent was paid by the Blackwell band's season at an Islington ballroom. An acquaintance, composer Lionel Bart, recommended Rory's new find to Britain's foremost pop impressario Larry Parnes, who always began by renaming his proteges after some emotional facet — Marty *Wilde*, Johnny *Gentle*, Dickie *Pride*, Nelson *Keen* . . . . Discovering that his original choice had already been taken by Pye's Lance Fortune, Parnes rechristened Clive Powell, 'Georgie Fame'.

However, when 'Georgie's' humble solo spot on one of his new manager's BIG BEAT SHOWS was not immediately impressive, a contingency plan was formulated. Why not create a band under Georgie's leadership to back another Lancashire lad, Billy Fury?

Fame vamped triplets behind Fury for two years until the band, the Blue Flames, was superceded by the more robust Tornados in 1961. Fame, with bass guitarist Ray Slade and drummer Red Reece, worked US air bases before being approached by promoter John Gunnell and his songwriting brother Richard to get a bigger band together for a residency at their London Soho club, the Flamingo.

From September 1962, it soon became evident that Georgie was no longer the rock'n'roller he'd never been. He'd ditched the pumping piano for the warmer sounds of a Hammond organ which had set him back £825 (a fortune in days when a ten bob note was considered an adequate consolation prize in a TV quiz).

On his new keyboard, he was in a Jimmy Smith bag, fired by the Blue Flames rhythmic undercurrent. He'd also been listening to James Brown, Ray Charles, the Impressions and, most markedly, Mose Allison. From specialist record shops in the close proximity of Wardour Street came his most idiosyncratic influence, a massive injection of various shades of West Indian musics — ska, bluebeat etc. — which would amalgamate into the primeval atom of reggae by 1967 before fragmenting again. Under the sophisticated stylistic umbrella called 'Rockhouse', these tributaries flowed through Fame's smooth 'coloured' husk of a voice, incapable of taking too many harmonic risks.

While the art school mob and weekend dropouts headed for darkest Ealing and the gutbucket hollering of Blues Incorporated, Georgie Fame and the Blue Flames attracted a cooler, sharper bohemian, usually from a lower social caste (who would later coarsen under the general label of 'Mod'). Even in 1962, Flamingo regulars could identify each other by the neat, short haircut and a changeable dress sense, often sporting gear that only West Indians, G.I.'s on a pass, or homosexuals would be seen dead in — slim-hipped jackets, narrow lapels, tab collars, parallel strides — Italian one week, Ivy League the next, Frenchified the week after that. Preparing themselves for the night, they would be listening to the Dansette ambience of modern jazz or the hipper blackness of soul or bluebeat.

Not only was Fame's music made for this audience but his clean, short-haired image and perpetual Madras drape was sympathetic; no doubt because he was so intense about his music, he had little time to keep up with clothes. Just like a musician but you gotta respect a bloke like that, even if you can't really beat the Americans. A 1965 drug bust only deepened his coolness. Relaxing, he might stroll down the nearby Crazy Elephant, where he could be prevailed upon to jam with Rufus Thomas, the Animals or whoever else was around that night. He took to carrying a melodica in his pocket for that very purpose. With Zoot Money's tutoring, he'd also become a proficient rhythm guitarist. In 1964, he was the only white singer in a round-Britain Motown review.

Early recognising Georgie as the group's X-factor, the Gunnells' management agreement covered only him, leaving the nebulous Blue Flames to their own devices. Usually consisting of Fame plus a horn and rhythm section, with congas as icing, among those who served time in the band were guitarists John McLaughlin and Colin Green, as well as drummers Jon Hiseman and Mitch Mitchell, while Tony Makin replaced bassist Ray Slade, who turned up in the Alan Price Set in 1965. Another notable percussionist was conga player Speedy Acquaye (whose patois inspired McCartney's *Ob La Di Ob La Da*).

After two narrowly-circulated independent singles, Rik Gunnell delivered Georgie to Columbia in summer 1963. Instead of the expected debut single, recording manager Ian Samwell made the surprising suggestion that an atmospheric live album from the Flamingo would make more sense. Giorgio Gomelsky was already talking about doing one with his Yardbirds a stone's throw away at the Marquee Club. It was worth a shot.

The Flamingo wasn't the Harlem Apollo; neither was Fame a James Brown, but the recording of September 25th 1963 stands up as more than a mere period documentary. There is often much false bonhomie on live L.P.'s but the genuinely enthusiastic clientele lend an inspirational framework for the Blue Flames to power through a streamlined but representative set, the most conspicuous soloists being session guitarist Big Jim Sullivan and tenor saxophonist Mick Eve. With the expected hat trick of Mose Allison numbers were known crowd-pleasers like *Let the Good Times Roll* and *You Can't Sit Down* as well as the samba outing, *Eso Beso*. Acceding to a bawled request, Georgie introduced a token ska number, *Humpty Dumpty*, in his lingering Manchester twang before singing it in an accurate West Indian dialect. This summed up the record very well. Nevertheless, LIVE AT THE FLAMINGO was innovative in that it anticipated 'jazz-rock' by at least five years.

However, Fame was to wait in the wings for over a year after this before making any chart headway. Overlooking the more commercial *Shop Around* on the B-side, Columbia extracted Rufus Thomas' *Do the Dog* as a single. Though its passionate drive transcended the stupid words and indifferent live recording quality, "the Dog" didn't have its day. Another misguided marketing exercise was *Do Re Mi* backed by the superior reptilian crawl of Booker T. Jones' *Green Onions*, which became Fame's concert theme (to which he later added perfunctory lyrics).

Working on several fronts, Georgie devoted an E.P. each to two of them. As well as the self-explanatory RHYTHM AND BLUEBEAT, there was FATS FOR FAME, an affectionate tribute to his old idol with *Blue Monday* as principal selling point.

The usual excuse offered for Fame's flops was that he was 'too good for the charts'; but this backfired when he suddenly found himself at Number One with his fourth Columbia single in December 1964. Co-written by 'Jazz Sage' Jon Hendricks, the lustful *Yeah Yeah* began an erratic Top 50 performance from Fame spread over several years. Like the similarly-placed John Mayall, Georgie was financially secure without chart honours, but it was still galling when the next three 45's all missed the Top 20, the highest flyer being the underrated *Something*, which managed No. 23. However, Fame's own *Getaway* (which began life in a petrol advertisement) displaced the Kinks from the top of the charts in July 1966, at which point Georgie dispersed his flexible Blue Flames to go solo.

This had been on the cards since the sarcastically-titled FAME AT LAST L.P., issued in the wake of *Yeah Yeah*, in which accompaniment was divided between the Blue Flames and a session band organised by musical director Earl Guest, who generally employed an enlarged horn section and female backing singers. These girls were particularly prominent on Marvin Gaye's *Pride and Joy* and Curtis Mayfield's *Monkey Time*. This zoological strain persisted on William Bell's *Monkeying Around*, as did a Bacchanalian tendency on *Pink Champagne* and *Gimme That Wine*, from the Flamingo repertoire which best suited Fame's regular band. A distinctly ambitious choice here was the jazz soliloquy *Moody's Mood for Love*.

The Blue Flames presence was less felt on the valedictory SWEET THINGS L.P. of May 1966. With its firmer emphasis on soul, this was more or less a Georgie Fame solo album (but then, weren't they all?). For many SWEET THINGS sessions, Fame had collaborated with big band conductor Harry South,

A day at the races: Georgie Fame glorifies his guitar tutor.

who further encouraged his jazz aspirations. These came to the fore a few months later with the daring, self-financed SOUND VENTURE L.P., with jazz veterans like Tubby Hayes and Stan Tracey. This confused many fans, who could not grasp that their Georgie's sights were now set on a higher showbusiness plateau far removed from tearing it up in a grotty dive in Soho.

At 23, he had been the youngest performer to play a solo concert at the Royal Festival Hall. Even so, it was with trepidation that he accepted an invitation to sing with the legendary Count Basie Orchestra at the Albert Hall in May 1967. Light years away from parochial old Harry South, Georgie nervously endeared himself to the tuxedoed audience with the self-effacing introduction 'Welcome to my dreams'.

Though he acquitted himself admirably on these prestigious occasions, his income still hinged on the daytime mundanities of record sales. Losing his grip on the album charts by the close of 1967, he was still able to clock in with five consecutive Top 50 singles chart entries culminating with a Christmas Number One in *The Ballad of Bonnie and Clyde*. Other hits included two American covers, Bobby Hebb's *Sunny* and *Sitting in the Park* from Billy Stewart. Since *Yeah*

Yeah had percolated slowly to No. 21 in the Hot 100, the US charts had given increasingly slight cause for optimism, making it quite in order for Fame and his advisors to plunder the American soul chart for likely material with which to clean up on home ground.

After some lean hit parade years and an intrinsically middle-of-the-road alliance with Alan Price, Georgie recruited top sessionmen for a Blue Flames rebirth in 1974. These included saxophonist Alan Skidmore, sometime Shadow Brian Bennett and the only original member, Colin Green. However, after recording an album and promoting it with a few exhilarating but shambling gigs (including a Reading Festival with Traffic), the project fizzled out with nobody rediscovering any roots. One wag put it down to too much Pink Champagne.

Apart from his Maxwell House coffee adverts, Fame wasted valuable time in a 1983 BBC 2 television series plugging a Hoagy Carmichael tribute album in collaboration with Annie Ross, one of his smart jazz friends. Yet no matter how much he smothered you with worse pap (like 1973's GEORGIE DOES HIS THING WITH STRINGS) there was always the knowledge that, without warning, he could still hit a groove with *Let the Sun Shine In* or a steaming *Green Onions*. All would then be forgiven and Georgie Fame would once more be the coolest cat of them all.

Eric, Rick, Wayne and Bob — it's Wayne Fontana and the Mindbenders

On Saturday 4th of May 1963, Decca's soul-tortured Dick Rowe (The Man Who Turned The Beatles Down) was judging a dire talent contest at Liverpool's Philharmonic Hall with one of his failed supplicants, George Harrison. That same evening, Fontana Records talent scout Jack Baverstock was also scouring the Lancashire hinterland to find, if not *The New Beatles*, then *A New Beatles*. Alighting on Manchester's Oasis club, he liked what he saw on stage there. The band was pretty rough and ready, but it still evoked more than passive attention from the girls near the front, and the lads too seemed to enjoy the unpolished enthusiasm of the familiar repertoire. Before the night was out, Fontana had made another snatch from the Northern goldmine — Wayne Fontana and the Mindbenders.

Only afterwards did Jack learn of the group's ad hoc nature. At the sound check, only the lead vocalist and Rick Rothwell, the drummer, had materialised; the rest presumably had more important things to do. Frantically, Wayne and Rick hauled in a couple of substitutes, guitarist Eric Stewart and bass player Robert Land, to make up numbers. Keeping the set plain and simple, this motley crew, fronted by charismatic Wayne and coalesced by Rick's beat, put up a brave show for an A & R man about to end his quest.

Wayne Fontana's walk with destiny began with a school skiffle group, the Velfins, organised by singer Glyn Geoffrey Ellis in the late 1950s. Deciding on a career in music, Glyn kept the wolf from the door as a telephone engineer before forming his first semi-professional group, the Jets, in 1961, adopting 'Wayne Fontana' as his stage name and rattling the tambourine as his gimmick.

Wayne and the Jets were nothing special. Taking their cue from Merseybeat, they stuck mainly to *Love Potion Number Nine*, *Some Other Guy*, *Skinny Minnie* and all the rest of them. To this was added a dash of pure pop — *Swinging on a Star*, *Locomotion* etc. They were also fond of the call-and-response style of American girl groups like the Dixie Cups and Marvellettes.

By 1963, they were fixtures on the Manchester to Liverpool beat circuit, a favourite stomping ground being the Savoy in Oldham; but the Jets were becoming increasingly unreliable. This culminated in the aforementioned near-disaster at the Manchester Oasis club, where a record contract was signed from the jaws of defeat and a slate-wiping new name chosen from a current horror film.

In the cold light of a London studio, Jack Baverstock realised that what he had grabbed was a competent set of musicians a little short on imagination. True, they had developed a line of unison harmonies topped by an unearthly falsetto and, yes, they had written a few derivative songs, but really they were no better or worse than any up-and-coming dance band to be found anywhere in the country.

Their first four singles did little to contradict this supposition, yielding as they did two minor chart entries with Merseybeat accelerations of Fats Domino's *Hello Josephine* and Ben E. King's *Stop Look and Listen*. Though Fontana thought it worthwhile to issue an E.P. in March 1964, if the next single failed, it was likely that Wayne and his group would be consigned to the haphazard oblivion from which they were still emerging.

They got lucky with *Um Um Um Um Um Um* penned by Curtis Mayfield, which entering the chart at No. 34, put Major Lance's original up Queer Street. Within seven weeks, it had peaked at Number 5. No one-hit wonders, they struck again in January 1965 with *Game of Love* which, propelled by rudimentary drumming and a *basso profundo*, was not merely their biggest British hit, as it also seized the top slot in the States. A chance to capitalise on this was thwarted by US immigration authorities who, while allowing respectable actors like Robert Morley to enter, temporarily refused visas for any more degenerate Limey pop combos to infiltrate Uncle Sam's fair land.

On the heels of the hits came the debut album, consisting largely of items from the stage act, plus a couple of originals — notably Eric and Wayne's *One More Time*, which sounded like Little Anthony and the Imperials. This L.P. sold quite well but trouble loomed with the next 45. Staying with the devil they knew, *Game of Love* composer, Hank Ballard Junior's *Just a Little Bit Too Late* only led to the edge of the Top 20, a serious mistake in those days. Doubtless they kicked themselves when another Ballard song on which they had first refusal, *I'm Alive*, eased to Number One having been picked up by fellow Mancunians, the Hollies.

During an Independent Television song contest in September 1965, Wayne endeared himself to neither the Mindbenders nor the viewers at home by bawling 'the winnaaaaaaaah!' as the group completed their self-composed entry *She Needs Love*. Scraping into the

Wayne Fontana backstage at ITV's Wembley studios, May 1966.

chart at No. 32, this single set the seal on the inevitable. Star and group separated a month later, blaming each other for their declining fortunes. 'All we've lost is our tambourine player', sneered a Mindbender to a *Disc* journalist.

With Eric Stewart in the catseat, the Mindbenders made their first (and greatest) impact when the lightweight ballad *A Groovy Kind of Love* rose to Number 2 on both sides of the Atlantic. Though they went off the boil in America almost immediately, the UK charts were game for two more lesser offerings, *Can't Live With You* and *Ashes to Ashes*. Using the same songwriting team of Carole Bayer and Toni Wine, these sob-stories belied the Mindbenders' half-serious specification that all their A-sides should have lyrically happy endings.

This optimistic desire was not fulfilled in real life. Apart from one more minor entry, even a cameo role in the feature film To Sir With Love, starring Sidney Poitier, could not resuscitate them as chart contenders after 1966. They initially took a dive with *I Want Her She Wants Me* from the pen of Rod Argent, whose Zombies were already out in the cold. Another strategy was covering a Robert Knight number, *Blessed Are the Lonely*, thus taking a leaf from Love Affair's more successful book.

A cover of the Box Tops' *The Letter* was produced by an old Manchester friend, Graham Gouldman, who also contributed two of his own songs to the growing pile of flops — the suggestive *Schoolgirl* and the innocent *Uncle Joe*, whose poor sales effectively killed off the Mindbenders. A grey eminence of the 1960s pop scene (though his own bands, the Whirlwinds and Mockingbirds, were unable to get off the ground), Gouldman's compositions provided hits for other artists, notably Freddie and the Dreamers, the Hollies, Herman's Hermits, the Yardbirds and — Wayne Fontana.

After the bust-up, Wayne vaguely followed Cliff Richard's example by tidying himself up a bit to become an altogether smoother pop "entertainer".

With accompaniment directed by the syrupy Les Reed, a missing link was a version of Garnett Mimms' *It Was Easier To Hurt Her* which made a modest No. 36, nipping Chris Farlowe's intended cover in the bud. A further advance was made back to the Top 20 with *Come On Home* by Jackie Edwards (then on the crest of a wave with Spencer Davis). Though Wayne projected a likeable personality well on TV, his third solo effort *Goodbye Bluebird* paid only a cursory visit to the Top 50. His oscillating chart performance highlighted his difficulties in establishing himself outside the group environment. His only L.P. without the Mindbenders, touchingly titled WAYNE ONE, uneasily mixed crooning standards such as Alberto Dominguez's *Perfidia*, with soul ballads and a quota of his own songs. Despite this identity crisis, Wayne still showed his teeth when Gouldman's sentimental *Pamela Pamela* left a wound at No. 11. Though its B-side, Wayne's own *Something Keeps Calling Me Back*, with its clichéd horns and girlie chorus, inadvertently found its way onto Wigan Casino's turntable to become a much-requested Northern Soul classic, after *Pamela Pamela*, neither love nor money could get Wayne back into the charts.

The Mindbenders meanwhile wound things up low on the bill at the Liverpool Empire on November 20th 1968. The final line-up was Eric Stewart with Graham Gouldman on bass, Birmingham organist Jimmy O'Neill, and ex-Chicken Shack drummer Paul Hancox. By this time, Rothwell was in antiques while Land sold stereo equipment before joining Racing Cars in 1976.

Awaiting their lengthy chart future with IOCC (which began in 1972), Eric and Graham plunged into session work, accruing capital to expand their Strawberry Studio project, then humbly situated above a Stockport hi-fi shop. Among their clients were Solomon King, Dave Berry and Wayne Fontana, with whom the hatchet had been buried.

Time had been rather unkind to Wayne, attacking his hairline as it had his father's before him. For a while he'd put much of his energy into songwriting, but in 1973 he took to the road again with a New Mindbenders. Highlights of this period were two 'British Invasion' revival tours of the USA with several old cronies. On the first, he opened with Gilbert O'Sullivan's *Get Down* before actually doing so with the expected oldies. In 1982, he turned up on the HEROES AND VILLAINS nostalgia concert, which celebrated fifteen years of BBC Radio One. Afterwards, like many of those who shared the stage with him on that night of nights, he vanished back into the cabaret nether-world that has since been his lot.

Across the Mersey with Gerry and the Pacemakers

With the Beatles, Gerry and the Pacemakers were arguably the prime exponents of Merseybeat. For a time, both groups were on terms of fluctuating equality; both cut their teeth in Germany before building a solid reputation back in Liverpool. By 1962, it was a foregone conclusion that they would seize the top two positions in *Merseybeat's* popularity poll. Shortly afterwards, the two bands signed with Brian Epstein who steered them into the charts within twelve months, with records produced by George Martin. Here Gerry's success was the most immediate, hitting Number One with each of his first three records (a debut unequalled until the coming of another Merseyside group, Frankie Goes to Hollywood, twenty years later). In the New Musical Express points table for 1963, the victory belonged to the Beatles with Gerry's lot coming third. However, considering the Beatles' head start of six months, their rivals' eleven chart-topping weeks suggested a prospect just as rosy. But at this point, their paths diverged; the Beatles shook the world, while the Pacemakers plodded a known path from maturity to dreary repetition, making the most of every chance that came their way. Finally, with their very name a mill-stone round their necks, they packed it in.

Unlike the Beatles, there was a sharp distinction between star and backing group. Gerry as guitarist and singer carried the show single-handedly while his Pacemakers laboured away behind him. With his impish geniality and intuitive crowd control, Gerry Marsden was a showbiz natural of the boy-next-door Tommy Steele stamp. By 1964, he'd already led the group into pantomime, royal cabaret, and charity football matches. Though removed from rock'n'roll, these ventures accurately indicated future developments.

However, there were no such portents in Liverpool's tough Dingle suburb in 1956, when 14-year-old Gerard Marsden joined the short-lived Red Mountain Boys, a youth club skiffle combo favouring the country style of Hank Williams. Two years later, as a British Rail delivery boy, he and his elder brother, Freddie (who bashed the drums) formed the Mars Bars. Adding bass guitarist Les Chadwick, a clerk like Freddie, they became the Marsden Trio. Mutating into 'Gerry and the Pacemakers' by 1960, they began making local headway, championed by Bob Wooler, master of ceremonies at Holyoake Hall off Penny Lane. On his recommendation, Gerry and his boys were a last minute booking at a prestigious promotion starring Gene Vincent at the 6,000 seat Liverpool Boxing Stadium. Earning unexpected acclaim during their spot, Gerry and the Pacemakers arrived in the first division of Merseybeat popularity.

Turning professional, the next step was a five week season at Hamburg's Top Ten Club in early 1961, where they took over from Ian Hines' Jets as Tony Sheridan's backing band. They were to perform a similar function for Fats Domino three months later. Most of their repertoire was founded on the R'n'B classics that were the backbone of Merseybeat; but beyond *Dizzie Miss Lizzie*, *Sweet Little Sixteen* etc., they cranked out mainstream pop such as Presley's *Got a Lotta Livin' To Do*, as well as perennial mainstays like Nat King Cole's *Pretend* and *You Make Me Feel So Young*. They also began composing songs in collaboration with Sheridan taping *Going On Home*, *Why* and others as demos for Merseyside impressario Sam Leach.

During a brief respite from the Grosse Freiheit, the group was augmented by pianist Les Maguire, formerly a Cheshire joiner. Prior to the electric piano's commercialisation, the frequent absence of even the most abused uprights at many home venues and the idea of three months using the same instrument attracted Maguire — who doubled on sax — to Hamburg as a Pacemaker. He was not informed of Beatle Stuart Sutcliffe's practice of removing piano strings to repair bass guitar breakages.

Each Pacemaker wore a monogrammed blue blazer with gold buttons. Gerry took the trouble to learn announcements in German. While these were interrupted in heated moments by English swear words, unlike macho leather boys the Searchers or Beatles, Gerry and the Pacemakers were purposely a polished and respectable act.

Coming on strong as Mr. Nice Guy, the focus of Gerry's vibrant cheerfulness was crucial. Without it, the band would never have become the live draw that led to their national breakthrough. The only example extant of their attractive concert style is a 1965 E.P. recorded before several thousand berserk teenagers in California. With Marsden's compelling scouse patter evoking audience participation, the group drove through four numbers that would have wowed 'em at the less salubrious Aintree Institute or Ellesmere Port Civic Centre three years earlier.

Friendly competition rather than bickering animosity existed between the Pacemakers and Beatles. They even combined as the 'Beatmakers' on one remarkable occasion at Litherland Town Hall, all eight musicians

*Gerry rocks while the Pacemakers roll (*left to right) *Gerard Marsden, Freddie Marsden, Les Chadwick and Les Maguire.*

swapping instruments and stage costumes. At one Beatles Cavern bash, Gerry deputised for an absent Lennon where it was noticed that, like John, he had copied Sheridan's high-chested guitar stance.

Teaming up with Epstein in June 1962 at first made little difference to Gerry and the Pacemakers, who continued traipsing round the familiar parochial gig circuit while Brian concentrated on launching the Beatles on a first-come-first-served basis. After angry confrontations born of Pacemaker frustration, he persuaded George Martin to visit Birkenhead, where he'd hastily arranged for Gerry and Co. to play a children's dance at the Empire Ballroom. This yielded the desired E.M.I. audition, leading to an assignment to its Columbia subsidiary in the spring of 1963.

A highlight of the Birkenhead showcase was a song called *How Do You Do It*, which George Martin had intended for the Beatles after its rejection by Adam Faith. Treating the Beatles' malcontented try-out as a helpful demo, Gerry's effervescent adaptation justified Martin's faith by galloping to Number One in April 1963. This spearheaded the Merseyside chart invasion, but before the deluge, Gerry moved in with another

Mitch Murray opus, *I Like It*, in similar bouncy vein, this time taken from a demo by the Dave Clark Five.

Though barely outstripping the Pacemakers in chart terms, the Beatles' composing abilities and their more balanced image affirmed early on that Gerry was to be Bill Haley to their Elvis. This meant that on a package tour with Roy Orbison, Gerry's mob were third on the bill while the Beatles, supplanting even Orbison, closed each evening's proceedings with *Twist and Shout*. But Gerry and his group had given a good enough account of themselves to headline in their own right a few months later with 'special guest' Kathy Kirby, whose star was on the wane.

The main purpose of the latter jaunt was to promote two new products. An album, HOW DO YOU LIKE IT, set the seal on Gerry's aspirations to be an 'all round entertainer', with the expected R'n'B mixed with orchestrated standards like *Summertime* and a solitary Marsden composition for good measure. Lifted from the L.P. was Rodgers and Hammerstein's *You'll Never Walk Alone*, the ballad that stole the show from Gene Vincent in 1960. Voicing doubts about its viability as a 45, Epstein was stunned when, prodding a sentimental public nerve, it went straight in at Number 7, to capture the top slot within a fortnight. Of course, this CAROUSEL song penetrated folklore, as the Liverpool Football Club anthem. Twenty years later, Gerry serenaded the Liverpool Cathedral congregation at team manager Bill Shankly's memorial service. Tears filled the eyes of grizzled, elderly supporters — for some, *You'll Never Walk Alone* was the only pop record they ever bought.

In June 1985, Marsden took it to Number One again as leader of 'The Crowd'.

Gerry's own song, *I'm the One*, was a return to his jaunty old fashion. Miming it on READY STEADY GO he was mobbed as usual by a rugby scrum of fans, extricating himself minus four shirt buttons. Nevertheless, there were perceptible signs of danger as *I'm the One* was blocked at Number 2 while the next single, *Don't Let the Sun Catch You Crying* stalled at Number 6, a real comedown by previous standards. At grassroots, they'd already dropped several places in *Merseybeat's* poll, having been overtaken by chart newcomers like the Merseybeats who were advantaged by continued omnipresence in Liverpool.

A belated attempt to stay further decline was FERRY ACROSS THE MERSEY, very much a period film set in the fast-fading 'Nashville of the North'. Squeezing the blood from Gerry and the lads' economic acting ability, the plot builds round a Battle of the Bands tournament. After shutting down a host of other opponents, the Pacemakers ultimately crush the bad guys, the

Blackwells (distinguished by aberrant bleached white hair). With Gerry's screen Mum cheering them on, the winners launch into their hopeful new single *It's Gonna Be All Right* over the closing credits.

In real life, it wasn't all right — it was the first serious flop. Another excerpt from the soundtrack, Gerry's evocative title song (revived, ironically, by Frankie Goes to Hollywood) extended a Top 10 farewell for the entire Merseybeat movement in January 1965.

Two stops on the way down were covers of Bobby Darin's *I'll Be There* and the tearjerker, *Walk Hand in Hand*, trying again for the Kop Choir market. The crunch came on SUNDAY NIGHT AT THE LONDON PALLADIUM with the second-billed Gerry pouring his heart and soul into the crass *La La La* with his Pacemakers less prominent than a line of choreographed Tiller girls.

There were still outstanding mopping-up operations overseas. In 1966, they still managed to shift *Girl On a Swing* in sizeable quantities in Europe while in Australia, they lasted even longer than they had in America. Considering the group's affinity to the Beatles, US advancement had been surprisingly sluggish until *Don't Let the Sun Catch You Crying* came to rest at Number 6 in the Hot 100. Backtracking, reissues of *How Do You Do It* and *I Like It* consolidated this breakthrough. With the film on general release and the band's actual presence in the USA, *Ferry Cross the Mersey* made the biggest chart strike before the foreseeable slide downhill. Still, it had been a reasonable run.

In 1967, Gerry made an unfruitful bid for solo stardom with CBS, though he did his bit for England with a Belgium song contest victory later in the year. By 1970, he indeed became an 'all round entertainer', initially on children's television where his unforced scouse urbanity was ideal. In more adult spheres, he gladly took over the male lead from Joe Brown in the West End musical comedy CHARLIE GIRL which ran and ran. Occasionally, he would hit the road with a revised Pacemakers to relive his past glories in Australia and wherever else he was fondly remembered. Even in Britain, millions tuned in to TV's UNFORGETTABLE to witness a middle-aged Dad — still holding his guitar like Tony Sheridan — get the studio jumping with a couple of his more inconsequential but maddeningly catchy classics.

Identified with and dependant on a certain media-defined sound, Gerry was unable or unwilling to transcend his origins, unlike fellow travellers the Beatles. Even so, there is a lingering moment of British pop's most unpretentiously optimistic period that is forever Gerry and the Pacemakers.

Billy J's Secret

Bastille Day 1984 was rather a soap opera for me. In the morning I'd fathered a son. By late afternoon, a bus had shaved the side of my car. At 10 p.m., I was chatting to a tired Billy J. Kramer shortly before his cabaret spot at Out of Town, a plush Padworth country club on the Bath Road. In his pop star prime, he'd had a pleasant croon which, when required, could turn into a polite growl. He didn't write songs or have any unusual sidelines. He d been boyishly handsome with a shadow of a double chin — all in all, a bit of an Average Joe. In the club ante-room in his vineyard-mauve suit, he was tanned and taper-thin, though his face was scored with deep lines that were less apparent when he bounced into the spot-light later, and his voice had dropped about an octave. His forty years hadn't been quiet ones.

It was a curate's egg of a set. As an overture to Kramer's entry, the New Dakotas rambled through what was vaguely recognisable as the original band's only hit in its own right — 1963's *The Cruel Sea*. The dressing

After splitting with the Dakotas and EMI, Billy updated his image and material but without chart success.

room had reeked of . . . . smoking, which may have explained why the New Dakotas were stone cold. A contributory factor may have been the attitude of the young Mancunian guitarist who admitted beforehand that backing Billy J. held little job satisfaction for him but the money was good.

Opening with a Beatles number, the Man Himself made his presence felt among the diners who filled every table. Pausing for them to bawl the hooklines during a succeeding classic rock singalong, Billy knew he had them — a pushover as usual. Not for nothing had he spent years perfecting his craft. Within minutes, I too was involved; worrying when he flagged, cheering when he rallied, glowing when he ultimately went down well. It was like the pity felt for the only talented member of a ghastly repertory company.

Nevertheless, he was often banal, vulgar and fake in the highest tradition of supper club pop. Though more Hamlet than Falstaff, Kramer was genuinely grotesque when, after the birthday request spot, a prearranged waitress minced forth to sit on his lap during a leering execution of *If I Were a Carpenter* which owed more to Dave Dee than Tim Hardin. He knew what he was doing, though; the rude backchat was appreciated by the customers, who were above bingo but a long way from Glyndebourne.

Billy leaned heavily on the old Beatle connection. Thanking us for buying the records they wrote for him, he added to these *I Wanna Hold Your Hand*, *I Feel Fine* and *Lady Madonna*. Two other numbers he 'had the pleasure of recording' were, of course, Mort Shuman's jogalong *Little Children* and his final chart entry *Trains and Boats and Planes* that, flying to Number 4 for its composer Burt Bacharach, left Billy stranded eight places lower in May 1965. He suffered a like defeat in France at the hands of the Claude Francois translation, *Quand un Bateau Passe*.

Among the many encores were a skank-hopped *Great Balls of Fire* from his first, and best selling, L.P., and a stirring *The Sun Ain't Gonna Shine Anymore* (leading to speculation as to whether Kramer had been sniffing round it before the Walker Brothers moved in too quickly).

Unnerved by the contretemps with the number 15 bus, I'd been driven to the venue by my photographer who, with six gin-and-tonics on board, wanted to go during Billy's fevered *Suspicious Minds* to avoid prowling police squad cars. The immediate impression of what we'd just seen was that, though it wasn't Zappa jamming with Hendrix, it was much livelier visually and more vocally expressive than when, as a nervous 19-year-old, a more conservatively-dressed Billy had first hit the Big Time in 1963. Smiling wanly, he'd seemed oblivious to the commotion round him as police frequently stopped the show when his girl fans lost control.

With journalists, he'd make much of his Mum and docker Dad who had reared him in Hankey Drive, Bootle, as William Howard Ashton, the youngest of their seven offspring. No long term plans for a showbusiness career were formulated though he did travel to Blackpool as part of a festival choir, and was once employed to pose as a Robinson's Golly — the stereotyped but affectionalely regarded marmalade motif — at an advertising conference. At St. George of England Secondary Modern he hacked inadequate rhythm guitar with Billy Ford and the Phantoms, mutating his name to 'Billy Kramer' after consulting a telephone operator about the relative attractions of random surnames picked from the directory.

As nominal leader of a new group, the Coasters, he passed an audition at the David Lewis Theatre in Liverpool 8. Though the dozen bookings gained from this boosted confidence, a more sordid event was of greater portent. Billy Kramer and the Coasters were

Billy J. Kramer relaxes before his cabaret spot at Out Of Town country club, Padworth, 1984.

primarily an instrumental act but when some dastard stole Billy's guitar one night, he agreed after much persuasion to front the band as lead singer.

He just about cut the mustard in this unfamiliar turn. Local impressario Edward Knibbs endeavoured to improve Billy's onstage projection by insisting he practice his singing whilst standing on a chair. Suddenly things became serious. Like many hip Merseysiders, Billy had witnessed the Beatles 'Direct From Hamburg' wipe-out at Litherland Town Hall on December 27th 1960. With such a buzz in the air, Billy and his boys so traced the Beatle scent that within two years, though still amateur, they shot from 19th to 3rd in *Merseybeat's* annual poll. Their music was less hard on the ear than most rival groups because Billy, swallowing dust behind more grizzled opposition on ravers, was born to sing ballads like *Twelfth of Never*, *Twilight Time*, and *Beautiful Dreamer*, plus passing joys such as Presley's *Anything that's Part of You* from 1962. He was also quite effective in medium-paced items of the *Under the Boardwalk — Da doo ron ron* canon, and at his wildest with Marvin Gaye's *I'll be Doggone*.

Though moderated by fame, his outrageous wardrobe did not endear him to the more bigoted of Liverpool's heterosexual chauvinists, but he became the darling of the ladies who saw beneath the gold

lamé exterior a little-boy-lost type who, like Johnny Ray and Scott Walker each side of him, needed mothering. During the working week, he pursued a more butch vocation as a British Rail apprentice fitter. The crunch came when a transfer to Crewe was in the offing — decisions, decisions. . . .

Ted Knibbs invited Billy to lunch at a posh restaurant, where Brian Epstein joined them. He had previously arranged a Scottish tour for the group as an award for their *Merseybeat* poll progress. Over the main course, a transfer fee of £50 delivered Kramer into Mr. Epstein's growing N.E.M.S. empire.

Unlike the captain of the side, the Coasters weren't assured of a fixed wage to placate anxious parents. With guitarist George Braithwaite as the main protagonist, the quartet left Kramer to offer themselves to a less ambitious local entertainer, Chick Graham, another Knibbs protégé. From Manchester, another backing group, the Dakotas (who included Elkie Brooks' brother, Tony Mansfield on drums) were such an improvement that Billy suffered initial twinges of self-doubt. However, under Epstein's guidance, they proved to be a competent team.

Mooted as first single was *She's My Girl* by Liverpool composer Ralph Bowdler, but a demo of this (with the Coasters) was rejected by George Martin who was frankly unhappy about Kramer's pop star potential.

Reluctantly trusting Brian's judgement, he tried Billy's slower treatment of an appealing Lennon ballad that had given George Harrison a piece of the action on the Beatles' debut album. *Do You Want to Know a Secret* was issued on May 26th 1963 after a harrowing recording session where double-tracking and Martin's patchy piano tinkling hid a nervous Billy's shortcomings, particularly on the falsetto line, 'I am in love with yoooooou'. On the Parlophone label, his name was now divided by a non-signifying 'J' (an adornment suggested by Lennon presumably to remove associations of weakness and add the ferocity that similar alterations had provided for older celebrities like Cecil de Mille and Edward Robinson).

John was also commissioned to write *Bad to Me* which went one better than its demanding predecessor when it snatched the top slot from the Searchers in August. Another Beatle-penned hit, *I'll Keep You Satisfied*, saw the year out in fine style as did a high placing in the *New Musical Express'* chart survey and its prediction of a golden future for Billy J., specifically on the silver screen.

With the confidence of the newly-famous, Kramer himself chose his fourth 45, *Little Children* which, to

Billy J. and his New Dakotas sock it to 'em, 1984.

JUNE 14
BILLY J. KRAMER
AND THE DAKOTAS
at the
Out of Town
Tel: Woolhampton 713282
Bath Rd, Padworth
Nr. Reading

his relief, knocked another N.E.M.S. star, Cilla Black, from Number One in March 1964. Coupled with *Bad to Me*, this was also Billy's biggest hit in the USA, where he and Epstein had paid an exploratory visit in 1963. His less anonymous return was a large scale re-run of British beat hysteria with even more rows of cripples, presentations to civic heads and their pert daughters, high jinks in hotels, and louder screams every stop of the way. (Peculiar to Billy and his band was an incident on the TV show SHINDIG when Chief Shooting Star of the Dakota Sioux debased his culture by relinquishing a Red Indian headdress to Kramer, who said he planned to write a song in the tribe's honour. Words are cheap.) In the midst of this madness, Billy and Gerry Marsden relaxed momentarily for an evening at Sunset Strip's Whiskey-a-Go-Go. Both cut live recordings at a Long Beach concert next day before flying home.

Plugging the next single, McCartney's *From a Window*, Kramer pioneered a Merseybeat probe into BBC TV's traditional Billy Cotton Band Show. However, when the next A-side could not crack even the Top 50 the rats started leaving the sinking ship, beginning with bass guitarist Ray Jones. Advantaged by a TV spot on READY STEADY GO, a Surrey band 'the Game', featuring a Jodrell Bank-eared singer, won a Pyrric victory over Parlophone's pressing of *You Make Me Feel Like Someone* which was Billy J. Kramer and the Dakotas' final record together.

By neglecting to renew his contract in 1967, E.M.I. indicated that Billy hadn't a hope in hell of making the charts again. Reaction, thinking otherwise, released several Kramer solo discs including the Bee Gees' *Town of Tuxley Toymaker* and *1941*, an undeserved flop. After a stint compering LIFT OFF, a children's television series, Billy roamed the Earth in cabaret and nostalgia revues where others of his standing would regale anyone who would listen with endless anecdotes about what Ringo said to Rory Storm at the Blue Angel in 1962.

Kramer's Katastrophe: author Clayson delivers judgement

FANS WALK OUT ON SIXTIES STAR

Kramer was not drunk, says agent

Sober Billy
SIXTIES pop star Billy J. Kramer denied yesterday that he was drunk during a concert at Reading, Berks, when 100 members of the audience walked out. He said : "I had a glass of wine and a can of lager, that's all."

Angry walk-out as Billy J sings
BOOS and jeers greeted 'sixties pop star Billy J Kramer when he took part in a concert at Reading, Berks.
More than 100 of the 1,000-strong audience walked out, many of them complaining he was drunk.
Promoter Peter Braham said yesterday : "I can only apologise for Billy J's very poor performance. He let everybody down.
"I understand he received sad personal news a couple of hours before the show. He took it badly and hit the bottle."
Kramer, 40, returned to Manchester after the Tuesday night show without comment.

HUNDREDS of people walked out of a concert by Sixties star Billy J. Kramer at the Hexagon last night amid claims that he had been drinking.
The audience jeered and booed Kramer and his backing band, the Dakotas, who were topping the bill of the evening of nostalgia.

Dale Martin presents
28 Mon 7.30pm PB **Wrestling Spectacular**
Arena £3 Stalls £2.50
Balcony £2.50, £2 Choir £3

29 Tue 8pm **60s Special**
presented by Alan Freeman
Billy J Kramer and the Dakotas
The Marmalade
Dozy, Beaky, Mick and Tich
Arena £5, £4 Stalls £5 Balcony £5, £4

WEEKEND POST Saturday February 9 1985
In defence of pop star
I WRITE in defence of Billy J. Kramer to whom I was speaking 10 minutes before the show...

...end surplus grain ...ks to Sudan

The Many Faces of Manfred Mann

Manfred Lubovitz was born in 1940 in South Africa. It was later alleged by his publicist that, though the security of his father's Johannesburg printing firm beckoned, young Manfred's musical precociousness won him academy places in Vienna and New York. In fact, he studied music briefly in the Transvaal under John Mehegan from New York's Julliard School of Music — a fellow student being jazz trumpeter Hugh Masakela — before moving to England in 1962. There he maintained himself by teaching music, playing piano and writing for *Jazz News* — for which he came to adopt the *nom de plume* Manfred Mann — 'Like . . . . what's your name, man?' 'They call me "Manfred", man.'

Later that year, he was employed in the same holiday camp jazz quartet as vibraphonist Mike Hugg, who was moonlighting from his jeweller's apprenticeship. Sharing the same musical passions, it wasn't surprising that, before the season was out, the pair planned a less arbitrary partnership. With Hugg exchanging vibes for drums and Mann piano for organ, the 'Mann-Hugg Blues Brothers' also included bass guitarist Dave Richmond, multi-instrumental civil servant Mike Vickers, and a horn section consisting of trumpeter Ian Fenby with Tony Roberts on tenor sax. Despite the name, the group betrayed strong jazz leanings, particularly in the Roland Kirk-Charlie Mingus direction. However, much of their work was found in the Home Counties R'n'B scene around London. This had overtaken trad jazz as an underground cult, becoming less the property of a student clique by 1963.

At London's Marquee, the Brothers became entangled in a dispute over cash with their support group, the Roosters, who were derived from a musical fraternity loosely centred in Oxford where English literature undergraduate Paul Pond met pianist Ben Palmer in 1961. Through a mutual interest in Chicago Blues, they tried to form a band — Thunder Odin and the Big Secret — but the transient nature of the remaining personnel precluded anything beyond rehearsal. An attempt at forming a group with asthmatic guitarist Brian Jones — future Rolling Stone — faltered likewise. Via a *Melody Maker* advertisement, they came across unemployed Tom McGuinness, who had been guitarist with three obscure groups — the Ravens, the Talismen and the London Thunderbirds. However, beyond a solitary engagement at a pub in Collier's Wood, South London,

*A curiously balancing effect (*left to right*) Tom Mc Guinness, Mike Hugg, Paul Jones, Mike Vickers and Manfred Mann.*

this collaboration failed even to decide on a name.

Studying at Kingston College of Art, Tom's girlfriend introduced him to a fellow student, one Eric Clapton. With Palmer, guitarists Clapton and McGuinness formed the Roosters with singer Terry Brennan and drummer Robin Mason. Unlike the Mann-Hugg merger, they were enthusiasts with no financial gain in mind beyond beer and petrol money. Though they were well-received at bookings as far afield as Guildford's Wooden Bridge Hotel and Uncle Bonnie's Chinese Jazz Club (!) in Brighton, their humble aspirations and lack of leadership — as well as a glaring lack of a bass player — made inevitable their disintegration within six months.

McGuinness and Clapton then threw in their lot with the Engineers, who backed Liverpudlian vocalist Casey Jones. Wearying quickly of riding this Merseybeat bandwagon for £3 a night, Tom was obliged to surreptitiously heist his own equipment from a Reading ballroom engagement before giving notice.

No longer able to afford their horn section, times were tough for the Mann–Hugg men too, even though they had enrolled a promising singer Paul Jones — formerly Paul Pond — who had been sent down from University to hover in the wings of showbusiness belting out Top Ten requests with a Slough dance band. However, everyone's luck changed when publicist Kenneth Pitt became the Brothers' manager. Under the less cumbersome banner 'Manfred Mann,' he secured them a recording deal with H.M.V.

producer John Burgess, who also worked with Adam Faith. Though the instrumental *Why Should We Not* — with Jones on maraccas — neglected to roar up the charts, their second single *Cock-a-Hoop* in October 1963 made sufficient impact to procure 'the Menn' a commission to compose and record a new theme for READY STEADY GO to replace *Wipeout* by the Surfaris.

With lyrical references to the Crimean War and the siege of Troy, what emerged was a fictitious musical autobiography built round Manfred's organ vamping and Paul's harmonica obligato. Though Mann stressed his preference for its more sophisticated B-side, the highly commercial *54321* cracked the Top Twenty before it was even heard on the programme. In a like vein, *Hubble Bubble* further established the group's viability as a long term chart act. Though they squeezed into uniform stage outfits and Paul went in for a lot of spasmodic crouching and leaping about, they exuded a 'Powerful Intellectual Aura' by pop standards. After all, for all his rugged vivacity, Jones was still a Varsity chap, dammit. Didn't he wear a Campaign for Nuclear Disarmament badge? He definitely read books. He'd even married a novelist. Also, Tom McGuinness and Mann both wore spectacles. Manfred had a beatnik beard too — and if that isn't Intellectual, then I don't know what is. (A cruel necessity had been the sacking of Richmond, whose egghead pate, unlike tousle-headed Jones's

On one notable TV appearance, Manfred was stranded on his organ rostrum for ten minutes, mobbed by fascinated female fans.

acne-pitted complexion, lacked 'teen identification'. On Paul's recommendation, he was replaced by the more youthful McGuinness in December 1963).

Visually, the line-up caused a curiously balancing effect. The front cover of their debut L.P. revealed that McGuinness looked like Mann — and Hugg like Vickers, thus emphasising the taller Jones's central position as Ace Face. Nonetheless, though the fans went wild over Paul on the group's tour with the Crystals, Mann, ostensibly the leader, was a good second, becoming patron saint of all homely boys in glasses who now had licence to chat up girls on the 'intellectual ticket'.

Hubble Bubble was the Manfreds last original A-side. However, though financially dependant on the singles chart, they were able to indulge themselves more on B-sides and album tracks where, to their credit, hardly anything was throwaway. In particular, they were foremost advocates of the E.P. as a worthy product in its own right rather than as an album chaser or regurgitation of four ancient favourites. In hard commercial terms, Hugg was the most enduring songwriter. Most renowned was his astute *You're a Better Man Than I* which began life as a Yardbirds flip before its hit revival by Sham 69 twelve years later. McGuinness provided much comic relief, best instanced in the overdubbed derisive laughter on his *What Did I Do Wrong* — though most of the group's humour went above the heads of the majority of their screaming audiences — hiatus maxime deflendus.

The most celebrated of the Manfreds' own songs was Paul's *The One In The Middle* a self-glorifying irony which, inchoately performed on READY STEADY GO in 1965, inspired the show's later all-live policy. It also precipitated disqualification from an Independent Television song contest for this unfair preview. Nevertheless, as lead track of an E.P., it sold enough to enter the singles charts.

On the same record was the first of their many Dylan covers, *With God On Our Side*. More important chartwise was his suggestive *If You Gotta Go, Go Now* a few months later, as was *Just Like a Woman* from 1966, and their worldwide smash *The Mighty Quinn* in 1968. So stimulating were their arrangements that Dylan himself was of the justified opinion that they were the most effective interpreters of his work.

Though their basic stylistic determination was R'n'B, the Manfreds were versatile enough to span other idioms from the mainstream jazz of Herbie Hancock's *Watermelon Man* to schmaltzy evergreens like *Autumn Leaves* and *Tennessee Waltz*. They also took on Motown and Ray Charles as well as good old

100 Club. 100 Oxford St. W.1.
Tues. 16 May 1972
7.30 till late. Admission 50p.

Jo-Ann Kelly, John Dummer
Blues Band, Brunning/Hall,
Brewers Droop, Paul Jones,
Tom McGuinness, Hughie Flint,
Mike Cooper & The Machine
Gun Company + other guests

Back to the blues: Paul Jones and Tom McGuinness reunited for this remarkable engagement in 1972. Eight years later, a more permanent liaison took place with the Blues Band.

rock'n'roll. Anything was considered, as long as it was good.

Nobody surfaced as a virtuoso, but each Mann was a first-rate musician. Even Paul was in demand for sessions as a harmonica player. Tellingly, the group cut a large proportion of instrumentals; enough, in fact, to fill an entire L.P. (SOUL OF MANN). They even had the satisfaction of a Top Fifty placing in this genre with *Sweet Pea*. Beyond technical ability, they also actually enjoyed playing. In 1963, Manfred remarked to a journalist, 'Whatever happened — even if we had a Number One — we would insist on one night per week doing a West End residency in a jazz club.'

They had *three* Number Ones, beginning in August 1964 with a version of the Exciters *Do Wah Diddy Diddy* which was forever on Top of the Pops. As well as

shifting a million in Germany, this disc also gave them the distinction of being the second British Invasion group to top the US Hot 100. Though the follow-up *Sha La La* made Number 12, further American success was sporadic, especially when the Yardbirds ungratefully queered the pitch with their wily US cover of *Ha! Ha! Said the Clown* in 1967.

At home, they remained hit parade fixtures until their disbandment. However, there were a number of personnel changes starting with Mike Vicker's departure in November 1965. Tired of a travelling life, Mike found a vocation in the field of film soundtracks, the most memorable being his score for Karel Riesz's *Morgan: A Suitable Case for Treatment*, though he stayed in touch with pop, chiefly in orchestral arranging. One of his solo singles, 'Eleventy-One,' was written by Tom McGuinness and became the theme tune to Independent Television's evening wrestling showcase in the later 'sixties.

The Manfreds closed ranks by enlisting the talented Jack Bruce from John Mayall's Bluesbreakers. This caused some embarrassment as Mayall, a near neighbour of Mann, was reluctant to lose Bruce. However, this enabled McGuinness to play guitar onstage — having only shared this role in the studio with Vickers previously — though it was he who pioneered the group's idiosyncratic rhythm guitar sound achieved by using a steel-plated National Duolian as early as 1964. Around this time, the band was briefly augmented by saxophonist Lyn Dobson and trumpeter Henry Lowther. This Manfred Manifestation was responsible for the second chart topper *Pretty Flamingo*.

As 1966 wore on, the expiry date for the H.M.V. contract loomed nearer. Jones saw this as an opportunity to try his luck solo. Always mature and professional about his colleagues' career decisions, Manfred took formal leave of Paul from the Marquee stage before the flash bulbs of the press.

By the end of the year, the charismatic Jones had rung up two fast Top Five entries, mainly on the strength of his Manfred Mann reputation. On one session, he was assisted by two ex-Yardbirds, Jeff Beck and Paul Samwell-Smith, with producer Peter Asher's sister's fiancé, Paul McCartney on drums (*sic*). These eminent musicians were paid the standard session rate by E.M.I.'s Accounts Department before they knocked off for the night. Nevertheless, as Paul became attracted to a more generalised showbusiness orbit, hit records became less important. An indication of this was his last chart entry, a version of *Aquarius* from HAIR with Geoff Love and his Orchestra.

Manfred's Menn, 1966 (left to right) Mike Hugg, Klaus Voorman, Michael d'Abo and Tom McGuinness.

Starring in the art film PRIVILEGE, Paul followed Adam Faith into the exacting role of Thinking Man's Pop Star. It must be said that, unlike Pete Townshend, he was among the more qualified holders of this title. As his spots in discussion programmes and highbrow newspapers tailed off, he found his feet in West End shows, light opera and periodic TV appearances, such as storyteller on the children's programme Jackanory. He even starred on Broadway in the early 1970s in CONDUCT UNBECOMING. He flirted with pop again in the 1970s with a short lived blues group and an extraordinary rendition of the Sex Pistols' *Pretty Vacant* but only when he and Tom McGuinness organised the Blues Band in 1979 did he make any progress.

Back in 1966, as H.M.V. spitefully issued the sub-standard *You Gave Me Somebody to Love*, Manfred was looking for likely lads to fill Paul's shoes on the group's new label, Fontana. After vacillating between Rod Stewart and Long John Baldry, he alighted on Michael d'Abo, leading light with A Band of Angels who had almost-but-not-quite-made-it with d'Abo's *Invitation*. Their gimmick had been the Public School bit — straw boaters, posh accents and toffee noses asking to be punched. Despite this, Michael's voice was a cross between Jones and Elton John, and he was charming enough at an interrogatory meal with Mann and McGuinness plus their wives, to be invited to join the Menn.

Another vacancy had been created by Jack Bruce, who quit shortly after Jones. His Celtic severity was exchanged for the Teutonic elegance of Klaus Voorman from Paddy, Klaus and Gibson (and also a close friend of the Beatles, designing their REVOLVER L.P. sleeve).

Though d'Abo wasn't an exact biological duplicate of Jones, the Manfreds' chart fortunes remained unaltered — albeit orientated towards the more direct pop of writers like John Simon (*My Name is Jack*) and Tony Hazzard (*Fox On the Run*, *Ha! Ha! Said the Clown*). Even d'Abo submitted his rapt *Vicar's Daughter* for consideration as an A-side. The group only missed once when Randy Newman's *So Long Dad*, with its lengthy melody line, faltered outside the Top Fifty. This apart, the hits kept on coming. The most outstanding was *Semi-detached Suburban Mr. James* — purposely altered from 'Jones' in deference to Paul (though its reference to a 'Mr. Most' did not pass unnoticed). On the flip of *Ragamuffin Man* was the atypical *A 'B' side*, credited to Emanon ('No name'); this re-emerged as *Travelling Lady* when Hugg and Mann's new band Chapter Three, came into existence after Manfred Mann officially folded in June 1969 (though Manfred did not symbolically shave off that famous beard for another three years).

Tom McGuinness kept the faith with two big hit singles resulting from his work with drummer Hughie Flint, singer Dennis Coulson and Scottish songwriting team, Benny Gallagher and Graham Lyle. Sticking closest to the old Manfred tradition, the team — under the name McGuinness-Flint — replaced the Pictish element with bass guitarist Dixie Dean before cutting an entire L.P. of Dylan numbers, LO AND BEHOLD, which was arguably a classic of its kind.

At a time when groups were 'Only As Big As Their Latest Single', Manfred Mann were too early for 'progressive music'. This is why the necessary balancing of cash amassed in the hit parade and their self-picture as innovative musicians was less obvious to outsiders than the policies of later and less well-loved examples like Jethro Tull or Fleetwood Mac, who convinced their fans that TOP OF THE POPS excursions were trivial tangents to their main body of work. At least Manfred was no snob; he couldn't afford to be. Plugging *Mighty Quinn* on The Basil Brush Show — a children's TV programme starring a puppet fox — was all part of a day's work.

Boulevard de la Moody Blues

From the remains of three Birmingham skiffle groups — the Ramblers, the Saints and Sinners and the transitional El Cats — evolved El Riot and the Rebels who, like another Brum band the Rockin' Berries, specialised in the classic rock of Jerry Lee Lewis, Gene Vincent *et al*. Though their sole demo tape of two rockabilly favourites reflected this, by 1962 their act contained a significant amount of R'n'B. El Riot's mainstays were bass guitarist John Lodge and singer Ray Thomas, who also played various woodwind instruments. Road manager Mike Pinder joined in on piano whenever it was possible to mike one up. When able to afford a direct input electric model, he became a full band member. Despite local popularity, an unsuccessful E.M.I. audition caused the group's disbandment in February 1963.

Under parental pressure, Lodge remained semi-professional in the interests of higher education, while Pinder and Thomas as members of the newly-formed Krew Cats elected to serve a different sort of apprenticeship in the clubs of Hanover and Hamburg, where there was continued demand for British talent. Whereas scanty regional opportunities had motivated this self-imposed exile, on their return from the Fatherland in November they were astonished to find that the city's beat scene had exploded.

Though this development was triggered by Merseybeat, Birmingham was unable to emulate its cohesion and depth. Largely because it mushroomed on the crest of a craze within months, it lacked the unique brand of enthusiasm matured over years of cultural isolation that was Liverpool's. Scavenging recording managers found precious few hit-makers among the many competent but derivative combos operating in the Second City (though there were heroic failures like the Lawmen, fronted by hip-shakin' Nicky James, 'the Elvis of the Midlands'). Mike Sheridan, the noblest Brummagem rocker of them all, despite a potent brew of comedy, surf and Top 20 preferences, led his Nightriders through six flop 45's for Columbia. Not as well loved were Carl Wayne and the Vikings who, adding Sheridan's lead guitarist and Dusty Springfield impersonator Roy Wood, metamorphosed into the Move. Another Move guitar picker, Trevor Burton, was shanghaiied from rock revivalists Danny King and his Mayfair Set.

For a hot Brum band, consolation for not Making It nationally was a full work schedule guaranteed within easy reach. From Dennis Detheridge's shortlived *Midland Beat*, the reader could select a night out from multitudinous parochial jive hives from the Cedar Club on Constitution Hill to Pershore Street's Silver Blades. Nearer the city centre stood the Carlton, the Rum Runner and the Elbow Room. Further afield lay Bilston Town Hall and Wolverhampton's Lafayette.

From this shared stamping ground, rivalry would dissolve into cameraderie at Alex's Pie Stand on the Queensway; on Saturday nights many bands would congregate there after completing bookings. Ambling down the row of parked Bedfords, Commers, and the infrequent posh new Transit, small talk was exchanged, rumours spread, equipment borrowed, information elicited . . . . boasting . . . . wishin' and hopin' . . . .

A familiar figure at these midnight meetings was singer Brian Hines, alias 'Denny Laine', who led the Diplomats, formed at school with future Move drummer Beverley Bevan in 1962. Laine's band were not as concerned as its contemporaries were with pandering to the crowd's desire to hear current hits. A

recognised lay expert on pop's obscurer trackways, Denny chose to draw his repertoire from the archives of R'n'B. That this daring approach also proved successful with audiences earned him the respect of less sophisticated musicians.

With musical visions held in common with those desperados from Germany, Pinder and Thomas, who were at something of a loose end, a pie stand plot was hatched by Laine for the three of them to form the nucleus of a Birmingham supergroup that would surely get somewhere if there was any justice in the record companies of London. With this contingency plan in mind, Denny left the Diplomats in April 1964, having made no headway with E.M.I. for whom they had cut several demos.

Starting rehearsals in May, Laine, Pinder, and Thomas recruited drummer Graeme Edge from the Avengers and bass guitarist Clinton Eccles, whose nom de guerre, 'Clint Warwick' was softened by his genteel nickname 'Whiskers', for his luxuriant sideburns.

*Mike Sheridan and his fabulous Nightriders (*left to right)
rhythm guitarist Dave Pritchard, drummer Roger Spencer,
Sheridan, lead guitarist Big Al Johnson (later replaced by Roy
Wood) and bass guitarist Greg Masters.

Rejecting the hit parade assortment that people knew and wanted to dance to, the quintet veered further towards the modern black sounds of James Brown, Irma Thomas, Bobby Parker, Jackie Wilson, and vocal groups like the Drifters and Impressions. They also refined urban and country blues as well as trying the odd diversion like a treatment of Gershwin's *It Ain't Necessarily So*.

Functioning as 'The Moody Blues', they re-entered the trivial round of local gigs where their professional ring of confidence won them the strongest possible Midlands reputation. The next logical step was to slither round 'Spaghetti Junction' towards Coventry and down the unfinished M.1 motorway to the Smoke.

Thanks to the persistence of newly-acquired manager Tony Secunda, the group replaced Manfred Mann as Monday night residents at the Marquee. From this prestigious showcase, they speedily attracted the attention of Decca who issued the debut Moody Blues single, the uptempo *Lose Your Money*.

And lose their money they did until the second release, the slower *Go Now*, topped the UK charts in January 1965. Penned by soul star Bessie Banks, this stately lament was well-suited to Denny's wounded voice, enhanced by Clint and Ray's background wailing. As well as epitomising the hard-won sunshine of Birmingham Beat, *Go Now's* descending ostinato and instrumental interlude restored the electric piano to pop prominence after a lengthy absence (possibly caused more by its expensive filling of valuable van space than for any musical reason).

As guest stars on Chuck Berry's British tour in February 1965, high-pitched fan adulation gave false impressions of the group's standing in market terms. This became painfully evident when corroboration of their chart conquest suffered a setback when *I Don't Want To Go On Without You* barely rippled the Top 30. This Drifters number from the previous year had also been simultaneously covered by the Searchers and Escorts, making it a poor choice (however skillfully executed) compared to the *Go Now* triumph.

In addition, the Moody Blues were a motley crew visually. Many felt that they seemed unbalanced and cluttered what with Laine hogging the lead vocal and guitar spotlight while Ray Thomas merely bashed a tambourine and went 'aaaaaah' into a microphone. Actually, as general instrumental factotum, Ray was invaluable in adding the icing that gave the band distinction. It would not be too presumptuous to say that he bore the same relationship to the Moody Blues as Brian Eno did to the embryonic Roxy Music eight years later.

As a detour from this gloomy outlook at home, the group embarked on a short promotional trek to the USA where *Go Now* had reached Number 10 in the Hot 100. Sharing the bill with the Kinks, they opened at New York's Academy of Music on June 9th as their fourth single peaked at No. 93. This show had been organised by Sid Bernstein, who had undertaken a similar office for the Beatles in conjunction with Brian Epstein. Epstein was now handling Moody Blues affairs in place of Secunda who had jumped onto bandwagons new.

A further change of staff had occurred in the studio where Denny Cordell, who also worked with Georgie Fame, now occupied the producer's chair. Foisted on them by Decca, the services of Alex Murray were best demonstrated in the abrupt fade of *Go Now*, which provokes thoughts of Laine being suddenly hooked offstage like a music hall warbler getting the bird.

Belatedly, Pinder and Laine made tentative steps as a songwriting team. One early effort, *From the Bottom of My Heart*, was the group's entry into an ITV-sponsored song contest won by Kenny Lynch's bland *I'll Stay By You*, though the Moody Blues emerged as chart victors clocking in at No. 22, eight places above Lynch. From the menacing piano introduction to the 'Hammer House of Horror' coda, this was the most exquisite record any incarnation of the Moody Blues ever made. Yet, despite acclaim, it seemed that the lads had had their fifteen minutes. They were to be admired for overlooking outright commercial concerns, electing instead to experiment stylistically; but with Epstein increasingly less available and Decca only interested in successful acts, they were obliged to drastically reduce their engagement fees and soon the inevitable cracks appeared.

First out was Clint Warwick, unable to face another moonlight mile. The vacancy was filled by ex-El Riot Rebel John Lodge, now sufficiently schooled, and a veteran of the Carpetbaggers and the John Bull Breed, both denizens of the Warwickshire gig circuit. So anxious was Lodge for the high life that he sold most of his equipment to finance the Moody Blues' forthcoming tour of Europe where it was still possible for them to break even.

A more injurious departure was that of Denny Laine in March 1967. He had become very much a face of the London 'In Crowd,' haunting the Scotch, the Ad-lib, and any clubs where the bright young things were. With the Moody Blues nearly as redundant as the Diplomats became, he couldn't be worse off solo. For a few months, he was backed by the Electric String Band, an amplified string quartet. Impractical in a concert

Underneath the arches: Ray Thomas, Clint Warwick, Graeme Edge, Denny Laine and Mike Pinder in the latest double-breasted style.

situation, Laine's single with this band, *Say You Don't Mind*, was still a courageous move whose advanced nature was evidenced when Colin Blunstone's exact copy crept into the hit charts in 1972.

Arriving on the off-chance on his distant manager's tasteful Belgravia doorstep, Laine received no answer to his knock. Inside, Brian Epstein was expiring in a drug-induced slumber. With this door closed, Denny wandered into the wilderness of ad hoc get-togethers, sessions, studying flamenco guitar, and other furloughs until invited by another Epstein protege, Paul McCartney, to join Wings in 1971.

Meanwhile, his former colleagues had brought in a good-looking Southerner called Justin Haywood who had an obscure Pye single to his doubtful credit. He had also been one of Marty Wilde's Wilde Three who recorded the mawkish recitative *I Cried* for Decca. Nonetheless, as a composer, Haywood was to be a catalyst in the chart revitalisation of the Moody Blues.

His arrival did not improve matters immediately until, at their lowest ebb, there came a most unexpected encounter. After a routine cabaret spot at the Cavendish Club, Newcastle, the group were professional enough to be civil to a Frank Sinatra fan named Derek who, apparently impressed beyond his wildest comprehensions, bought them all a drink.

Mr. Derek McCormack had become a millionaire with the growth of his heating and ventilating business on Tyneside. It was his cash that rescued the Moody Blues from their thankless slog round the northern clublands. In *Teenbeat Monthly* earlier that year, Pinder had complained, 'it's difficult to get the time and put everyone to the expense of sitting in a studio dreaming up different sounds and styles'. With time and the latest facilities — including a Mellotron — now available, courtesy of Mr. McCormack, it seemed that the days of such frustrations were past.

Correlatively, Decca had created a subsidiary, Deram, to cater for a swing towards 'progressive' music with 'meaningful' lyrics. Having written off the unviable Moody Blues as highbrow R'n'B connoisseurs, it was now felt that, in their happier financial circumstances, they warranted a niche on Deram's roster, even though their new music had been developing since *From the Bottom of My Heart*. Restored to public favour with DAYS OF FUTURE PASSED, a grandiose conceptual L.P. with the London Festival Orchestra, an excerpt, Haywood's *Nights in White Satin*, returned them to both the UK and US charts. Its B-side *Cities*, with its tango mode, was in direct descent from *Boulevard de la Madeleine* from the Denny Laine period.

From then on, it was plain sailing as platinum albums breathed mystical chords in the hearts of millions of others who shared Derek McCormack's partiality, revering the Moody Blues as 'the Word made vinyl.' There were, however, times when the effect was so excessively grandiloquent that unintended humour resulted as 'poetic' gems were declaimed in vile Birmingham accents over a thick orchestral backwash. However, the Moody Blues can be seen as precursors of a complex, elegant style so nebulous in scope that such diverse organisations as Yes, King Crimson, and Roxy Music were all irregularly cited as being variants of their blueprint.

A Touch of Brian Poole and the Tremeloes

Brian Poole and the Tremeloes were the only new group from the south of England to present any immediate challenge to Merseybeat in the UK charts of 1963. Nevertheless, as a result of rediscovered evidence they will be principally remembered as the ones Decca Records chose instead of the Beatles. This is like thinking of Chuck Berry as merely the *Ding-a-Ling* man.

Brian Poole, son of a Dagenham butcher, liked Bobby Darin but was obsessed with Buddy Holly. In March 1958, through his black-framed spectacles, he saw his idol and the Crickets in concert during their only British tour. Brian's path became clear. He decided to form his own Crickets with himself as Buddy. Though he had studied piano and guitar as well as purchasing a Fender just like Holly's, he had to overcome a natural shyness before approaching the lads at his Barking secondary school with his idea. After a while, he recruited Graham Scott, another guitarist, and talked the very musical Alan Blakely into hitting the drums. Alan Howard honked bass lines on his tenor saxophone until able to afford an electric bass like that of Cricket Joe Mauldin.

As Blakely's talents were wasted behind the kit, school boxing champion David Munden was roped in for percussion duties. Blakely was then free to hold things together on rhythm guitar or keyboards depending. Top-heavy with guitarists, Brian very professionally elected to leave his Fender at home so that he could concentrate on lead vocals. At this point, they became the 'Tremilos', after the note-bending handle on some electric guitars. Later to please Brian's Mum, her son's name was given its familiar prominence.

When Scott left in 1961 an old classmate, Richard Westwood, who had had classical guitar lessons, made the transition to electric, truncated his surname and threw in his lot with Poole and the Tremilos. He also had a useful high-pitched singing voice to add to Munden and Blakely's backing harmonies.

With a competent mixture of current favourites and the inevitable Holly catalogue, the group acquired a manager in former Dublin greengrocer Peter Walsh, who took them beyond local hops to better paid work in US air bases, a Butlin's holiday camp season in Scotland, and southern county ballrooms. At one Southend engagement, BBC Radio's Light Programme producer Jimmy Grant was impressed enough to offer them a regular spot on SATURDAY CLUB, which often booked bands yet to make a record. Here they achieved some national recognition; but the fateful Decca audition came about through Brian scraping acquaintance with the company's young A&R assistant Mike Smith, who shared the same optician.

Crawling down from Lancashire in a freezing van the night before, the Beatles weren't at their best when *they* nervously performed for a tardy Smith on the morning of New Year's Day 1962. Needing only to cut across London, the more relaxed Barking band were in a fresher frame of mind for their afternoon session. Only budgeted for one signing, Smith settled for Brian and his boys, who were further advantaged by closer proximity to the West Hampstead studios and, of course, their SATURDAY CLUB reputation.

The recording career of Brian Poole and the 'Tremeloes' — more symmetrical but still incorrectly spelt — began as accompanists on such masterpieces of song as *Ahab the Arab* by Jimmy Savile and a Vernons Girls cover of *The Locomotion*. On their own, things got off to a quiet start with a version of *Lost Love* from US vocal group the Superiors, coupled with *Twist Little Sister*, a nod towards prevailing trends. The next single, *Keep On Dancing*, cobbled together by Poole, Blakely, and Smith, sold fractionally more (aided by a makeweight plug in the conveyor belt pop feature film, JUST FOR FUN with the Tornados, Joe Brown, and many others). They also released BIG HITS OF 1962, a cut-price L.P. of medleys from that year's Top 20, a forerunner of the 'Stars on 45'-type discs that infested the charts in the early 1980s.

With the surfacing of Merseybeat, Brian invested in contact lenses as his group was promoted as the London wing of the movement, the word 'Poole' being so effective that four years later, a French publication *Special Pop* began a Tremeloes article with the sentence, 'Brian Poole vient de Liverpool'. They made the grade with their fifth single, *Twist and Shout*, which shimmied to Number 4 in July 1963, Poole doubtfully pleading ignorance of the Beatles' slower but more frantic version.

Two months later, the Tremeloes and Brian earned a chart topper with *Do You Love Me*, taken from a promo copy of the Contours' US original. Simultaneous covers of the same song were not unusual in the 1960s; therefore, Decca weren't surprised at having to fight two other labels pushing their own artist's version of this number. In fact, they cancelled Bern Elliott and the Fenmen's rendition so that Brian's group could have a clearer run. As they had just left the Top 10, the Tremeloes had the edge over the main enemy, hitless fellow Londoners the Dave Clark Five. Faron's

Brian and his Tremeloes in festive mood (back, left to right) Ricky West, Brian Poole, Dave Munden, (front) Alan Howard and Alan Blakely's version of Twist and Shout *was the first record ever played on RSG.*

Flamingos Liverpudlian adaptation was so vanquished that it was relegated to a B-side.

However, the wind was taken out of their sales when the follow-up *I Can Dance* trickled miserably to Number 31, rehashing as it did the salient points of the two previous smashes. Other like retreads such as *Why Don't You Love Me* and *I Wish I Could Dance* turned up less blatantly on B-sides and E.P.'s dubiously credited to group members. Though they had their moments as composers, no-one expected Brian and the Tremeloes to be the next Lennon and McCartney.

A hasty album, TWIST AND SHOUT, was pushed out to cash in on what seemed a perishable commodity. Eight of its numbers had already appeared the previous year on a well-received Canadian L.P. There were also stage favourites like *Alley Oop* and other items going the rounds with scores of rival groups. A comedy element emerged in West's shrill lead vocal outing, *Peanuts*, and a version of *You Don't Love Me Any More*, Dave Curtis' paean to snowblinded masochism.

Taking stock, the Essex boys showed they weren't quite the pigs in a poke Decca imagined they were. Although they couldn't guarantee delivering every time, it was only around late 1965, after two consecutive 45 failures, that they could be legitimately written off. A rendering of Roy Orbison's *Candy Man* made Number 6 but Brian felt more personal elation when *Someone Someone* stopped only one position short of the top slot in May 1964; this was also the only Poole record to generate any American interest. Like the Stones, Poole had plundered a Crickets B-side, albeit a more sombre example than *Not Fade Away*. They even netted the practical approbation of the song's composer and original producer when Norman Petty — surely the next best thing to the deceased Buddy — volunteered to tinkle the ivories on *Someone Someone* and several other Poole tracks.

This was the final big hit. From their obligatory B-feature, A TOUCH OF THE BLARNEY, came *Twelve Steps to Love* which trudged up to a meek Number 32. More respectable was a revival of the Browns' biographical *Three Bells* at Number 17. Next-up was a frenzied *I Want Candy*, a US hit for the Strangeloves, reaching Number 25 in Britain in the hands of Poole and Co. Seventeen years later, Bow-Wow-Wow did only a little better with their version.

By early 1966 it was every man for himself, as singer

Brian stole the show in Nottingham, 1984.

and backing band recorded separately. However, it wasn't until a Birmingham University booking that Brian finally parted from the Tremeloes, who were on the verge of a 'Second Coming.' By this time, Alan Howard had quit to set up a dry-cleaning business. His place on the Tremeloes first single without Poole, Paul Simon's *Blessed*, was taken by Mike Clarke, who saw the Decca contract out before being supplanted on the CBS follow-up, *Good Day Sunshine* (a Beatles cover), by ex-carpenter Len 'Chip' Hawkes. An adequate bass player, Hawkes was also blessed with a strong lead voice and was considered handsome — sexy even.

The REVOLVER song received airplay on pirate radio but was not a hit. Nevertheless, it suggested a new direction for the Tremeloes. Growing their hair and catching up with the latest psychedelic gear, they updated the fun-loving, beery atmosphere, tinged with sentiment, that they used to create with Brian at the Ayrshire holiday camp in 1961. This reaped immediate dividends when their third effort, *Here Comes My Baby* repeated history when, like their chart debut with Poole, it swept to Number 4. But unlike the previous incarnation it also took the group high into the American Hot 100. After a troubled tour with the Hollies (punctuated with murderous arguments about which of them would play *Reach Out I'll Be There*), the Trems worked the old revamped B-side routine, gaining a chart topper with *Silence Is Golden* from the other side of the Four Seasons' *Rag Doll*.

With this new lease of life, the group yielded twice

as many hits as they had known with Brian. Though there were some miscalculations, it was only in the early 1970s that they really met trouble when, foolishly, they killed the goose while the eggs were still golden by casting aspersions in the Press about the I.Q.s of those who had put their 'rubbish' into the Top 20. They had their last chart entry soon afterwards with the country-flavoured *Hello Buddy*. It wasn't luck that passed them by, but diplomacy.

Supper club audiences don't read music papers and were, therefore, unaware that the Trems had insulted them. With their 'progressive' sounds receiving lukewarm acclaim, the group's latent pop star tendencies resurfaced too late to keep them from the cabaret circuit. During the later 1970s, all the Tremeloes bar Munden took a sabbatical; Hawkes, for instance, sojourned in Nashville for a while to cut a solo L.P. Blakely went into production with, among others, Brian Poole.

Brian's solo career comprised four orchestrated ballad A-sides. Although the second of these, the lachrymose *Everything I Touch Turns to Tears* was voted a hit on JUKE BOX JURY in November 1967, none had so much as a sniff at the Top 50. By 1968, it was possible to buy a pound of sausages from Brian, now back behind the counter of E. Poole and Sons, Family Butchers. But nothing could stop him singing and, sure enough, he was fronting a band again down the local boozer. With the best of intentions, he'd try sticking to current preferences but he knew he'd have to give 'em his old hits before chucking-out time.

When his Tremeloes climbed the charts, Brian characteristically wished them all the best and kept in touch, which is why Blakely dropped by in 1983 to help his old boss with remakes of *Do You Love Me* and *Twist and Shout* as well as proffering advice about a projected new album, SECOND TIME AROUND. Alan knew the game; hadn't the Trems themselves committed the cardinal sin of issuing a clap-trapped medley of their old hits, *Tremelodies*?

In April 1984, Brian Poole was thought by most to have put up the best show at a celebration of thirty years of rock'n'roll at a Nottingham theatre with Dave Berry, the Swinging Blue Jeans, and the Dave Dee group. In those three decades, his hair had gone quite grey. It was as if he'd always been old. Nineteen years earlier as he and the Trems were fading from the charts, he'd taken it philosophically, 'We've had a good run. . . .and even without the hits we have managed to convince most people that we are a good enough band to book'. Without being over-modest as usual, the butcher's boy told it like it was.

Pretty Things in Print

On virtually any Tuesday during 1984, anyone could have seen the Pretty Things perform in the functions room of the Bridge House pub in London's Little Venice free of charge. Word of mouth ensured the place was packed each week as a rough and ready but proficient group backed Phil May who, with shorter hair and rampant good health, became very much the darling of the ladies of Maida Vale. His diction had gained greater clarity (presumably forged of necessity through variable P.A. systems during earlier periods of his wild career). From a ringside table a beardless Dick Taylor, to whom time had been less merciful, would leave his drink to join in numbers he remembered from when he and Phil had first groped at the brittle fabric of fame.

Dick's R'n'B pedigree was already impressive when the Pretty Things began rehearsals in 1963. Graduating from Dartford Grammar School, where London dissolves into Kent, to Sidcup College of Art, he discovered that other graphics students shared his enthusiasm for Chuck Berry, Bo Diddley *et al*. From impromptu jam sessions in common room, toilet (for echo), and his Bexleyheath bedroom, evolved Little Boy Blue and the Blue Boys. The mainstays over a two year privatised regime were guitarist Keith Richards and Dick, who was later persuaded to switch to bass. The singer was a bloke he knew from school called Mike Jagger. More a musical appreciation society than anything else, the lads compounded their blues obsessions when they renamed the band after a Muddy Waters song in 1962.

With a Royal College of Art scholarship pending, Taylor baulked at the idea of 'the Rolling Stones' going professional. Besides, a chance to revert to his natural role as guitarist when a vacancy arose had been thwarted when Mike and Keith, taking advantage of his amenability, had their eyes instead on a fellow from Gloucestershire named Jones. An earlier choice, Reading slide guitarist Mike Cooper, lost interest for the simple reason that he didn't like Chuck Berry.

Conflicting emotions at the unforeseen rise of the

Rubbing shoulders with the clergy may have occasioned the high moral tone of some Pretty Things recordings — Judgement Day, Death of a Socialite *and their Top Fifty swansong,* Ray Davies' House in the Country. *Emotions had some startling moments such as Phil's breathy understatement in* The Sun *and an unprecedented Beach Boys touch in* Children.

100 CLUB

100 OXFORD ST., W.1
7·30 to 11 p.m.

THURSDAY, October 8th
THE GRAHAM BOND ORGANISATION
THE BLUES BY SIX

FRIDAY, October 9th
SANDY BROWN'S JAZZ BAND

SATURDAY, October 10th
ALAN ELSDON'S JAZZ BAND
MICK EMERY'S FOLK GROUP

SUNDAY, October 11th
TERRY LIGHTFOOT'S JAZZMEN

MONDAY, October 12th
THE BIRDS
THE WESTSIDERS

TUESDAY, October 13th
THE PRETTY THINGS
THE BLUES BY SIX

WEDNESDAY, October 14th
THE BACK O' TOWN SYNCOPATORS

THURSDAY, October 15th
THE TRIDENTS
THE EPITAPHS

Full details of the Club from the Secretary, 100 Club, 8 Great Chapel St., W.1 (GER. 0337).

THE CRICKETERS
THE OVAL, SE11 Tel: 735 3059

Wednesday 1st August
THE CARDIACS and THE FERRARI BROTHERS

Thursday 2nd August
CAT TALK

Friday 3rd August
LAVERNE BROWN

Saturday 4th August
GASPER LAWAL

Sunday 5th August
(lunch) **THE ZODIACS**
(eve) **T. S. McPHEE** and **SAM MITCHELL**

Monday 6th August
MYRIAD

Tuesday 7th August
CHRIS THOMPSON BAND
(Ex-Manfred Mann)

Wednesday 8th August
IMMACULATE FOOLS

Thursday 9th August
HERE AND NOW

Sunday 12th August
THE PRETTY THINGS

Around and around: two London club calendars twenty years apart. In 1964 (left) the Pretty Things were on the same week as Ron Wood's Birds and Jeff Beck's pre-Yardbirds Tridents. In 1984, they were preceded by Tony McPhee, former member of John Lee Hooker's UK tour backing group, the Groundhogs.

Stones in 1963 motivated Dick to organise his continued musical activities more earnestly. With Phil May, a younger acolyte of the Sidcup blues crowd, the Pretty Things took recognisable form with the addition of bass guitarist John Stax, fresh from a building site, and rhythm guitarist Brian Pendleton, who answered an advertisement. That no Pretty Thing (or Stone) was a virtuoso did not preclude acceptance — even popularity — in the specialist clubs and college circuit of London's Home Counties. Taylor, for example, had more in common with Hilton Valentine than, say, Jeff Beck; May was no Caruso but, as a latter day manifestation discovered, the concept of a Pretty Things without his frail, straining vocal attack was unthinkable.

The group's abandoned attitude towards R'n'B standards such as *Help Me*, *I'm Ready*, and, of course, *Pretty Thing*, was reviled by purists as being even nearer the knuckle than that of Mike and Keith's band who'd also insolently sucked Berry into the vortex of blues. Mike Cooper, who paid five shillings to see the Pretty Things at the 100 Club on February 28th 1964, wrote in his diary: 'Don't be misled by the name. This group are all atrocious musicians led by a sickening effigy of Mick Jagger. . . .Jagger and the Stones have just succeeded in making a name for themselves and already some maniac, an anaemic-looking little punk, is on his tail'. Unlike the Stones the Pretty Things, in scorning Motown and adopting a less contrived, rawer approach, did indeed give the impression that everything could fall to bits at any given moment. In fact, they were undiluted exponents of art school blues from 'the Medway delta,' patron saints of legions of also-ran 'revolting' R'n'B groups of the Primitives-Beat Merchants ilk.

They might have remained cult celebrities had the same sounds been made by such as wholesome Ian Stewart or Blues Incorporated saxophonist Dick Heckstall-Smith with his galloping alopecia. The Pretty Things' first permanent drummer Viv Andrews was dismissed because his extreme Christian commitment jarred with the post-Beat, anti-everything angle outlined by their management. They peddled a demo of *Route 66* round A&R departments pressurised from above to find their own long-haired, moronic money-makers to combat Decca's Stones coup, the Pretty Things' Stones connection being a handy bartering factor.

However, before a drunken manager signed them after a Central School of Art performance (their fourth paid booking) they had briefly fermented in underground security where among their afficianados were the young Malcolm McLaren, punk Methuselah Charlie Harper, Van Morrison, and an old Bexley Heath and Sydenham acquaintance of Phil's, David Bowie.

Originally involved with the nascent Bonzo Dog Band, who also attended the Royal Academy, managers Bryan Morrison with Jimmy Duncan, though lacking the flash of an Andrew Loog Oldham as managers Bryan Morrison and Jimmy Duncan, though lacking the flash of an Andrew Loog Oldham, were sensible enough to leave their rough Pretty Things made their chart debut). Unrealised by more illustrious pundits than the Club Noreik impressario was that the group's aggressive untidiness and, most spectacularly, the famous hair, were what sold them to the teenagers. They were unlike other pop stars who had merely let their D.A.'s go to seed. The devastation caused by a screeching Phil May on *Top of the Pops*, his cascading, girlish tresses flickering across a surly, blemished complexion, was most keenly felt by those lace-curtained, acned middle-class boys who had previously gazed with yearning at the shadowy sleeve of WITH THE BEATLES — if only Mum and Dad would let me have my hair like George Harrison's then I wouldn't go on about it any more.

Mum and Dad might have chuckled incredulously when these cartoon beatniks flashed into the living room as Phil, by slightly overdoing the obnoxiousness, somehow gave the impression that he too was aware of and revelled in his repellent fascination. Others, however, failed to grasp this underlying humour, a common opinion being that, put bluntly, them Stones may look like ponces but they ain't half professional — not like 'them other hairy gits' in the Pretty Things. Beyond verbal abuse, this was projected by last minute cancellations by hoteliers expecting trouble and punch-ups with provincial cowboys, which in its extremity included some unpleasantness with a shotgun at one particular cultural backwater. But attempts to evict them from their Belgravia flat (13, Chester Street) were nipped in the bud after a CHECKPOINT-type investigation on ITV.

As Britain's overseas representatives, the story was much the same, their exile from New Zealand soil being an ultimate instance. However, US radio censoring of the line 'I laid her on the ground' from their biggest hit, the quintessential *Don't Bring Me Down*, and the issue of a 'clean' version by an outfit called On Her Majesty's Service backfired, when the Pretty Things' notoriety was emphasised to such a pitch that adolescent America and its exploiters hungrily anticipated a freak carnival of greater magnitude than even those far-out Rolling Stones. Appetites were further whetted with filmed TV snippets including a group interview direct from Dick's parents' front room. No time was better for the Pretty Things to clean up in the States — tours were negotiated, trade mag adverts were designed ('proof positive that long hair *can* be popular'). Dollars danced before their eyes but Morrison and Duncan dithered until the thrill had gone.

Back home, there were questions in Parliament, God slot TV discussions, and hellfire sermons concerning the depth to which pop music had sunk with its championing of such filthy, shaggy degenerates. On one such screening where the group were invited to answer their clerical critics, their verbal contributions were hastily restricted in case they upset the programme's intentions by using long words and acting intelligent. Still it added to turnout at gigs. Bemused by sudden infamy, it became usual for Pretty Things engagements to be filled to overflowing mainly by curiosity-seekers with only the vaguest notion about the music they had paid to hear.

The group enjoyed one good year before record sales took a dive, though their music acquired a less derivative sophistication as Phil and Dick found their feet as songwriters. In June 1967, their final Fontana L.P. EMOTIONS contained some startling moments but

The Pretty Things in a hotel foyer in January 1985: (left to right) *Joe Shaw (guitar), Jon Clark (drums), Dave Winter (bass), Kevin Flanagan (sax), Dick Taylor (guitar), Phil May (vocals) and Dave Wilkie (Keyboards).*

its programming was such that after a few passable tracks, the group ran out of creative steam. Underneath the desperate overdubs of bandstand brass and tea dance strings was a London R'n'B group in uncertain transition, which is why, as a musical faux pas, EMOTIONS is worth listening to for that reason alone.

Clutching at unlikely lucrative straws, the acceptance of offers to churn out incidental music for films led to further involvement in cinema such as an appearance in the finale of 1980 horror spoof THE MONSTER CLUB. More renowned was their part as token reprobate pop group in WHAT'S GOOD FOR THE GOOSE fourteen years earlier. As it became obvious that its star, Norman Wisdom, was failing in his attempt at becoming a second Rudolph Valentino, the Pretty Things' contribution to the film was considerably increased beyond that of the sideshow originally required.

By 1969, the group was on its knees. Stax had emigrated. Pendleton had vanished without trace. Drummer Viv Prince embarked on a brief solo career before an unhappy association with the Hell's Angels. Though the band's most experienced musician, his dedicated unreliability sweetened the pill of his passing. The most vital source of new personnel was from the ranks of Kentish group the Fenmen, who had created an overlooked minor key classic in *Rejected*.

Dick Taylor had thrown in the towel in 1969 but by

the turn of the decade, they'd all had enough. No longer an overnight sensation, it was still necessary to maintain the trappings of a shooting star reputation whilst holding creditors at arm's length. With slender margins for progression and dogged by an abysmal distribution set-up in America, there was also a sobering undercurrent in the knowledge that the next bite of the apple, if it ever came, would never be as big as in 1964.

Nevertheless, beneath pop's capricious quicksand was a sufficient bedrock of encouragement assuring them that this was always just around the next bend of the freeway, even if everyone else was presently deaf to meisterwerks like the *Defecting Grey* single, S.F. SORROW and the critically-acclaimed PARACHUTE. After a US tour supporting the Kinks in 1976, there was a three year lay-off until a reformation for a solitary Dutch concert sponsored by a fan was stimulating enough to give it yet another go.

This brings us back to the Bridge House where the evening closed with a driving *Gimme Some Lovin'*. That they were still able to whip up the old vicarious excitement after an age of struggle and heartache placed them outside the realm of heroic failures. Pop is an unfair, erratic business. Arbitrary isolations — a producer's stomach ache, a manager's procrastination, a drummer's hangover, an agent's extended lunch break, an amplifier packing up, parental pressure, a flat tyre — all these unrelated trivialities can trigger changes effecting the whole course of a band's career even one with the tenacity and class of the Pretty Things.

The Searchers Play The System

With two smash hits in rapid succession, the Searchers caused the Beatles some nervous backward glances by the close of 1963. Making their Top 30 debut in the summer, they soon closed the gap of Gerry and the Pacemakers' head start as leading pretenders to the Beatle crown. As MEET THE SEARCHERS shut down HOW DO YOU LIKE IT in the L.P. lists, a Searchers E.P. generated enough interest to rate in the singles chart. Even an ancient live recording from one of their Hamburg visits warranted an entry. Even so, the Beatles felt secure enough to be magnanimous on their celebrated JUKE BOX JURY service in early 1964. Voting *Needles and Pins* a 'ding!' the kings of the jungle declared the Searchers their favourite Liverpool group.

This compliment was fully deserved by a band that with the merest skiffle prelude had only been in existence since 1960, when 18 year old guitarist John McNally was asked to form a backing unit for singer Johnny Sandon. From his old school he enlisted drummer Chris Crummy and Michael Pendergast, another guitarist. The line-up was completed by an older boy of formidable local reputation, bass guitarist Tony 'Black Jake' Jackson. To complement their mixed repertoire of American pop and country, they named themselves 'the Searchers' after a 1956 John Ford western. By 1962, they had amassed a potent enough following to justify a high placing in *Merseybeat's* annual popularity poll. However, shortly afterwards, the Searchers and Sandon parted company, Black Jake's strong personality possibly forcing the issue. At any rate, it was he who supplanted Johnny in the lead vocal spotlight.

The Beatles may have ruled the Cavern but the Searchers' standing at the Iron Door in similarly mildewed Temple Street was such that the club hosted their fan club convention in January 1964. This drew coach parties from distant London as well as being blessed by the presence of singer-comedian Ken Dodd. Only three Searchers attended, their lead singer being stranded on the wrong side of the North Sea.

*Meet the Searchers (*left to right*) John McNally, Chris Curtis, Mike Pender and Tony Jackson.*

131

Like other Merseyside acts, the group had regular bookings in clubs in the red light district of Hamburg 4. At their Star Club residency in spring 1963, they were housed in the crowded but homely Pacific Hotel (which was a far cry from the stinking dungeons provided for the Seniors, Beatles and other Reeperbahn pioneers over two years earlier). Though time could hang heavy between sets, the actual hours spent playing were greatly reduced from the punishing eight hour shifts of 1960. Though the overwhelming Grosse Freiheit toughened them up, the Searchers became exceptional for their less frenetic versions of Merseybeat standards like *Money* and *What'd I Say*. They could rock out with the best of them but the overall impression was that they preferred a more subtle approach. A comparison could be made between the smooth precision of their *Twist and Shout* and the Beatles almost uncontrollable version. The Searchers' approach paid dividends in lighter selections like their good-natured update of Don and Dewey's *Farmer John*, though they were weak on more intense items like their gutless rendition of Ben E. King's *Stand by Me*. Much more successful were their adaptations of discs by female artistes such as Laverne Baker's *Bumble Bee*, Brenda Lee's *Sweet Nothings* and, from the Orlons, *Shimmy Shimmy* and *Don't Throw Your Love Away*.

Even more far-reaching was their fusion of Merseybeat and contemporary folk. They frequently stole the show from wilder co-stars with the maudlin sentimentality of *All My Sorrows* or *Where Have All the Flowers Gone*. With the uniquely circular effect of fingerpicking two electric guitars, this trademark was later broadened by using 12 string models. Of equal importance were the distinctively melodic three- and four-part harmonies developed during battles with primitive house P.A. systems over hundreds of hours onstage. This was the richest legacy given by the group to their transatlantic cousins in 1964. Listening consecutively to their *When You Walk In the Room* and the Byrds' *Don't Doubt Yourself Babe* (both Jackie de Shannon songs) the sounds of the two groups merge until they become interchangeable.

Back in Britain where the Beatles, Gerry, and Billy J. were tearing up the Top 20, the Searchers correctly anticipated a demand for more Liverpool groups. In cleaning up their act, having been no better than they ought in Hamburg, Pendergast and Crummy also seized the opportunity to alter their respective surnames to the more glamourous 'Pender' and 'Curtis'. Sure enough, by May 1963 the Searchers had acquired Tito Burns, a London manager who had come to stake his claim in the musical diggings up North. That Brian Epstein did not sign them is surprising as, more than any other Merseyside band, they exemplified ideally the two guitars, bass and drums archetype of the British Beat explosion.

Within a fortnight, Burns had them under contract to Pye Records who also drained Liverpool of the Undertakers, Chants and (by coincidence) Johnny Sandon and his new band, the Remo Four. The job of producing the Searchers fell to Tony Hatch who was more accustomed to the easy-listening sophistications of the Wally Stott Orchestra or Petula Clark. Nevertheless, with his assistance, the group were home and dry by August with an exuberant reading of a little-known Drifters track, *Sweets for My Sweet*, booting Elvis from Number One. While the iron was hot, Hatch under a pseudonym reworked the song as *Sugar and Spice* which only failed to match its predecessor because of the inconsiderate Beatles' Yuletide offering, *I Want to Hold Your Hand*.

The Searchers' elevation was not quite the walkover it seemed. From the moment the Pye agreement was inked, they plunged into an exhausting but exhilarating schedule of zigzagging one night stands, TV and radio spots, and other promotional necessities. Among high points were a weekly Radio Luxembourg series and package tours on the scream circuit with Roy Orbison, Freddie and the Dreamers, and Tommy Roe where mobbing by fans was a pleasurable hazard. They also contributed to two film soundtracks, *Saturday Night Out* and *The System*, starring Oliver Reed.

One onerous obligation was an outstanding engagement at the Star Club but, in the long term, this had hidden blessings emerging from social and musical exchanges with another club attraction of December 1963, Cliff Bennett and the Rebel Rousers. By the time of their return to their disturbed UK sales campaign, the Searchers' sparser arrangements of two Bennett crowd-pleasers had been incorporated into the act. One was Stephen Foster's *Beautiful Dreamer*, the other was to become their second chart-topper and the song that most people would forever associate with them. The unhappy outcome of a studio rehearsal of *Needles and Pins* (another de Shannon number) was an irrecoverable schism within the ranks leading to the first major group personnel change of the Beat era. Tony Jackson's growing unease with his colleagues' musical preferences had come to a head when Pender was elected to sing lead on *Needles and Pins*.

During his six month layoff following the split Jackson had his nose remodelled before fronting a London backing band, the Vibrations. A less

Crummy's Last Stand, 1964: nineteen years later, the Searchers suffered a certain loss of dignity when they were involved in a TV send-up of When You Walk In the Room *with comedians Little and Large — the 'Syd and Eddie' of this poster.*

pugnacious Tony enjoyed a minor hit with a cover of Mary Wells' *Bye Bye Baby* backed with Bobby Parker's *Watch Your Step* from the Iron Door days. Both sides, however, radically departed from the old group's sound with Martin Raymond's Farfisa organ and girl background singers highlighting an aggressive lead vocal. Sadly, times got tougher for Jackson and, in extremis, he even re-recorded an old Searchers' track, *Love Potion Number Nine*. After his seventh single made its depressingly familiar journey to the bargain bins, Black Jake was lost to the archives of oblivion.

Back on the ranch, the Searchers had spirited the less volatile Frank Allen (Francis McNiece) away from the Rebel Rousers. This transition enacted, it seemed that no harm had been done as *Don't Throw Your Love Away* tramped the well-trodden path to Number One in April 1964. However, the end of the Searchers' high summer was nigh. Peaking at Number 11, *Someday We're Gonna Love Again* was a comparative non-event, possibly because current releases from the Beatles, Stones and new sensations the Animals deluged this run-of-the-mill effort. Rallying, the Searchers returned to the Top 3 with their pièce de resistance, *When You Walk in the Room*, aided by a promotional film shot outside Sydney Opera House. Nevertheless, it was clear that their records could no longer be assumed to automatically chart.

Much of the fault lay with Pye who, predicting only fleeting prosperity for Merseybeat, rush-released as much Searchers product in the first fiscal year as the traffic would allow. By April 1964, supplementing the singles were three L.P.'s — with attendant E.P.

133

off-shoots — compared to the Beatles' two and Gerry's one. This meant that after a fat twelve months, the arrival of newer bands such as Pye's own Kinks made the concept of collecting Every-Record-The-Searchers-Ever-Made economically unsound for the average teenager.

Also, as they had doggedly stuck to the same safe 45 formula since *Sweets for My Sweet*, they were starting to sound dated. One exception, the 'protest' song, *What Have They Done to the Rain*, ironically offended hard-line Searchers purists with its use of strings. In Britain they had become strictly a singles act by 1965 and in the States, this story was being repeated on a grander scale.

In a continent gone crazy about Liverpudlia, even a malfunctioning amplifier went unnoticed amid uncritical audience hysteria during the Searchers' USA television debut on the ED SULLIVAN SHOW. While they were kept busy on a coast-to-coast tour with the Supremes, their US label, Kapp, began saturating the market with Searchers' records with much the same result as Pye had had in Britain. With the foreseen signs of flagging in autumn 1964, Kapp countered by issuing the group's catchy treatment of the Clovers' aphrodisiacal *Love Potion Number Nine* with Jackson singing. Previously unavailable in the US, this antique album track at Number 3 in the Hot 100 was the band's biggest American smash. Resuming their chart decline, P.F. Sloan's *Take Me For What I'm Worth* was their Hot 100 swansong from this period though *Desdemona* managed a modest Number 94 as late as September 1971.

Ending a world tour with a long British trek with the Zombies, a shattered Chris Curtis collected his cards. From being rather a practical joker, he had grown into a withdrawn, disillusioned neurotic. After a failed solo single — appropriately entitled *Aggravation* — he dabbled in record production before an unlikely role as lead singer with Roundabout. When this group ground to a halt in 1967, three of its number, including Chris's flatmate, Jon Lord, became the nucleus of Deep Purple, while Curtis quit showbusiness altogether becoming Chris Crummy again in the security of the civil service.

He had been the Searchers' most prolific composer although all group originals were restricted to B-sides and album fillers except for *He's Got No Love* which, though only a moderate seller, was a personal triumph for Chris and his collaborator, Mike Pender. The rest of the group's output consisted mainly of revivals, covers and items specifically written for them by professional tunesmiths like Burt Bacharach, the aforementioned

Hatch, and his wife, Jackie Trent. From the pens of other artists came examples like *Ain't Gonna Kiss Ya* (P.J. Proby) and *Take It or Leave It* (Jagger and Richard).

Unlike Manfred Mann who likewise depended on outside help, the Searchers lost the knack of picking hits. Their final Top 50 placing was with the risqué *Have You Ever Loved Somebody* which found itself fighting a rival version by Paul and Barry Ryan which, by chance, happened to have been produced by Chris Curtis. Their deterioration was worsened by periodic absences from the recording scene arising from legal problems after Pye allowed their option to expire in 1968.

Spending most of the 1970s in a cabaret rut, the Searchers nonetheless accrued more cash than they had ever realised as serious chart contenders. An ugly surtax demand in 1973 made it prudent for them to join the bill of a British Invasion Reunion tour of the States. On this trek, Neil Young got what he deserved with the Searchers' fifteen minute extrapolation of his *Southern Man* diatribe, an attempt by the group to show that though they'd never worn headbands or played Woodstock, they were still hip. However, all they did was confuse people.

Six years later, *Melody Maker* editor Allan Jones reviewed a more typical Searchers engagement at Rhydyfelen Non-political Club in his native Wales. This wasn't as novel an expedition as it seemed because, having been signed to the mainly New Wave Sire label, the Searchers were no longer quite the has-beens previously imagined. This venture was well-received critically and a single from one of the two albums almost charted. But at a showcase at London's Nashville Rooms, the audience found juxtaposition of the remembered classics and all these new-fangled numbers by the likes of Tom Petty and Bob Dylan unsettling. Some clever dick asked Pender how the new boy was settling in, referring not to Billy Adamson, drummer since 1967, but to Frank Allen, a Searcher for nigh on twenty years.

The real benefit from this episode was the broadening of the group's work spectrum, especially into the lucrative US supper clubs and invitations to appear on television again for the first time in years. On a Sunday in May 1984, they showed up on ITV's KNEES UP, a pub-style singalong, where they ran through a medley of their best-loved songs while the patrons danced, sang and clapped in time. Considering the fate of most other Merseybeat groups — including the Beatles — being on such a programme wasn't such a bad place for the Searchers to finish up.

All or Nothing for the Small Faces

Blue note Mods really existed only in London and the bigger cities where it was easier to keep apace with the times, as did prototypes like David Bowie whose prissy Mod coiffure adorns the cover of his first L.P. His friend Marc Bolan even aspired to be a 'Face' — a self-appointed Mod leader who wantonly redesigned the image from tailor to dance floor. Unlike Sloane Rangers who are ruled by seasons, real Mod was open-ended and in constant flux. Everything had to be just so; all or nothing. Back vents were precisely five inches one week, seven the next. How wide are lapels now? I only bought this shirt six days ago but I can't ever wear it again.

With their deepest musical roots in an alien US culture, the Who were tolerated even though they were always half a step behind fashion-wise and were regarded as 'Mods' by yokels in Uxbridge and Staines. Zoot Money and Georgie Fame were fair interpreters of the Americans but who could like Long John Baldry? Should I buy Dobie Gray or Betty Everett this Friday? Don't tell me you haven't heard *Whatcha Gonna Do About It* from Doris Troy! Talking of which, don't miss the Small Faces on READY STEADY GO this week. They're Mods like us; the genuine article. You better believe it.

Like Herman Noone, Jimmy Langwith and Steve Marriott were both child actors. Jimmy had bit parts in many feature films while Steve was in the West End in 1962 as the Artful Dodger in Lionel Bart's OLIVER!. After eighteen months of *Food Glorious Food*, his voice broke. Not liking to see this public exposure going to waste, Decca engaged 15 year old Marriott as a pop singer. After two solo singles (including a very Buddy Hollyish *Give Her My Regards*) died a death, Steve, who played a bit of guitar, formed the Moments with Langwith on bass, future Animal John Weider on rhythm, and passing drummers. In a futile attempt to put one over on the Kinks, the Moments' window-rattling version of *You Really Got Me* was issued by World Artists purely for the US market. Then followed Steve Marriott and his Frantic Ones (amended to just 'the Frantics') who added no further depth to the vinyl oceans.

By this time, the ex-Dodger was serving behind the counter at the J60 Music Box equipment workhouse in his native East Ham. One afternoon is Spring 1964, this geezer comes in looking for a Harmony bass guitar. . . .

In the ensuing conversation which continued after hours 'round Steve's gaff,' it turned out that this Ronnie Lane from Plaistow worked in quality control at Fender where one of the perks was that he could borrow amplifiers, etc. to use with his band, the Pioneers, formerly the Outcasts, who happened to have a pub booking that very evening. While sifting through Steve's erudite record collection for keys to character, Ronnie decided to invite his fellow Mod along for a blow. The resulting performance, made chaotic by an illicit chemically-induced haze, caused the under-age Pioneers and Marriott to be barred by an outraged landlord. The next day, within the cool of hangover logic, the Small Faces were conceived.

From the Pioneers came Lane and Kenneth Jones, a drummer discovered in a Stepney pub duo by Ronnie's barman brother, Stanley. The late Frantics contributed Marriott and, having changed both instrument and surname, organist Jimmy Winston né Langwith. Their stylistic determination was to be like an English Booker T and the MG's with vocals.

With a name adopted at a girlfriend's suggestion, the Small Faces dry-ran a courageous extrapolation of a mere half-dozen numbers at Club 60 in remote Sheffield. By June, they had gained a residency closer to home at the 'Cavern' in Leicester Square. Included in their repertoire were passionate interpretations of the Miracles' *You Really Got a Hold On Me*, Brenda Holloway's *Every Little Bit Hurts* (current Spencer Davis A-side) and Marvin Gaye's *Baby Don't You Do It* which eclipsed the Who's version.

At this venue, they were spotted by Don Arden, an impressario of extreme strategy and a fast mouth. Becoming their manager, he swept aside obstacles like demos and auditions and had the group signed to Decca purely through their pressure-cooker reputation in central London clubland. Dispelling any small clouds of doubt, the Small Faces were secure in the Top 50 within eight weeks. With a chord sequence lifted from a Solomon Burke number and a title from Doris Troy, *Whatcha Gonna Do About It* was knocked together by producer Ian Samwell who had also penned Cliff's *Move It* in 1958. Actually playing their own instruments in the studio, the group aided by a session tambourinist (!) and Samwell's console twiddling, truly earned their tea break. Like Booker T's band in a Cockney brainstorm, a foundation was laid for Steve to regurgitate his lot, his heart-failure soul bandit vocal anguish matching the feedback scrawl of his electronic guitar.

Unfortunately, the buoyant optimism of this initial breakthrough was temporarily dampened when the follow-up, Lane and Marriott's *I Got Mine*, took a dive. A sober, introspective ballad, this might have been by a different group. Though a musical progression, it was issued too soon for Mr. Average to appreciate that the Small Faces, with only a Number 14 hit to their credit, were anything other than that lot with a knock-kneed, strangulated singer who, with a finger in his ear, screeched himself black in the face.

In the light of this failure, Jimmy Winston was not particularly bitter when fired after a harrassed READY STEADY GO appearance in which his vainglorious keyboard posturing had drawn audience attention away from Marriott. Dark nights of the ego apart, it had been felt for some time that he was too tall and burly anyway to be a proper Small Face. From the Who's end of London came a replacement of more suitable build, Ian MacLagen who, studying industrial design at Twickenham, had waxed a version of Howlin' Wolf's *Back Door Man* with the college band, the Muleskinners with ex-Rooster Terry Brennan. However, it was as a member of Boz People that he came to the notice of the Small Faces.

On the rebound, Jimmy re-recorded *Sorry She's Mine* from his last Small Faces session. Though this single sank without trace, a song co-written by the same composer, singer-comedian Kenny Lynch, was to put Winston's old group back on course. Both dinky little pop songs, *Sha-La-La-La-Lee* (for every boy with marriage in mind) and the lesser *Hey Girl* were better fitted to, say, Herman's Hermits or Adam Faith but the Small Faces dealt with them commendably. Both B-sides were off-the-wall instrumentals revealing a mature absorption of the Stax-Jimmy Reed genre.

Their only Number One, *All or Nothing*, was a million soul miles from any costermonger's christening and, aided by a strong flip in *Understanding*, fully restored any lost Mod credibility. Nonetheless, the next brace of 45's rested on its laurels. With a weather eye on Christmas, *My mind's eye* — derived from *Ding Dong Merrily On High* — made the Top 10 on earlier merit; but this was not the case with 1967's first effort, *I Can't Make It*, which despite outlaw chic gained from an arbitrary BBC ban fell far short in chart terms of what *Relax* achieved in later years (although it was, in fact, less suggestive than the similarly-arranged *All or Nothing* which had somehow slipped the censor's net). At one point, the B-side, the whimsical *Just Passing* sung by Ronnie Lane, was given preference in a salvage attempt.

However, this aberration notwithstanding, the Small Faces were chart fixtures for three years when singles mattered most. That they also did well in the album lists was gratifying as confirmation of deeper popularity but the financial and artistic arrangements made by Arden and Decca were so unsatisfactory that the group's allegiance to both was faltering by winter 1966. Yet, despite possible economic repercussions, it was feasible that management and corporation were just as sick of the Small Faces. Their isolation from everyday life, prompted by stardom, gave vitality to rude, disrespectful behaviour towards important executives in the music industry and media who, despite finding them personally objectionable, were obliged to promote the Small Faces' continued chart success in order to cater to a considerable and, in many cases, equally repulsive, teenage following. In this respect, Marriott and his cronies anticipated by over a decade the prevalent attitude of the Sex Pistols and their disciples — the Pistols' early sets actually including an updated *Whatcha Gonna Do About It* ('I want you to know that I *hate* you baby'.)

After an apocryphal period with the Harold Davidson firm, the Small Faces came under the aegis of the formidable Andrew Loog Oldham, mentor of Immediate, Britain's first major independent record label. He was also manager of the Stones who, though tied to Decca until 1970, were associated by affinity to Immediate and in close social contact with the Small Faces; Marriott, for example, had been romantically linked with Jagger's former girlfriend, Chrissie Shrimpton, and had attended a few SATANIC MAJESTIES sessions. Oldham, supported by Jagger and Keith Richards, lent a sympathetic ear to sad tales of Decca's indifference, stinginess and general lack of understanding. Gradually it was made clear that the Small Faces — hot property for any UK company — would be an even greater proposition on Immediate, where everyone fired on all cylinders, than if they re-signed with uncool, staid old Decca.

They had been able to conduct some minor experiments, such as the police whistle that punctuated *Understanding*, within the limited studio time granted previously, but their entire period with Immediate represented an unrestricted creative peak. However, much of the rough edge and drive born of earlier conditions was tempered as Steve's voice was now able to float effortlessly over layers of treated sound, courtesy of Immediate's sophisticated eight-track desk.

Co-related with this episode of imagination and invention was evidence of the group's drug experiences. Not yet versed in hip jargon, BBC narks passed their first Immediate single, *Here Comes the Nice*, celebrating the energising effects of amphetamine sulphate. Indication of L.S.D. usage — which started as early as 1965 — emerged on *Itchycoo Park* with its effervescent phasing and surreal

The Rodgers and Hammerstein of Mod: Lane and Marriott promote Hey Girl *on RSG, May 1966.*

invocation of light and space which even the *omnes fortissimo* 'it's all too beautiful' chorus could not mar.

Hallucinatory influences were less pronounced on *Lazy Sunday Afternoon* which best summed up the Small Faces dialectic by merging their R'n'B roots, gorblimey chirpiness and psychedelic trendiness with a wash of sound effects for good measure. Thankfully, this pot-pourri, by avoiding over-arranged affectation, was a deserved smash hit inexplicably stopped at Number 2 by the 'Young Girl' warbling of Gary Puckett and his Union Gap. *Lazy Sunday* reappeared in context on the best-selling OGDEN'S NUT GONE FLAKE two months later in June 1968. This album wears much better than other 'concept' artefacts from the same period even if Stanley Holloway's linking verbal gymnastics are not exactly conducive to mirror freaking.

In common with major group songwriters of the Davies-Townshend proliferation, Marriott and Lane earned pin money by composing for other artists. However, monetary rewards were meagre in this direction beyond two minor chart placings for Immediate playmates Chris Farlowe (*My Way of Giving*) and P.P. Arnold (*If You Think You're Groovy*), who later sang on a Small Faces single, *Tin Soldier*. There were also rumours of a Salvation Army choir recording of *Happydays Toytown* from OGDEN'S.

The group made their unsweeping exit at Alexandra Palace on New Year's Day 1969 when Marriott stumbled offstage in a daze as they jammed *Lazy Sunday* with special guest Alexis Korner. A break-up had been first mooted on an exhausting Australian tour with a newly-acquired horn section while, on the other side of the globe, the unusual *Universal* — nodding vaguely towards Dylan's *Tombstone Blues* — was having a hard time in the summer charts. They had also been unable to cross the Atlantic when *Itchycoo Park* made their biggest strike in the US Hot 100. When they finally played the Fillmore East in the latter half of 1968, their UK chart seniority did not prevent Birmingham newcomers the Move from topping the bill.

The following year, Jones, Lane, and MacLagen with two likely lads from the Jeff Beck Group, built on this small beginning in the States, eventually abbreviating the name to just 'Faces'. Marriott too lit out for America with Humble Pie after pushing a nondescript single into the UK chart and achieving slight notoriety for boorish behaviour on TOP OF THE POPS.

After a shallow megastardom accrued over 22 US tours, Steve began thinking aloud about reforming the old firm. The others were high and dry after Ron Wood and Rod Stewart's defections to the Stones and Hollywood respectively and a reformation seemed a natural regression, especially as the Small Faces were among the few 1960s acts tolerated by the mushrooming New Wave. The only fly in the ointment was nomadic Ronnie Lane, who, having quit the Faces before the rot set in, was content with the modest acclaim realised by his new band, Slim Chance. He agreed to attend rehearsals but left after a fracas with Marriott. A replacement was found in time for the Small Faces British tour which, symbolising the desired rebirth, began in Sheffield. However, it soon became painfully transparent that all their fans, old and new, wanted were the sounds of yesteryear, as poor sales of the two 'comeback' albums against healthy chart performances of the reissued *Itchycoo Park* and *Lazy Sunday* testified. It was no longer so easy to bounce back.

Rather than milk nostalgia, MacLagen got himself temporarily enlisted into the Stones and Jones into the Who, thus affirming the respect still held in musical circles for former Small Faces. It had been on the cards for Marriott to join the Stones in 1974 in place of the departed Mick Taylor but in the 1980s, tempted by the distant roar of the crowd, he would materialise in London pubs fronting pick-up bands with funny names. Almost without fail, he could still belt out the old magic even if nobody was getting any younger.

From Andover — the Troggs

Seventy miles west of the Chiswick flyover in west London is the farming town of Andover on a tributary of the River Test. Here in 1965, friction existed between two home-grown groups — Ten Foot Five (who had made a record) and the Trogdolytes (who went in for a lot of instrumentals). Eventually the former gave up the ghost and the other lot, adopting a more diminutive name, continued traipsing round St. Anne's Institute, the T.A. Centre, Wallop Village Hall and other familiar venues within spitting distance of Andover.

The Troggs originally consisted of guitarists David Wright and Howard Mansfield, bass player Reginald Ball, and drummer Ronnie Bond, a trainee jockey. However, with the absence of rivals taking the fun out of the game, Wright and Mansfield both left to be replaced from the ranks of the defunct Ten Foot Five. The first of these was Peter Staples who had been taught bass in a Boy Scout band. He had known Ball and Bond when all three attended Andover Secondary Modern. The odd Trogg out was Chris Britton, a younger boy from the Grammar School who had exacerbated his implied intellectual superiority by studying classical guitar for four years. Not such a snob that he couldn't transfer to electric, he was a competent enough rock'n'roller to allow Reg Ball to front the band as lead singer rather than undertake guitar chores himself.

Beginning with the less complicated material from the repertoires of the Stones and other metropolitan R'n'B combos, the Troggs worked backwards to cruder influences like Chuck Berry, Little Richard, Muddy Waters and Slim Harpo as well as trying Stax and Motown items going the rounds like *Ride Your Pony* and *Knock on Wood*. Weary of brittle parochial fame, they voyaged over the edge of the world to tape demos at one of these here fancy London studios. Hawking the results round West End publishers, the Trogg treatment of *You Really Got Me* chanced on the ears of Kinks manager Larry Page who, like other music business entrepreneurs, was no longer so dismissive of pop groups from the sticks. Though the Troggs had exceeded his own protegés primitive exuberance, Page was only able to secure his new clients a one-off deal with CBS, who issued the first Troggs single in February 1966.

Though she was never found in Britain, *Lost Girl*, written by Ball, entered the Dutch Top 10; but opportunities for CBS to take up their option were thwarted when the Troggs were signed to a long term lease contract with Fontana. By process of elimination, choices for the next release boiled down to either a safe Lovin' Spoonful cover or another American song, *Wild Thing*, which walked a tightrope between inspiration and rubbish.

They decided to plunge in at the deep end. Despite uncertainties about its lyrical content, the group punched out *Wild Thing* in one take in the fifteen minutes of studio time left after an orchestral session directed by Page. Like film stars obliged to act a nude scene, Pete, Ronnie, and Chris — though only semi-pro — ignored the supercilious grins of departing classically-trained musicians as the number's pulsating three chord trick framed Reg's transatlantic-Hampshire drawl which extended from monotonous snarl to sensual mutter. He also replaced the whistling of James Voight's demo with a remarkable ocarina solo. The Troggs even found time to have a go at another one of Reg's songs, *With a Girl Like You* before knocking off for the night.

Prior to the campaign to launch the record, Page suggested that Reg's surname did not have quite the same ring to it as, say, 'Jagger', 'Starr' or even 'Winwood'. Taking this to heart, Reg settled for an affinity to the most famous pop star of all time.

Though myth later intimated that Reg Presley had

been part of the research team that invented the motorway fog warning light, he was employed on a building site when *Wild Thing* began to catch the imagination of young England in May 1966. One day as the sound of the Troggs penetrated from a workmate's transistor, Reg downed tools to make a frustrated 'phone call to Page. By the evening, the group had gone professional. Before long, they had appeared on THANK YOUR LUCKY STARS and SATURDAY CLUB and were off on a package tour with the Dave Dee group, where their rustic charms won more hearts.

The general reaction of the music industry to the Troggs retrograde simplicity was one of bemusement. After all, 'progress' was in the air in 1966; even old Tich from Dave Dee's mob was using a balalaika. The Yardbirds with almost the same instrumental line-up as the Troggs had gone far beyond the 12-bar blues band they once were. As Graham Nash explained, the Troggs were so far behind, they were ahead.

Mick Jagger was intrigued enough to proffer advice during a fruitless attempt to improve upon *With a Girl Like You*, chosen to follow *Wild Thing*. Ironically, it

Wild Things: so Far Out, they're In. Who else but the Troggs?

In 1966, there was a 'security leak' that Chris Britton (blond) was quitting the band — though contractually bound till 1971 — because of his profession's association with illegal drug-taking. This served the dual purpose of facilitating quicker customs clearance and assuring parents that the Troggs were decent, clean-minded lads. The other fellow is Pete Staples.

was the first rough and ready version of this song that pushed Jagger's production of Chris Farlowe's *Out of Time* from Number One in August.

The Troggs time in the sun lasted until 1968. Until then, every record they made was a world-wide smash. The only exception was *Hi Hi Hazel* lifted from the year old L.P. From Nowhere to steal some of the thunder from Geno Washington's version, which likewise rose no higher than Number 40 in Britain. One of the biggest sellers, *I Can't Control Myself*, was the subject of a total ban in Australia because it contained the word 'hips' though nearer the knuckle was what was almost said in its lewd, minor key middle eight. The more explicit *Give It To Me* six months later somehow escaped unscathed. Casting Reg as a sort of bumpkin Heathcliff, the rush-released *Night of the Long Grass*, loaded with sexual innuendo, suffered airplay restrictions in the States on the ridiculous premise that it referred to drugs ('grass' and all that).

Though these sanctions bolstered the Troggs' rebel rocker image, there was an increasing tendency to slow the tempo down, the obvious example being the placatory *Anyway That You Want Me*. Like the Stranglers after them, the sales angle was that of hard men with a romantic underbelly; their UK chart swansong, *Love Is All Around* was even regarded by some as a flower power anthem. Using the well-tried limited chordal range, this softer side was intensified with fairy dust strings though Reg's nasal intonation could not be mutated electronically or otherwise to sound like Scott Walker, a singer he much admired.

Presley's vocal shortcomings, if anything, added to the overall attraction, especially in the United States. After *Wild Thing* hit Number One there, much impetus was lost through legal wrangles between Fontana and US label, Atco, both of whom claimed the rights to release Troggs records in America. Though their Hot 100 placings dwindled, they accumulated a large following during two nationwide tours, the first supporting the Who, the next in their own right. However, in the long term, it was their instrumental directness coupled with Reg's whining, sneering style that encouraged hundreds of minor US groups from ? and the Mysterions to Mouse and the Traps to borrow aspects of the Troggian dialectic. Overlooking the group's capitalistic contribution to a Miller beer advertising exercise, even the radical MC5 paid their agitprop tribute in their mangling of *I Want You*, a Troggs B-side. There was also a drivelling 28-page eulogy of Presley and Co. by the late journalist Lester Bangs in a US fanzine.

Larry Page, who co-wrote *I Want You* and other Trogg tracks, was the antithesis of the revolutionary ideologies of the MC5. His royalties enabled him to finance his own record company, Page One, in which the Troggs were the main money-spinners. Other Page One ambassadors of the non-existent 'Andover Sound' were the Nerve and Loot, who featured Dave Wright from the Trogdolyte era.

In decline, the Troggs clutched at dubious straws such as a few 'psychedelic' experiments like the self-explanatory *Maybe the Madman* or, more bizarre, *Purple Shades* (where old Reg goes on about 'the bamboo butterflies of yer mind'). In 1970, a muddled endeavour to relaunch themselves back into the hit parade yielded instead an insight into their recording methods. During a session for *Tranquillity*, an intended A-side, an enterprising engineer left the tape running during a studio discussion. The group had occasionally consumed needle time with rehearsed dialogue tracks such as *Off the Record* from the L.P. MIXED BAG, but the notorious 'Troggs tape' was much more interesting. In a conversation riddled with swearing they and their entourage argue at cross purposes about hiring an independent producer before trying to sort out the mess themselves. The high point of this unconscious humour is when Ronnie almost comes to blows with the patronising Reg over a one-bar drum fill. If nothing else, it proved that the band's naive peasant image was not entirely contrived — though such a session was not untypical of many other groups. Whatever did their mothers think?

Chris Britton was allowed to abandon the sinking ship when his contract expired in 1971. Possibly seeking a scapegoat for their broken fortunes, the rest thought it timely to sack Britton's best friend Staples, whose playing had long been found wanting. He doubtlessly felt vindicated when his former colleagues placed the Troggs in neutral a few months later.

After short-lived solo careers, Bond and Presley drifted back under Page's wing with a new band. Expected to do no more than churn out the old classics, the Troggs were now seen as lovable curios as they roamed the trackless wastes of cabaret and the college circuit. However, there was life in the old dogs yet as they scored a South African smash with the song *Feels Like a Woman*, as well as doing likewise in Europe with *Strange Movie*, a number they also performed as guests on David Bowie's American TV special in 1974 with Wayne County, Marianne Faithful and stranger bedfellows. There was also their revival of *Good Vibrations* which approximated closely to the original bar Presley's half-spoken Andover twang. What next, Reg? *Bohemian Rhapsody*?

Following a German tour where the presence of Ian 'Tich' Amey in the Troggs provoked audience requests for *Xanadu* and the like, a lucrative US excursion was undertaken in the light of Presley's £23,000 tax bill. With the reinstatement of Britton, bored with running his club in Portugal, the capacity crowds witnessed a middle-aged joviality in place of the previous angry scowl as the Troggs spiced-up their still-rivetting act with all the good old good ones from *Hound Dog* to *Satisfaction*, which Reg delivered as though he were Robert Newton telling a dirty joke.

The Zombies Begin Here

North America, having lost its marbles over the Beatles in 1964, was still vague about regional differences in Britain a year later — Freddie and Herman were 'scouse'; Mick Jagger and Dave Clark were 'cockney'. Other English pop stars had girlie Public School accents like the Zombies or Ian Whitcomb: the Church clock stands at quarter to three — I wonder if there's jam for tea.

The Zombies hit the States at an optimum moment when the lunatic bin was on its second turning. They epitomised well-mannered, educated choristers straight from Tom Brown's Schooldays. After all, they came from St. Alban's on the site of the ancient Roman city of Verulamium which, as far as the US was concerned, was a feudal rurality of Merrie England; the rich man in his castle, the poor man at his gate. What America found so attractive about them was what exhausted the Zombies' momentum at home. Without the novelty of being foreign and talking funny, the 'scholarly' gimmick of their collective 50 'O' level examination qualifications wouldn't wash back in Blighty. Unlike Manfred Mann, the Zombies, though also having two bespectacled members, still looked like the callow, provincial sixth formers they were — out of place in pop's vulgar realms. Not exactly snooty, they nevertheless lacked the common touch.

Their predominantly introspective, romantic approach was the antithesis of the blueswailing aggression of the Small Faces or Pretty Things. It felt especially uncomfortable when they actually attempted R'n'B. The debut album of both the Zombies and Pretty Things opened with a version of Bo Diddley's *Road Runner*. Comparing the two, the Zombies more intricate arrangement pales beside the lean and hungry drive of the Sidcup quintet. *Road Runner* just didn't suit Colin Blunstone's elegant vocal style whereas it was perfect for a lesser singer like Phil May. If British pop fans thought at all about the Zombies after 1965, it was that they were too clever by half, and it was this attitude that caused their innovative music to be appreciated only in retrospect. At the time, they often got the bird as their UK engagement fees dwindled, driving them into exile to keep their self respect.

In 1962, 17-year-old Colin Blunstone was Hamilton House sports captain at St. Alban's Boys Grammar School in Clarence Park. He was a mainstay of the Rugby XV and such an athlete that he represented Hertfordshire in a national championship. As a prefect, he was permitted to punish younger boys with detention. Academically sound too, young Blunstone could expect a favourable valediction from his headmaster, Mr. Ronald Bradshaw, when he left to become an insurance clerk after the 'A' levels.

In a more select part of the town near the Roman ruins, Rodney Argent attended the fee-paying Abbey School where he had studied violin, clarinet and, crucially, keyboards to scholarship level. Though his preferences lay in jazz and the classics, he was broadminded enough to consider a career in pop. From an Upper Sixth cabal, he rehearsed with drummer Hugh Grundy and guitarist Paul Atkinson. A year below was Paul Arnold who played a home-made bass guitar. A barrier to going public was Rod's finding it difficult to sing and vamp simultaneously. Arnold said he knew a fellow called Colin from the Grammar who could sing a bit.

With the addition of Blunstone's exquisite tenor, the Zombies hawked their musical wares round the colleges and sports club socials within an area roughly outlined from Dunstable to North London, Aylesbury to Hertford. Their primal set necessarily contained Cliff Richard and Buddy Holly favourites but they also acquitted themselves adequately with other numbers common to beat groups everywhere like Rosco Gordon's *Just a Little Bit* and a medley of *You Really Got a Hold On Me* with *Bring It On Home To Me*. A guaranteed showstopper was Colin's breathtaking treatment of Gershwin's *Summertime* from PORGY AND BESS. Sometimes they slipped in the first ever group original, Rod's *It's All Right With Me*.

The rest of the group finding Arnold's condescension towards rock'n'roll tedious, a grocer's son, Christopher White, from Markyate near Luton, was chosen to replace him in 1963. Apart from his superior bass playing, another advantage was the use of a room above the shop for rehearsals and equipment storage. At White's suggestion, the group entered a 'Herts Beat' contest sponsored by the *London Evening Post*. With *Summertime* as the clincher, the Zombies won an audition with the mighty Decca. With their parents' blessing, they took the plunge and went professional having gained both a manager in Tito Burns and the Decca contract in June 1964.

Surprisingly, their assigned producer, Kenneth Jones, was so taken with an eleventh hour composition by Argent that plans to release *Summertime* as first single were scrapped. The arresting minor key *She's Not There* had no obvious precedent. Like most of their subsequent pigeon-holed efforts, it was propelled by Argent's idiosyncratic, vaguely jazzy keyboard ramblings and Blunstone's

*Grundy goes for the Big One: the Zombies at play (*left to right*) Paul Atkinson, Colin Blunstone, Hugh Grundy, Chris White (sans spectacles) and Rod Argent.*

spell-binding vocal supported by precise backing harmonies on critical lines. An unrealised classic of dramatic restraint, its unusual atmosphere amid more extrovert offerings of the day pushed it to a grudging Number 12 before it quietly died its death.

After catching up on medical and dental treatment, the boys' showbusiness baptism of fire came low on the bill of a seven week package tour with the Isley Brothers and Searchers during which they weren't too busy to note that their second 45, White's *Leave Me Be*, was thought too wantonly melancholy for much airplay. One sympathetic Radio Luxembourg D.J. even gave the more animated B-side, *Woman*, a few halfhearted spins.

With another suspected one-hit-wonder on their books, Decca hustled the group into West Hampstead studios for an album padded with The Hit, a royalty-earning instrumental by Ken Jones and one-take standbys from the stage act, including the most horrendous *I Got My Mojo Working* ever heard. However, some new originals compensated for most deficiencies.

Decca's forebodings were confirmed when *Tell Her No* teetered on the edge of the Top 30 before falling backwards — and that, as far as Britain was concerned, was that for the Zombies.

Three months earlier, the local boys had truly made good when *She's Not There* topped the US charts (news that Mr. Bradshaw saw as unworthy of mention in school assembly). Many words were required from another elderly British man, Tito Burns, before American immigration, presumably worried about

Limey longhairs taking custom from home-grown acts, allowed the Zombies to take part in a Murray the K ten day package show in Brooklyn, New York, before a month's hard graft on the road with the Shangri-Las. Any subtlety packed into the Zombies' short spot was lost on screaming mid-Western audiences who, nonetheless, bought *Tell Her No* into the US Top 5. Buoyed by more tours, they did not vanish from the American scene with the same indecent haste as in Britain. *She's Coming Home*, inspired by the Nunc Dimittis, and a jazz-tinged waltz, *I Want You Back Again* were less spectacular hits, but hits all the same. Luckily, this winning streak was staggered to varying degrees in other sales territories such as the Phillipines and Scandinavia, thus holding an undignified demise back home at bay. A murky flash of screen stardom occurred in *Bunny Lake is Missing* with Laurence Oliver, in which the group's fifteen second excerpt from *Remember You* was lengthened for the trailer to suck in the adolescent viewer.

One rare flying visit to Britain was to vainly plug *Whenever You's Ready* on TV in August 1965. When its three successors joined it on the deletion rack, the Zombies twice resorted to that well-known strategy, The American Cover Version. The last of these, Little Anthony's *Goin' Out of My Head*, though augmented with brass, arrived too late to prevent a Dodie West rendering snatching the slight chart honours.

Too adventurous for the commonweal, not cool enough for the In Crowd, the Zombies were granted even less individual attention by Decca (who similarly dogged the careers of Them and the Moody Blues). It is intriguing to speculate the outcome had the Beatles passed *their* audition with the company. As it was, Decca's biggest earners, the Stones, made it clear that, when their time was up, they would sooner not record than re-sign.

The Zombies formulated the same opinion long before their own contract expired in June 1967. So disenchanted were Hugh and Colin that they considered jacking in music altogether. However, their agony was prolonged when the group was theoretically granted the final word over all future records by the new label CBS. Yet, despite this greater artistic freedom and promotional aid, there was no immediate sales animation, even for the commercial *Care of Cell 44* with its oblique chorale and adroit lyric.

Nevertheless, they went out with a bang when *Time of the Season*, spurred by accumulated American airplay, saw them back near the top of the Hot 100, shifting two million copies on the way. This elegy was taken from the bestselling L.P. ODESSEY AND ORACLE (*sic*

— a spelling error unnoticed by the lads with 50 'O' levels). The US wing of CBS almost rejected this refined meisterwerk but at the insistence of Anglophile producer, Al Kooper, it was issued with bad grace on a subsidiary outlet.

With CBS cap in hand for more product, the Zombies told the whole fairweather industry to get stuffed when they disbanded in late 1967. Neither wild horses or a £20,000 net offer for just one little concert could drag them together again. Showing the band's unfortunate facelessness, a rash of groups began illicitly accepting bookings under the Zombies' name. One UK Zombies was, allegedly, Johnny Carr and the Cadillacs; Perkin in the USA, another maverick combo got lucky with $7,000 a night until exposed at the Whiskey-a-Go-Go by socialite Rodney Bingenheimer and the visiting Move.

The public were more effectively misled when Rod Argent, in a CBS half-Nelson, falsely attributed the first two singles by his eponymous new group to the Zombies. To be fair, much of the band Argent's stimulus came from its leader's old group, to the extent of including a couple of real Zombies numbers in its early repertoire. By contrast, nobody was fooled when Colin re-appeared in the UK Top 30 under the guise of 'Neil McArthur' with a lusher, orchestrated revamp of *She's Not There* — still twisting the heartstrings.

The Zombies' legacy to pop is more insidious than two paltry British chart entries would imply. Apart from respects paid by Vanilla Fudge and Santana amongst others, with further remakes of *She's Not There*, an obscure San Jose band, People, earned a surprise US hit in 1974 with a version of an equally obscure Zombies B-side, Chris White's *I Love You*.

Less obviously, the Zombies' unpretentious creativity centred on conventional beat group instrumentation. Not for them were the self-conscious pastiches and funny noises of their more marketable contemporaries. The careering coda of *Indication*, for instance, conveys in pop terms a suggestion of somewhere in Araby without Atkinson thrumming some simplistic 'Lawrence of Arabia' riff on a hastily-procured lyre. This scorn of ostentation, and the strange contradiction of enjoyable depression that was the frequent aftertaste of their music, infiltrated the fertile vision of later British groups like Traffic and Procol Harum; it can even be detected in *Waterloo Sunset* — period Kinks, who recruited Argent's cousin, Jim Rodford, to their ranks in 1978. Across the Atlantic, it is questionable if pieces such as *Walk Away Renee*, *Do You Believe In Magic* or even *Bridge Over Troubled Waters* would have been envisaged as pop songs without the Zombies' ill-fated pioneering accomplishments.

MERRY GENTLE POPS

Through The Past Lightly

In 1979, a rumour spread that a surprise reunion of a famous '1960s group' would occur during an otherwise routine Hammersmith Odeon pop concert. Though Lennon was still alive, credulity wouldn't stretch that far. Who then? The Pretty Things? The Animals? The Zombies? On the night, Billy Connolly as ad hoc compere joked, 'I dinnae want tae raise yer hopes but I've just seen three ex-Applejacks backstage'. As the resulting derisive snigger testified, most recalled who the Applejacks were, but they and other alternatives for Connolly's twitting were of little cultural importance although they had hits. They were throwbacks to times when most British pop stars were exactly that; purveyors of popular songs which people would hum, whistle and partly sing incessantly over a few chart weeks while the powers behind them prepared another ditty for instant consumption by either the same act or a substitute with a new angle, such as: Adam Faith with his singularly odd pronunciation in 1959; the Honeycombs and their female drummer in 1964; the Pipkins with their clowns' trousers in 1970. By 1984, Black Lace were the most conspicuous custodians of this tradition.

Beatlemania gave Tin Pan Alley a nasty turn but why shouldn't business carry on as usual with the eternal verities of catchy tunes, harmless fun, scripted grinning and someone raking in a bit of cash at the end of the day? As for the artists, they'd come out of it with a backlog of hits and, thus, in a favorable negotiating position for personal appearances in variety, night clubs and, if of vibrant enough personality, TV shows or advertising. Furthermore, if they could actually sing and/or play their instruments, there was session work. Some could even get famous all over again as did the Ivy League, alias the Flowerpot Men, with the inevitable commercialisation of flower power.

A record of distinction: as well as two Ivy Leaguers, this single also featured future Pretty Thing Viv Prince and Yardbird Jimmy Page whose ice cream van guitar tone brightened the A-side Your Momma's Out of Town.

Ivy League

Of them all The League, a vocal trio with backing group, were the least naive and most professional. Two of them, John Carter and Ken Lewis, led the Southerners, whose most memorable release was *Your Momma's Out of Town* in 1963. Though this song was provided by the omnipresent Mitch Murray, Lewis and Carter's own collaborations were profitable, notably with *Will I What*, *Is It True*, inquired respectively by Mike Sarne and Brenda Lee, and later, *Listen People*, a US smash for Herman's Hermits. The third partner was another music business entrepreneur, Perry Ford (Brian Pugh) who, as well as vamping keyboards in Bert Weedon's group, had also turned his hand to composition, Adam Faith's *Someone Else's Baby* being his crowning achievement.

Setting themselves up as session singers, the Ivy League decided that it would do no harm to try some records under their own name — arguing that no-one within the spectrum of the Beat Boom had capitalised on the Four Freshmen-Hi-Los-Four Preps close harmony sound as the Four Seasons and Beach Boys had done in the States. After a non-starter with *What More Do You Want*, the League struck gold with *Funny How Love Can Be*, a well-crafted melancholia appealing to bedsit girls, grannies, and those too tough to admit they liked it. A TV plug on READY STEADY GO in January 1965 put the trio en route for the Top 10.

Taking a breather as *That's Why I'm Crying*, almost a 'Son of the Hit', moped at Number 22, their third single, *Tossing and Turning*, topped with Ford's soprano, panted to Number 3. Its B-side, *Graduation Day* — in grateful tribute to the Four Preps — was in the set as the League in imagined American college boy get-up (grey slacks, striped jackets, etc. — not really worn since 1900), took the product on the road backed by Division Two, led by ex-Tornado Clem Cattini.

Apart from a minor entry with *Willow Tree* in 1966, the League's chart time was up. Carter had been replaced by Tony Burrows who, significantly, went on to sing with the Pipkins among others. By the 1980s, *an* Ivy League was trundling the night club circuit peddling current smashes interspersed with camp comedy and a hit medley, but the last of the original makers of those hits, Perry Ford had left after the group had given viewers a rousing *Rock My Soul* on an ITV religious programme introduced by Andrew 'Dr. Cameron' Cruikshank in 1971.

Fame and Fortunes

Joining them in worship had been the Fortunes who, that same year, had shown class in the US Hot 100 with *Rainy Day Feeling* as well as breaking into the UK Top 10 with *Freedom Come Freedom Go* after a six year absence. They proved that it hadn't been a fluke by repeating this feat with *Storm In a Teacup* in 1972. Unlike others of their kind, they'd only struck cabaret after the first flush of hits on the understanding that another good song would come up — as good as Greenaway and Cook's *You've Got Your Troubles*, which had propelled them to Number 2 in 1965 after their first three attempts had done nothing.

The Fortunes began as a Birmingham-Welsh vocal trio fronting the Cliftones, whose repertoire centred around easy-listening sentiment like *September Song*, *Look Homeward Angel* and a tremulous *Maria* from WEST SIDE STORY. With the advent of the Big Beat the singers, Rodney Allen, Glen Dale, and Bert Weedon lookalike Barry Pritchard, now sporting electric guitars and bass, began holding auditions for an organist and drummer. Under the proprietory eye of manager Reg Calvert, they retained their smart suits and haircuts while scrutinising the latest 'quality' material by the likes of Gene Pitney and Dionne Warwick for inclusion in their act. Though they may have conceded to requests, they didn't go in for too much wild stuff.

After their debut single *Caroline* was adopted as theme tune of the radio station of the same name, it was a matter of a year before *You've Got Your Troubles*. Their second hit, *Here it comes again*, was once more heavily orchestrated by Les Reed and characterised by an overdubbed vocal counterpoint by Barry near the finale. It was unfortunate that, on this occasion, it seemed to fade in on a flatulent vulgarity which rhymed with 'heart' at the end of the next line.

Before this chart run ended with *This Golden Ring* in April 1966, the group chose to reveal that, though they were competent instrumentalists in concert, sessionmen were used in the studio. This mattered little in itself as their records relied mainly on massed strings and vocals anyway, but the realisation that Glen, Barry, and Rod were the only Fortunes actually heard on their A-sides certainly damaged their career at this stage. Though there were other exposés of British bands not playing their own sessions, such as Hedgehoppers Anonymous and, later, Love Affair, the media gave the Fortunes' confessions much unwelcome coverage, which could be linked with their failure to make the Top 50 again until 1970.

Their tenth 45, *The Idol*, was a fundamental departure from the orchestral slop that made them. Even aired by 'underground' D.J. John Peel, it was an intelligent effort in the Hollies style, and played by the Fortunes themselves this time. Co-written by Pritchard, the Aesop's Fable lyric could, in retrospect, be applied to the late Elvis. Luckily for them, the Fortunes didn't become superstars like 'The King' — in 1980, they were singing the praises of a fizzy drink in a TV commercial. Nevertheless, of all the groups presently discussed they emerge with the most credit, if only for sheer tenacity.

The Fortunes: you can judge a book by the cover.

Lulu and Her Luvvers

Less enduring were Lulu and the Luvvers, a septet from Lennoxtown just north of Glasgow. It was apparent from the outset that the 16-year-old singer Marie Lawrie ('Lulu') was the only one that mattered. With the candour of middle age, she would describe herself then as 'an obnoxious little cow' but any personal defects were belied by the ashtray rasp from her vocal chords — Ray Charles meets Katherine Hepburn. Kitted out by her manager in Angela Cash dresses, Lulu, bawling the Isley Brothers' *Shout*, escorted her Luvvers to Number 7 in summer 1964. On one TV plug, the B-side, *Forget Me Baby*, a duet with guitarist and maracca man Jim Dewar, was performed on an ice rink.

The next two singles crashlanded in the bargain bins. When a third, *Satisfied* (a *Shout* rehash) followed them in March 1965, Lulu and her Luvvers stopped going out with each other, though the group stayed on for live dates until 1966 when they cut one flop, *House On the Hill*. They never got over Lulu, though Dewar later played *bass* for Robin Trower and in Stone the Crows.

She who travels fastest travels alone. Lulu's patchy chart placings resumed with *Leave a Little Love* at Number 8 in September 1965. Other entries included Marty Wilde's *I'm a Tiger*, a Song For Europe contender in *Boom-Bang-A-Bang* and, at Number 3 in 1974, *The Man Who Sold the World*, which resulted from her friendship with its composer David Bowie. Lulu then settled down as a middle-of-the-road media personality on panel games and in women's magazines advertising fashion catalogues, the closest she ever got to her original intention to be a hairdresser.

The Honeycombs

While on the subject, let us peer through a hairdresser's window in Edgware, North London where, in 1962, Ann 'Honey' Langtree was putting the finishing touches to an aged crone's blue rinse. After work, Honey drummed in her brother's group the Sherabons, whom fate decreed would top the charts in August 1964 as the Honeycombs. They were pretty ordinary. They weren't even the first otherwise all-male band with a girl drummer — the Ravens who recorded for Oriole beat them to that one. However, the Ravens weren't blessed with the management and songwriting skills of Ken Howard and Alan Blaikley or the services of a producer like Joe Meek who, though not entirely in sympathy with the Beat Boom, still went beyond the call of duty. *Have I the Right*, owing more to Dave Clark's crude stomp than the Tornados otherworldliness, was Meek's last big fling before his brains splattered the stairs to his flat. It was backroom elements rather than the Honeycombs themselves that got them their Number One.

Like George III's conduct of the American War of Independence from Whitehall, the Honeycombs — committed to a lengthy Australasian tour in autumn 1964 — were ill-placed with regard to their UK chart campaign. The follow-up, the faster Latin-tinged *Is It Because*, came unstuck at Number 38 while their third 45, *Eyes*, lost sight of the Top 50 altogether. Even *Something Better Beginning* from the Kinks, with whom they had shared their fortnight of glory, only made Number 39.

Back from their Antipodean adventures, it was noted that L.P. track, the ambulant *That's the Way*, a duet by Honey and lead vocalist Denis d'Ell, had gone down well during the group's spot before the adverts on SUNDAY NIGHT AT THE LONDON PALLADIUM. Issued as a single it showed at Number 12 late in 1965. Of their last four 45's, only *Who is Sylvia* is conspicuous, with lyrics by some theatrical cove named Shakespeare with a tune by this German cat, Franz Schubert. On that horrendous note, the curtain started falling on the Honeycombs.

D'Ell, after an abortive solo career, represented the group on a TV nostalgia romp in 1982 but without Miss Langtree's presence the point of the exercise was lost. Replaced by a Peter Pye of the Skylarks after breaking his leg tripping off a Peterborough stage in 1964, simpering, bespectacled guitarist Martin Murray invited me to his Hendon home in August 1979 to 'discuss a recording contract' after I'd answered a *Melody Maker* ad requesting demo tapes. To my disgust, this turned out to be a projected agreement whereby Murray would shunt my tape round record companies in exchange for what he called an 'investment fee' of £500. A week later, I discovered *Have I the Right* in my record collection. Having nothing better to do, I childishly scratched a rude word on it with a screwdriver and, taking it into the back garden, sent it soaring like a discus over the rooftops into the endless blue.

The Honeycombs make the best of their fifteen minutes.

The Applejacks

A band with a lady less in evidence was the butt of Billy's quip. The Applejacks hailed from Solihull in the West Midlands where in 1960 guitarists Martin Baggott and Philip Cash were in a church youth club skiffle group, the Crestas. Drummer Gerry Freeman persuaded Megan Davies, a fellow Sunday School teacher (and, later, his wife) to come in on electric bass. Adding organist Don Gould in 1962, they went forth as 'the Jaguars', specialising in instrumentals. The following year with singer Al Jackson in their midst they started walking in the ways of Chuck Berry, the Coasters, Ray Charles and Little Richard.

On the lookout round Birmingham, Decca A&R man Mike Smith visualised the Applejacks in their bright red smocks as harbingers of a 'Solihull Sound'. Grubbing round publishers' offices, a commercial vehicle was found to project this — *Tell me when*, which would have also been ideal for a known entity like Gerry Marsden. Not possessing the vocal arsenal of the Ivy League, the Applejacks unison harmonies came and went behind Al's thick Birmingham lead. However, the instrumental track was lively enough round Gould's Noddy organ riffing. For first timers, their Number 7 position in March 1964 was no mean achievement.

For the next A-side, a bright spark at Decca blew the dust off McCartney's *Like Dreamers Do* from the Beatles' failed audition tape. Yet, despite this distinguished antecedent, it wasn't up to *Tell Me When* standard and consequently slumped at Number 20. After *Three Little Words* got tongue-tied at Number 23, it became clear that the 'Solihull Sound' era was past. Before signing off with the appropriately titled *I'm Through* in 1965, two noteworthy releases were *Chim Chim Cheree* which had the edge over Dick Van Dyke's Illinois Cockney original from MARY POPPINS, and Ray Davies' *I Go to Sleep* which generated some interest in the States. By 1966, though now above youth club bashes, the Applejacks were back on the Birmingham — Solihull orbit of engagements — a classic local group.

*The Sunday school party goes on forever (*clockwise*) Gerry Freeman, Megan Davies, Al Jackson, Don Gould, Martin Baggott and Phil Cash.*

JUST A LITTLE BIT

Cliff Bennett and the Rebel Rousers Do It Right

Clifford Bennett grew up in Maxwell Road at the heart of a West Drayton housing estate in outer London suburbia. In keeping with this lugubrious background, his early life was not remarkable. Leaving his Secondary Modern school, he followed his brother Ted into his father's Harmansworth foundry. 'Gone' on skiffle, he purchased a cheap guitar to make his first public appearance with a local group at a dance in Colnbrook at the age of 17. Searching for BBC Radio's Light Programme one day, he tuned into an Eddie Cochrane show on a foreign station. From that moment, skiffle died and Cliff's championing of rock'n'roll soon became audible to his family and their neighbours. The vital difference between Cliff and most other pop-mad teenagers of the 1950s was that he could sing American music in his Middlesex accent without departing far from the original in spirit.

Among his admirers was former Outlaw Chas Hodges, with whom Bennett would perform dangerous 100 m.p.h. stunts in an MG Sprite, thus enlivening the glum streets within the drone of Heathrow Airport. At Chas' prompting, he formed the first edition of the Rebel Rousers in 1961. Backing Cliff was a floating line-up of guitar, bass, drums, and pianist doubling sax. Later an additional pianist and saxophonist were hired. Among those passing through the ranks were future Searcher Frank Allen, from a Hayes band called 'the Skyways'; drummer Mick Burt, who joined Hodges in 'Chas and Dave' a generation later; and Roy Young, a Little Richard impersonator from television's 6.5 SPECIAL who was recording with David Bowie in 1979.

Emphasizing punctuality and discipline, Bennett once fired a horn player for drunkeness on stage. Although he rated the Stones as musicians, Cliff was a vitriolic critic of long hair. Nevertheless, neat coiffeur and matching tartan jackets gave Rebel Rousers a likeness to a Mafia hit squad with their vocalist as Don Michael Corleone — *me duce tutus eris* (Ovid). Particularly intimidating was burly, narrow-eyed multi-instrumentalist Sid Phillips.

Anchored to the works of Elvis, Jerry Lee and twist king, Joey Dee, they came to the attention of Holloway Road console boffin Joe Meek, who had also worked with Hodges in the Outlaws. Noting Cliff's Presleyesque intonation, Meek produced his group's first three Parlophone singles, beginning with the bathroom rockabilly of *You Got What I Like* in June 1961. *That's What I Said* four months later best captured the embryonic Bennett sound. A lengthy extrapolation, it featured Instant Karma flutter echo, wild drawing-pin piano, with overdubbed rudimentary sax from Phillips and Michael King's savage guitar interludes. No wonder the Rebel Rousers didn't catch on in a year ruled by the jellyfish flab of Bobby Vee and Acker Bilk's popped-up trad.

The strongest pointer to later tendencies was the flip of the third effort, *Poor Joe*. A soul-rock crossover co-written by Californian band leader Johnny Otis, the original version of *Hurtin' Inside* by Brook Benton was so precisely cloned in Meek's studio by Bennett and his group that it truly seemed American.

With failure in hit parade terms, records became a by-product of the Rebel Rousers' booking schedule via their Richmond agent, which found them in northern Europe by 1962. Morale was considerably boosted by a Hamburg Star Club residency where they were well-treated by both audience and Manfred Weissleder, the club's owner, who provided comfortable accommodation, requiring only two 60 minute sets per night six hours apart. With other southern boys like the Nashville Teens and Dave Dee's Bostons, the Middlesex lads rubbed shoulders with the prevalent Merseyside faction.

Though some numbers, such as Benton's *Do It Right* and Marvin Gaye's *Try It Baby*, came to be peculiar to Bennett alone, it was inevitable that many songs were showcased by more than one Grosse Freiheit act. Specifically, the Rebel Rousers shared *Dr. Feelgood*, *Stupidity* and *Everybody Loves a Lover* with Rory Storm, the Undertakers, and Kingsize Taylor, and *I'll Be Doggone* with Billy J. Kramer. Their *Steal Your Heart Away* was rendered less eerily by the Krew Kats (who were to mutate into the Moody Blues back in Brum). All British groups were in awe of visiting US idols like Ray Charles, the Drifters, and Sam Cooke. Therefore, Cliff was greatly flattered when Jerry Lee Lewis asked for an acetate of his arrangement of *Beautiful Dreamer* to take back to Louisiana.

Stunning 'em in Hamburg, the West Drayton rebels roused the interest of Brian Epstein who, encouraged by his runaway success with the pick of Liverpudlia, was eager to diversify. Engaging Bennett's band as support on his POP'S ALIVE promotion at London's Prince of Wales theatre where they impressed with a rendering of the Impressions' *Talking About my Baby*, Epstein afterwards added them to his roster of artistes.

With this entrepreneurial muscle behind them, Cliff Bennett and the Rebel Rousers made their *New Musical Express* chart debut at Number 29 on October 2nd 1964 with their seventh single, a tougher Anglicised copy of the Drifters' *One Way Love*. One unexpected plug was a peak hour BBC TV trailer for a pop series on its posh new second channel, which happened to feature Bennett's *One Way Love* spot in toto. After making the Top 10, the group stuck to the Drifters for the follow-up, *I'll Take You Home,* which made it to a paltry Number 42. This was to be their last Top 50 entry for nearly two years; as they toured relentlessly as special guests of the likes of Dave Clark, the Kinks, and Frank Ifield.

The most noble failures were Aaron Neville's *I Have Cried My Last Tear* (with characteristic querulous backing vocals) and *Hold On I'm Coming*, also a miss

for the Sam and Dave original. Most inexplicable was *Three Rooms With Running Water*, an emotional rockaballad devastatingly performed on the first all-live READY STEADY GO.

After promising Cliff a song since their common

Though they were short on 'teen appeal, Bennett's band grew to be appreciated by other artistes as a 'group's group' for their stylistic tenacity and exacting musical standards (back, left to right) Sid Phillips, Cliff Bennett, Ricky Winters, (front) Frank Allen (who switched to bass in the Searchers), Chas Hodges and Maurice Groves who doubled on sax.

Hamburg sojourn, Paul McCartney delivered the goods at last with a James Brown pastiche, *Got To Get You Into My Life*, which he also produced. Though Bennett was to cut at least two more Beatles tunes, only this penultimate REVOLVER track did the trick chartwise. Sweeping to Number 6, their biggest and final hit obliged E.M.I. to rush out the group's second L.P. DRIVIN' YOU WILD, — a pot-pourri of flop 45's, E.P. tracks, and recordings unreleased — on the budget Music for Pleasure label thus ensuring it a place in the album lists. Like other Rebel Rouser collections, it was a studio work-out of items from the stage act, principally taken from American soul R'n'B catalogues. The few band originals were B-side compositions by Cliff, either alone or collaborating with associates present such as Joe Meek or guitarist David Wendells.

It was their treatment of the Americans that made them and it was this that killed them off. By 1967, a group could either risk boring everyone to tears with an all-original or blues-derived set extended with endless soloing à la Cream, or else dive on Engelbert's saccharin bandwagon as did the Dave Clark Five. For Cliff Bennett, it was business as usual. This meant that he became to many a high-class plagiarist whose *C.C. Rider-Barefootin'* anachronisms worked their short-lived magic less and less.

With most of the remaining Rebel Rousers eventually defecting to Roy Young's leadership, among later incidents in Cliff's musical career were his recording of a nondescript film theme, HOUSE OF 1,000 DOLLS, before his involvement in Toe Fat, a heavy group in which he finally gave his defiantly short hair its head as well as standing further from his razor. With the band Shanghai in 1974, (with ex-Pirates Frank Farley and Mick Green on drums and guitar, respectively, and with Robin McDonald from Billy J. Kramer's Dakotas on bass), Cliff revived Johnny Kidd's *Shakin All Over* before they split after a disagreement over managerial finance and his intended record company's excessive thrift. Amid a shower of High Court writs, Cliff Bennett retreated from the music business. As his distant friend McCartney could have told him, a mere great voice wasn't enough.

In 1983, Cliff was sales executive with an aviation firm though his showbusiness connections had secured a secondary income in advertising voice-overs. Occasionally, he had trodden the boards again as in a Star Club anniversary show with P.J. Proby among others. In 1982, Dave Dee persuaded him to sing a couple of numbers in the celebrated 'Heroes and Villains' concert in Hammersmith where, according to a random survey, he stole the show.

The Art of Chris Farlowe and the Thunderbirds

Chris Farlowe always sounded as though he needed to clear his throat. Indeed it seemed at times he actually did so on disc. Whether as leader of one of his bands, in the rank and file of Colosseum or Atomic Rooster, or guesting on Jimmy Page's 1982 soundtrack of DEATH WISH TWO, Farlowe's vocal arsenal — from strangled gasp to anguished roar — displayed a strong musical personality beyond mere rhymes and chords. With the B-side *Treat Her Good* a laughable theft of *Treat Her Right*, a 1965 hit for Roy Head, Chris wasn't much of a composer, but that he could warp music as diverse as *Hound Dog* and Jon Hiseman's *Daughter of Time* to his own devices was as idiosyncratic an ability as that of any of his more technically-gifted rivals.

Born John Henry Deighton in 1940, he became proficient on guitar and keyboards as well as realising his vocal prowess. At 17, he and his steel-drivin' John Henry Group won an all-England skiffle championship at Tottenham Royal Ballroom. However, with Lonnie Donegan drowned in the rip tide of rock'n'roll, Deighton assumed his more familiar stage name while assembling a new backing band, the Thunderbirds. By 1962, he turned professional following a German tour during which his repertoire was injected with more than a shot of R'n'B, though he was never to be a purist of this genre.

In the Fatherland, Farlowe met guitarist Albert Lee, who became a Thunderbirds mainstay when the nucleus of a permanent line-up was founded. On Larry Parnes' books, the teenage Lee had backed the likes of Duffy Power and Dickie Pride before earning a crust with both Jimmy Justice's Jury, in a 21's residency, and the Don Adams Trio. With another member of the latter, Barry Jenkins, Albert drifted to Hamburg where he joined the Nightsounds in 1962. After replacing Jimmy Page in, respectively, Neil Christian's Crusaders and ex-Springfield Mike Hurst's combo, Lee emerged as an experienced musician whose harsh fretboard tone was ideally matched to Farlowe's style when the pair joined forces circa 1964.

Somewhere along the way, Lee had also played in Don Spencer's XL5 who enjoyed a minor hit with the theme tune of the TV puppet series FIREBALL XL5. Another XL5-er was Thunderbirds drummer Ian Mague, who was supplanted by 16-year-old wunderkind, Carl Palmer. Yet another figure from Lee's past, Duffy Power bass guitarist Richard Chapman, passed through the group, as did saxophonists Paul Carson and David Quincy, from both the Bo Street Runners and the P.J.

Chris Farlowe, 1966.

Proby Orchestra. Like Georgie Fame before him, Farlowe had accepted a management offer from the Gunnell brothers, proprietors of the Flamingo and Ram Jam Clubs. From the Flamingo house band the Wes Minster Five Chris acquired the services of organist Dave Greenslade.

Depending on whether soloists or groups were 'In' at any given moment, the Thunderbirds were sometimes not credited on Farlowe's records. The man himself wasn't even mentioned on two occasions when it was thought commercially prudent to use pseudonyms. Beginning in July 1963 with *Air travel*, a one-shot deal with Decca, it took ten more singles before Farlowe and his band cracked the top 20. Among these were Chris's only self-penned A-side, the forgettable *I Remember*, and *Hey Hey Hey Hey*, a retread of *I Wish You Would*. As 'The Beazers', they rode the Blue Beat craze ('the dance that everyone's doing') far less lucratively than later Tottenham Royal veterans, the

Migil Five. *Buzz With the Fuzz* achieved an unprofitable notoriety when belated executive appreciation of its drug-related hipster slang necessitated its deletion. On his lengthy reading of T-bone Walker's *Stormy Monday Blues*, it was a tribute to Farlowe's soulful delivery that under the guise of 'Little Joe Cook', he fooled most of the people into believing he was an obscure American blues shouter. Though this cult eagle didn't fly into the charts, it remained such an integral part of the Farlowe oeuvre that he was still declaiming it on TV's UNFORGETTABLE eighteen years later.

In August 1965, Chris signed with Andrew Loog Oldham's industrious Immediate label. Even so, success here was by no means instant — though a spirited revival of Sanford Clark's *The Fool* from 1956 created a stir. Capturing Farlowe and the group in top form, it was produced by Eric Burdon who had been sincerely loud in praising Farlowe after catching his act at the Flamingo.

A more powerful ally was Mick Jagger who took charge of all Farlowe recordings for the next two years.

Starting 1966 in fine style with *Think* — at last, his chart debut — another AFTERMATH selection, *Out of Time*, shot to kill five months later after Chris put down a vocal to Mick's fastidious satisfaction on a backing track prepared with arranger Art Greenslade (no relation), Dragging Georgie Fame from Number One on July 30th, Farlowe was deprived of lording it on TOP OF THE POPS by an industrial blackout. That same week in a *New Musical Express* article he alienated many potential buyers by ridiculing Bob Dylan's famous semi-surreal Berkeley press conference. An old rocker at heart, he was later outspoken in his contempt of the hippy lifestyle. When all was said and done, Chris's slit-eyed, short-haired, besuited bulk made him an unlikely-looking pop star at the dawning of the age of Aquarius. Indeed, when *Out of Time* fled the Top 50, Chris was exactly that — out of time.

Though the going got rough, Jagger and Farlowe plodded on, temporarily ditching the Thunderbirds. Of at least six more Jagger-Richard numbers Chris recorded only *Ride On Baby* got so much as a glimpse of the hit parade, though *Paint it Black*, an afterthought A-side of late 1967, was a magnificent effort, trading the sitar of Brian Jones for an eastern European orchestral setting complete with gypsy violins and syncopated bolero passage. The sitar did turn up, nonetheless, on another glorious flop, an extrapolation of the Jon Hendricks jazz standard, *Moanin'*.

On his brace of Immediate L.P.'s were mixed well-known soul classics, show-stoppers from musicals such as Anthony Newley's *Who Can I Turn To* and items written to order like *Life Is But Nothing* by Oldham proteges, Twice As Much. There were also oddities such as Johnny 'Guitar' Watson's *Cuttin' in*, with Lee's tingling obligato, and Dylan's *It's All Over Now Baby Blue* (a peace offering perhaps). The soul covers, of which there were many, suffered because even Jagger was unable to transform Pye studios into Stax-Volt or Motown. However, under the circumstances, some of them almost worked — *In the Midnight Hour* being the prime example though *It Was Easier to Hurt Her* wasn't bad. Besides, who wanted the warblings of a white boy from sleepy London town when the real black McCoy was so easily available?

Into Jagger's shoes in winter 1967 stepped Michael d'Abo, whose *Handbags and Gladrags* was given its definitive treatment by Farlowe. Contrasting Palmer's splattering percussion and his own piano with swirling strings and plaintive mouthorgan, d'Abo's arrangement allowed Chris to squeeze every emotional nuance from the lyric. Equally moving was an image of him emoting the later *Turn Out the Light* in a single spotlight on a rock'n'roll revival TV show. Unfortunately, even these notable 45's weren't enough to push Chris back into the limelight though they picked up moderate sales over a long period.

In 1968, the Thunderbirds were reconstituted as a trio with Lee, Palmer and bass player Peter Shelley. However, after a year, the band took its leave from Farlowe with an album suitably titled THE LAST GOODBYE.

Palmer was drawn into the Crazy World of Arthur Brown with organist Vincent Crane who, coincidentally, had co-written some material for Farlowe. Serving a term in Crane's next year's project, Atomic Rooster (who in 1974 also requested Farlowe's company) Carl joined a band with another keyboard player, Keith Emerson, and bass guitarist Greg Lake. Updating Emerson's previous group, the Nice, 'E.L.P.' became exponents of what was coined 'techno-rock'. Rolling in krugerrands, the three disbanded in 1975. Palmer then retired — and, after that lot, who could blame him?

Rightfully regarded as a prize acquisition by many noted musicians, Chris left his Islington military souvenir shop in neutral to front a group named 'The Hill', after a Sean Connery film, before being reunited with Dave Greenslade in Colosseum, in which he enlivened the more solemn aspects of the band with inspired off-the-cuff humour. In Atomic Rooster, he was a moderating influence on their heavy quasi-occult tendencies.

In 1975, as the reissued *Out of Time* was runner-up in a chart race with Dan McCafferty's (of Nazareth) Hibernian croak-out and the Stones' Decca original, Chris again teamed up with Albert Lee (by then a sessionman of great repute, having worked with Joe Cocker, Eric Clapton, and his old hero, Lonnie Donegan amongst others, as well as leading his own band, Head, Hands and Feet) for a few UK dates which brought forth a live L.P., from which a single of Alice Cooper's *Only Women Bleed* was extracted.

Since then, Farlowe has flitted fitfully across the music scene in nostalgia reviews, rare engagements with a pick-up band, and even rarer singles, such as a 1982 reworking of Long John Baldry's *Let the Heartaches Begin* of which great things were expected. Like the similarly-placed Cliff Bennett, his larynx was his fortune but it alone could not sustain a chart breakthrough. However, unlike the West Drayton tearaway, Chris Farlowe — with the patronage of Jagger rather than McCartney — got a Number One and, if that sort of thing matters to him, John Henry can die easy.

The Four Pennies Cash In

Forty miles north-east of Liverpool stands the smaller industrial settlement of Blackburn where, in the early 1960s, warehouses and obsolete machinery rotted near the railway track as clouds of factory smoke further stressed its glumness. Inland and undistinguished, it was hardly expected to contribute much to the Big Beat beyond copies of the seaport eccentricities of Merseyside. Nonetheless, Blackburn's only hit group the Four Pennies by this very isolation absorbed a style so peculiar to themselves that no concessions to Merseybeat trendiness could completely eradicate it.

For seven years, Lionel Morton sang in the city's new cathedral choir. At 16 with a voice broken but well-trained, he moved to a more secular musical sphere by forming the Lionel Morton Four in 1961, a hybrid of mainstream pop and skiffle's last stand. Not surprisingly, they had a strong emphasis on vocals through they were competent instrumentalists; drummer Allan Buck, for example, had worked with both Joe Brown and Johnny Kidd. With 'blond bombshell' guitarist Mike Wilshem and bass player Davĭd 'Fritz' Fryer (anticipating the 1984 Prince Andrew pin-up aesthetic) they also offered teen appeal and, therefore, an avenue for selling records.

Unaware of two American groups using the same name, they became 'The Four Pennies' in 1963 when their manager, Alan Lewis set the ball rolling by suggesting they scoused-up their accents prior to a descent on south Lancashire clubland. Here, their gaucher approach was a breath of fresh air at a time of tacit suspicion that if you'd heard one group with Beatle haircuts, you'd heard 'em all. Though the Pennies had, indeed, cultivated fringes, their repertoire did not include set works like *Money* and *Twist and Shout*. Instead they tackled items from the bedrock of their continued interest in amplified skiffle which ranged from the folk-blues of Leadbelly and Jesse Fuller to more Caucasian mainstays like *All My Trials* in well-defined three part harmony. More conventionally, they played a lot of Everly Brothers material minus the bluegrass nasal whine, one particular showstopper being a funereal *Crying in the Rain*. Better suited to Morton's chorister control were treatments of standards such as *My Prayer* and *If You Love Me*, revived in 1962 by the Bluenotes. The group were also exceptional in the performance of a large proportion of original numbers onstage, mostly from the pen of Fritz Fryer.

The Pennies infiltrated the Liverpool scene to such an extent that they qualified for a spot on Radio Luxembourg's SUNDAY NIGHT AT THE CAVERN. It was to be expected that the first two singles betrayed a reciprocal impression. Creeping to the charts' edge, the debut *Do You Want Me To* was the better seller until the ballad flip of *Tell Me Girl* picked up airplay. With *Juliet* promoted to A-side, the Pennies wended through the Top 50 to charm the Searchers from the top in May 1964.

As their companion E.P. and album titles reiterated, there was more than one side to the Four Pennies but it was the 'smooth' rather than 'swinging' angle that inflicted most chart damage. Though lost to the Top 10 forever after *Juliet*, the weepy *I Found Out the Hard Way* managed Number 14. By contrast, another chart killing four months later was an uptempo death disc, Leadbelly's *Black Girl*. Miming it on TV, Morton at his most rugged got so carried away he abandoned his guitar altogether during Wilshem's lead break, a display repeated during their UK tour with Freddie and the Dreamers, which followed a vexing attempt to shoot a promotional film in Paris.

Procrastination over suitable songs as well as a busy concert schedule occasioned a cessation of single releases for eight months. Ultimately, it was back to the ballads when the Pennies issued the first of many covers (including Elvis') of Buffy St. Marie's *Until It's Time For You To Go*. Like its two predecessors, it earned a respectable if unremarkable chart placing.

The Pennies were now on borrowed time as, during their sabbatical, new heroes had supplanted them and their Merseybeat contemporaries. Liverpool was dead and the Pennies were being buried with it. Apart from one more minor hit, 1965 was to be their last fat year. They bowed out in October 1966 with Tom Springfield's *No Sad Songs for Me* of which the final words were 'it's all over' — and it was.

Lionel announced he was leaving after a residency in Turkey. Encouraged by his first wife, film actress Julie Foster, he eventually became a children's TV personality though he continued to release records with decreasing frequency.

When the Pennies failed to find a replacement for Morton, Fryer — still stage-struck — formed 'Fritz, Mike and Mo' with Wilshem, but when this foundered he slipped behind the scenes to produce Motorhead and Squeeze among others before moving to Ross-on-Wye to derive most of his income from an antique lighting business.

After a period at Radio Luxembourg, Buck found freelance employment in the music industry at management level. He was most interested in reforming the Pennies for cabaret work in the 1970s but

this was scotched by Morton's desire to try new numbers. The principal advocate of this scheme, Mike Wilshem, was allegedly last seen on a Berkshire construction site.

Spinning both ways (left to right) *Lionel Morton, Mike Wilshem, Alan Bush and Fritz Fryer. The reason for* Juliet's *original burial on a B-side may have been its close melodic resemblance to a Ruby Murray hit of 1955.*

The Merseybeats' Merseybeat

It was Bingo that really counted at the E.M.I. Social Club in London Street, Reading, where the Merseybeats appeared in 1981 in their white Elvis-in-Vegas jump suits and pandering to assumed audience desires with slick patter and executions of *American Trilogy*, a Beatles medley ('where would we be without 'em?'), Gerry's *You'll Never Walk Alone* and other M.O.R. favourites. Ending the first set leader Tony Crane, unplugging his Gibson Firebird, was approached by a fellow expatriate Liverpudlian and genuine fan with a list of requests. Obligingly, the suntanned Crane ran through as many of these half-remembered artefacts as his subordinates could play. For the first time in ages, Merseybeats hits were regurgitated as detached entities

instead of being excerpted in the usual medley. After twenty years, it was the most they could do.

With bass guitarist Billy Kinsley, Tony had been a member of the Pacifics, formerly the Mavericks. On the suggestion of Cavern M.C. Bob Wooler, they became the Merseybeats in 1961, having gained clearance from the publication of the same name. Among the youngest of first wave Liverpool groups, they originally consisted of Crane, Kinsley, drummer David Elias and second guitarist Frank Sloane. However, by 1962, Elias and Sloane had been supplanted by John Banks and Aaron Williams respectively. For a while, they also showcased two guest vocalists in beauty queen Irene Hughes and comedian Billy Butler, a professional 'Liverpudlian' like Mickey Finn.

Toughened during the required Hamburg stretch, their local standing became such that they were granted a spot low on the renowned New Brighton Rock Spectacular bill in October headed by Little

The Merseybeats offstage (left to right) Aaron Williams, Johnny Gustafson, Billy Kinsley and Tony Crane in 1964. At this point, Kinsley had officially left the band. John Banks was presumably in another part of the studio.

Richard and the Beatles. At the start of 1963, they were rated tenth in *Merseybeat's* hierarchy of groups, just below the Spidermen.

They came to be represented by Les Ackerley, a northern variety agent, after a period with Brian Epstein was unsettled by a disagreement over image. You could see Epstein's point. In preference to macho leathers or Burton lounge suits, the Merseybeats' more gigolo tastes ran to bolero jackets, multi-ringed fingers and frilly shirts like whipped cream. As late as 1964, *Record Mirror* felt bound to comment on their 'bizarre' dress sense. Yet, after running the Merseyside hard case gauntlet, accused of being nancy boys, the Merseybeats' sartorial judgement proved to be correct as every night they made the little girls scream.

Their hit singles, produced by Jack Baverstock, were also directed at a doe-eyed female following. Most caught a romantic mood via a wistful Latinised shuffle with melancholy words, occasional tempo shifts and a staccato rhythm guitar style. Rather than a chorus, repeated hook lines — generally the song title — and a punchy riff on organ or low-register guitar were used. These records certainly contrasted with the heavy-handed ravers of many of their contemporaries.

As well as more common beat ballads like *Mr. Moonlight* and Arthur Alexander's *Soldier of Love*, they dared to peddle a gaucher brand of sentiment than other bands. Working from *Hello Young Lovers* from THE KING AND I and Vic Damone's version of GIRL THAT I WILL MARRY, they dipped into Mario Lanza's bag (*My Heart and I*) and even did an arrangement of *Lavender Blue*, a nursery waltz dating from the last century.

Beyond mining this fanciful seam, they were as capable as anyone else of powering through *Long Tall Sally*, Bo Diddley's *You Can't Judge a Book*, and any other lowdown rockers. In between lay first British versions of *Fortune Teller* and *Bring It On Home To Me*. Their record company, Fontana, was not ready to risk any group originals (all co-written by Crane) as A-sides, but though not prolific, the Merseybeats showed promise as composers, notably with the jaunty *Really mystified* and another flip, *Milkman*, to which they mimed in a 1964 pop film JUST FOR YOU directed by Douglas Wilcox.

Wanting a place in the murky Mersey sun, Fontana had clutched the Merseybeats to its breast in April 1963. Four months later, their cover of the Shirelles' *It's Love That Really Counts* spread itself thinly enough to sell 100,000 copies without rising above Number 24. In the New Year came their biggest smash in Peter Lee Stirling's *I Think of You* which pondered at Number 5 after an endorsement by the Beatles on JUKE BOX JURY.

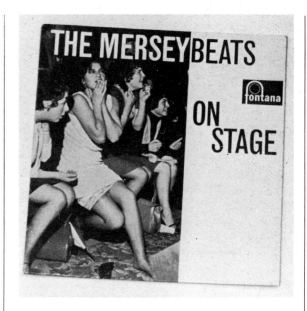

The only release representing their real onstage material.

Don't Turn Around and Bacharach's *Wishin' and Hopin'* both made Number 13. The latter was the nearest the group came to a US breakthrough but unhappily they were beaten to the punch there by Dusty Springfield's rendition.

With their fancy clothes and smoochy ballads, they were mobbed by young ladies whenever they appeared in public during this, the apogee of their career. A leitmotif of notoriety lent piquancy when a Sunday newspaper investigated their backstage frolics, characterized by the words 'Free love' scrawled on Banks' bass drum.

They lost momentum temporarily when, dogged by internal problems, the quartet lost Kinsley in February 1964 for several months. Robert Garner, later to join the Creation, filled in until a more suitable replacement could be contacted. Located in Germany, Johnny Gustafson, late of the Big Three, dived on a 'plane to Gatwick on the morning of March 2nd. There he hastily boarded the next flight to Newcastle where he stumbled into a theatre dressing room at 7.30 p.m. to honour his first official engagement with the Merseybeats.

It was only late in 1964 that any vinyl mishaps were suffered when *Last Night* and *Don't Let It Happen to Us* both stopped short of the Top 40. After a decent

Tony Crane with the New Merseybeats, 1984.

interval, *I Love You Yes I do* saw the year out at Number 25 though oblivion was in sight as the Mersey Sound faded taking with it its most direct associations. Revived in 1980 by Elvis Costello, the Merseybeats' final 45, *I Stand Accused*, with weird percussion effects towards the end, was unusually extroverted.

Aaron Williams wound up back in Liverpool where, though ostensibly retired from showbusiness, he grew a moustache and tried to make a go of it as a songwriter.

John Banks, on recovering from a nervous disorder, teamed up with Gustafson as 'John and Johnny' to cut a topical ditty, *Bumper to Bumper*, before going their separate ways. John was last seen in Israel while Johnny, after a brief solo attempt, formed Quatermass. Towards the 1980s, his pulsating bass style was heard in groups as diverse as Roxy Music and Uriah Heep. In 1982 a Gustafson opus, *Dear John*, was recorded by Status Quo.

Now managed by Who mentors, Stamp and Lambert, the old firm of Tony Crane and the prodigal Billy Kinsley, whose eponymous group had come to nought, hired a backing band who were unusual in their employment of two drummers. Unencumbered by instruments, Tony and Billy as 'the Merseys' now concentrated on two-part harmonies and onstage physical gyrations. With studio help from the likes of Jimmy Page, Jack Bruce and Clem Cattini, their big band scouse treatment — 'with yer long blonde *hur*' — of a McCoys B-side, *Sorrow*, climbed into the Top 5 in 1966; and the craziness of 1964 flashed before them as once again they packed auditoriums the length of the country. This Indian Summer broke as subsequent records flopped and the pair hit times so lean that in 1970, Kinsley was pressed into the Swinging Blue Jeans for a few months. When David Bowie resuscitated *Sorrow* in 1973, hopes were treasured that the Merseys would be the beneficiaries of a new Bowie hit song. However, this wasn't to be and the partnership was dissolved after a last single, *I Love Onions* credited to 'the Crackers'.

While Tony hit the chicken-in-a-basket trail with the New Merseybeats, Billy ticked over in Jimmy Campbell's Rockin' Horse and a band with ex-Undertaker Jackie Lomax. After taking part in a Merseybeat nostalgia show in the USA, he joined forces with Paper Chase led by Pete Clarke from the Escorts. As 'Liverpool Express,' this pure pop alliance twice got lucky, in the UK hit parade in 1976. When this ran out of steam, Kinsley organised another Merseyside outfit, the Cheats, for yet another crack at the Big Time in 1978.

The Nashville Teens Let It Rock

From the stockbroker town of Weybridge in Surrey came the Nashville Teens, brainchildren of Arthur Sharp and Ramon Phillips, lead singers of two rival groups of the parish who amalgamated in 1962. Of the two, Phillips was the more commanding, taking most of the weightier vocals leaving comic relief to the easy-going Sharp. In 1966, Ray declined Ginger Baker's invitation to sing with Cream. With his long-jawed, hunched stance, he came close to a 1960s Johnny Rotten, minus that punk gentleman's 'revolutionary' pretentions and loutish affectation. Even if, like most people, you were ignorant of his name, Phillips was always the most visually distinguishable Nashville Teen. This isn't much of a compliment considering that the second least nondescript member was prodigious keyboard player John Hawken, by virtue of his swot spectacles. The remainder of the original crew were guitarist Michael Dunford, drummer Roger Groom and bass player Peter Shannon.

Frustrated by the scarcity of local venues tolerating anything wilder than trad jazz, the possibility of a season in Hamburg sorted out the men from the boys. The band that climbed from the van outside the Star Club in May 1963 showed a radical personnel reshuffle. In place of Dunsford and Groom respectively were guitarist John Allen of Woking and drummer Peter Lace, who was soon succeeded by Londoner Barry Jenkins. Another addition was a *third* vocalist, Terry Crow, who decided to stay in Germany when the group's residency ended, Sharp nearly joining him.

A palpable Reeperbahn hit, the Teens had acquired class by their return to Surrey. With a non-specific, diverting style, among their repertory selections was a torrid rocking-up of Bing Crosby's *How Deep Is the Ocean* with Dylanesque harmonica. They regaled the Mods with this on their maiden READY STEADY GO TV slot. More conventional American preferences were *Hoochie Coochie Man*, *Searchin'*, *Let It Rock*, and *Hurtin' Inside*, shared with another Hamburg minstrel, Cliff Bennett. More erudite were *Nashville Blues* from the Everly Brothers and a note-for-note facsimile of Roy Orbison's *Crying*. With the Stones they shared *Mona* and *Chantilly Lace*. It was intriguing to compare similarities in arrangement when the Stones smashed out the Big Bopper monologue during their 1983 world tour.

Through the offices of manager Don Arden, the Teens gained a reputation as a reliable back-up group for visiting old tyme rockers from the States. As late as

Revived 45 Time: the Teens back Jerry Lee at the Star Club (above). Back in England (below), the hitmaking line-up was (left to right) John Allen, Barry Jenkins, Pete Shannon, Ray Phillips, Art Sharp and John Hawken.

1969, supporting Gene Vincent and Chuck Berry, they unfairly got the bird from ancient Teds baying for the reassuring original articles. Memories of a similar stint with Berry five years earlier were evoked for it was then that they first made the acquaintance of Aldershot-born vocalist with the Minutemen, Mickie Most.

Having notched up a hit with the Animals, Most sold himself to Arden and the Teens as a big shot record producer. The studio sessions began with a try-out of

Mose Allison's *Parchman Farm*, but another hard luck story, *Tobacco Road*, seemed a better proposition as debut single, with the band's hacked-up rhythm and throbbing pulse behind the strident vocal duet and barrelhouse piano interlude. Discovered by Sharp while serving behind a record shop counter, this song was composed by John D. Loudermilk from North Carolina whose relationship with the Nashville Teens was to become much the same as Dylan's with Manfred Mann.

Decca was not the wisest choice of record company. Saturating itself with beat groups, the label often neglected the publicity needs of all but its consistently best-selling acts — all pop groups are the same; let's sign as many as we can, see which racket catches on and cash in quick — none of them last long anyway so why waste resources trying to prove otherwise.

A world-wide smash, *Tobacco Road's* B-side, a rendering of Chris Kenner's *I like it like that* caused Columbia to withdraw their Dave Clark version of this for UK release. After overruling Ray's unease, the Teens revamped another Loudermilk opus, *Google eye*, a folksy tale of an unfortunate trout first narrated by Big Pete Deutscher. Even aided by a promo film, it made far less international impact than its predeccessor though its British Top 10 entry was respectable enough.

The outcome was possibly effected when US visa restrictions confined their American tour with the Zombies to New York State, quashing an eagerly anticipated trip to Nashville. However, from a Big Apple taping attended by the Drifters' Johnny Moore emerged a third single, *Find My Way Back Home*, which, finding its way to Number 34 back in Blighty, soured their partnership with absent Mickie Most. From 1965, the Teens were to run through seven more producers of the calibre of Shel Talmy, Mike Leander and Roy Wood — none with Mr. Most's chartbusting touch.

However, these good men and true were not entirely to blame for the Teens' Top 50 demise. In April 1965, Decca hedged its bets by simultaneously issuing both the group's and Marianne Faithful's pressings of Loudermilk's *This Little Bird*, each with the same producer, Andrew Loog Oldham. The British sales victory was Marianne's though the Teens' better version had the upper hand in the Japanese and Australian theatres of war.

In February 1966, Roger Groom was back in the fold when Jenkins transferred to the Animals, with whom the Teens had appeared in the 1965 movie, *Pop Gear*. The friendship between the two groups was emphasised when Eric Burdon's team segued into a

downbeat *Tobacco Road* at the marathon CHRISTMAS ON EARTH CONTINUED presentation in London in 1967.

The next two rats to leave the sinking ship were Shannon and the irreplacable Hawken, who had been asked to form Renaissance with ex-Yardbirds Keith Relf and Jim McCarty. In 1972, Art Sharp quit for a post as assistant to Don Arden, with whom the Teens remained on cordial terms even when he no longer represented them.

When *The Hard Way* departed the Top 50 in 1966, the Teens' living was to depend more and more on the road. Apart from a few B-sides, few publishing royalties were forthcoming though Hawken's *T.N.T.*, based on *Green Onions* three-note ostinato, was a Canadian A-side. *Revived 45 time* of August 1966 was either hopelessly outdated or too far ahead of its time; by contrast were the psychedelic meanderings of *I'm a Lonely One*.

Bearing the slings and arrows of fashion, the Teens, like Cilla Black and Alan Price, had a go at a Randy Newman song, *Biggest Night of Her Life*. Later, their perfectly credible job on Dylan's *All Along the Watchtower* was overshadowed by Jimi Hendrix's more upmarket rendition as was their worthy attempt at *Indian Reservation* by Don Fardon. More commercial was *I'm Coming Home* from the pens of Les Reed and Barry Mason though the opposite was true of their spooky deadpan arrangement of *Widdecombe Fair* (a nod towards Traffic's *John Barleycorn*). *Day and Night* ventured further into this territory while *Ex Kay One Ex* rode the Free bandwagon.

After an *in extremis* reworking of *Tobacco Road* was a four year vinyl silence until the single *Midnight* appeared on a Chichester independent label, 'Go'. By this time, the only original Teen left was Ray Phillips. In good shape for a man in his mid-forties, his vocation had led him to a semi-detached home near Weybridge by 1981.

On TV in UNFORGETTABLE, the Nashville Teens cut everyone else on the series to pieces. With a more contemporary sound, they scorned much of the cabaret security that beckoned other 1960s attractions, preferring to entertain the bikers at Angie's in Wokingham or the beer-swilling regulars of High Wycombe's Nag's Head. They even went down well at Dreamland in Margate where, in 1966, the entire group had a fist fight with local toughs the moment they arrived.

Blue Jeans A-Swinging

In the Merseybeat edition of *The History of Rock* magazine in 1982, the Swinging Blue Jeans were not mentioned once — an apposite omission as, twenty years earlier, they were also absent from *Merseybeat's* popularity poll even though they'd been around since 1957. Almost becoming the first Liverpool group to make a record, they were ditched by Oriole Records during a 1962 staff reshuffle for being 'too amateurish'. They'd also lost the interest of Joe Meek, for whom they taped an instrumental. Yet, this crestfallen headway at a time when the Beatles were barely surviving put them a cut above the rest. It may have also turned them into taciturn 'professionals' set in their ways, waiting for this Beatle-inspired rubbish to fizzle out so that 'decent music' could resurface. This attitude was exampled in their sneering at the Stones' scruffiness which precipitated a punch-up in the BBC canteen prior to the first ever TOP OF THE POPS. No wonder Bob Wooler, though admitting they were unique, referred to them as 'the Methuselahs of the scene'. When Merseybeat became more than a passing fad, that the Swinging Blue Jeans could adjust so easily to the new regime was admirable. That they endured as the most frantic archetype of the form showed that they weren't faking either.

The quartet that made its chart debut in June 1963 were the remaining travellers of a mighty rough road from Wilson Dance Hall in the grim suburb of Garston where Ray Ennis, a 15-year-old printer's apprentice, sang with his skiffle group in 1956. Among his admirers was a lad named Norman Kuhlke, who had spent part of his youth in Venezuela before returning to Liverpool to be a mechanic. Discovering that Norman was instinctively musical, Ray invited him to thrash washboard in a band which in July 1957 became the Swinging Blue *Genes*.

At a Liverpool Empire skiffle contest, the group defied all comers including the Ralph Ellis Group, whose leader further conceded defeat by joining the Genes in May 1958, shortly before cabinet maker Leslie Braid was hired to slap double bass. They began the 1960s as an instrumentally lopsided sextet with Braid on a new-fangled electric bass, banjoist Paul Moss, Kuhlke up to his ears in H.P. on a drum kit, and the other three on guitars. Trying to please most of the people, they wore a uniform of striped blazers and blue jeans and, having no horn players, walked an uneasy line between trad jazz and current favourites.

As a kind of backdated skiffle act who could afford proper instruments, the Genes were bland enough to

Surely some mistake: Good Golly Miss Molly Malone!

be an acceptable concession to pop at Liverpool's then jazz fortress, the Cavern. However, their days as the club's token pop group were numbered when, on March 21st 1961, the Beatles were booked as the Genes' 'guests' during the regular off-peak evening devoted to pop. Lennon and Co.'s sixty extra customers, by loudly voicing their preferences, abused the Genes' hospitality causing an after-hours protest to promoter Ray McFall for allowing such barbarians to invade.

The incident gave the group food for deep thought as did the exit of Moss to the marriage bed and their last impermanent third guitarist to a new life in Canada. Convinced that skiffle and trad would not recover from being dead, the less abstract Swinging Blue *Jeans* remained a quartet concentrating on the harder rock that had so eclipsed them at the Cavern — the wisdom of which was noted by no less a barbarian than John 'I'm glad they got rid of that banjo player' Lennon on JUKE BOX JURY two years later.

Though their manager John Ireland was proprietor of the Beachcomber and Mardi Gras clubs, it was the Downbeat that the Jeans were to rule as the Searchers did the Iron Door. Beyond Merseyside, they did the usual stretch in Hamburg but long absences down south may explain their poor showing in *Merseybeat's* survey.

Signed to H.M.V. within a year of their Oriole dismissal, the Jeans were assigned to producer Walter Ridley and arranger John Chilton; significantly, a jazz buff. As well as engineering the sponsorship of Lybro denim manufacturers, Ireland had paved the way by convincing Radio Luxembourg that the Jeans would be

The Jeans in cabaret, 1984 (left to right) Colin Manley (ex-Remo Four), Ray Ennis and, obscuring drummer John Ryan, Leslie Braid.

ideal for their own show SWINGTIME every Sunday at 9 p.m. These efforts resulted in the polished *It's Too Late Now*, composed by Ennis, reaching Number 30 — not a bad start.

In favour of the nondescript *Don't You Know*, faint H.M.V. hearts effected the flipping of the follow-up, Tom Springfleld's *Angie*, in the light of a rival version by Pye's Gregory Philips. Consequent confusion and meagre sales put the Jeans back at square one but from a fifty minute session in late 1963 emerged their best-remembered hit. From Bob Wooler's erudite record collection, Chan Romero's *Hippy Hippy Shake* from 1958 boomed over the Cavern speakers to be absorbed into the sets of dozens of Merseyside bands but, though Pat Harris and the Blackjacks had a complacent vinyl stab at it in October 1963, the Jeans' exciting, definitive treatment crashed in at Number 18 to eventually threaten *I Wanna Hold Your Hand* at the top slot in January 1964. Apart from normal TV plugs, the group's cameo role in BBC police series Z-CARS as well as a real life part in the SOUND OF A CITY documentary supplemented endless cross-country one-nighters and tours with Marty Wilde and the Stones, with whom differences had been settled.

Overworking a successful formula, Little Richard's *Good Golly Miss Molly*, daughter of the *Hippy Hippy Shake*, only made Number 11 on the rebound. A recovery was made with a worthy revival of Betty Everett's downbeat *You're No Good* which got to Number 3, but the fifth 45, *Promise You'll Tell Her*, was the leveller that reduced the Swinging Blue Jeans to also-rans.

Retreading old ground, *It Isn't There* by *You're No Good* composer Clint Ballard was too déjà vu but its tearjerking harmonica obligato gave it such period charm that, more than *Ferry Cross the Mersey*, it served as a requiem to Merseybeat's passing. Having previously attempted to distance themselves from it, the Jeans leading position among Mersey groups ensured that they would never leave the leaking ferryboat. Though they were prolific songwriters, their own material lacked the depth of even a Gerry Marsden to sustain interest, and their over-caution in repeating tried and tested procedures exacerbated this. Also, though their handling of R'n'B was often exhilarating, newer, wilder acts caused them to undeservedly get the bird as on their 1964 Chuck Berry tour with hit parade newcomers, the Animals. The L.P. BLUE JEANS A-SWINGING encapsulated all these traits loaded as it was with hoary old rockers, jumped-up Garston chestnuts, and a brace of substandard originals.

The string-laden *Don't make me over*, penned by Bacharach and David, coasted to the brink of the Top 30 in 1966, but, to all intents and purposes, the Jeans' axe fell when *You're no good* ended its thirteen week run in July 1964.

In the USA, their first chart entry had been by proxy when *It's Too Late Now* was flatteringly covered by Tina Robbins. *Hippy Hippy Shake* sold well enough but, after 1964, little was forthcoming until 1969 when *Hey Mrs. Housewife* paid an astonishing flying visit to the Hot 100.

Back home, they maintained themselves on such

carrots before the donkey as a 1966 'Tip for the Top' spot on TOP OF THE POPS and futile nods to transitory crazes like the psychedelic symbolism of *Don't Go Out in the Rain, Sugar, You Might Melt* which was crushed as a fellow Liverpudlian David Garrick's equally laughable version picked up more airplay. The Jeans were more comfortable (though outdated) with *Tremblin'* of 1967, influenced by the Hollies. More intriguing were the B-sides, *What Can I Do Today* being particularly strong with rumbling tom-toms and hard riff based on the Animals' *It's My Life*.

That the group's final endeavour *What Have They Done to Hazel* was attributed to 'Ray Ennis and the Blue Jeans' emphasised what a burden their very name had become. Lead singer Ennis warranted such prominence because, after years in his shadow, Ellis had quit in 1966 for a securer haven in an insurance office, closely followed by Braid. The vacancies were filled by guitarist Terry Sylvester and bassist Michael Gregory, both from the Escorts. The former stuck three years with the Jeans before joining the Hollies. Ironically, Gregory had earlier rejected an offer from the Mancunian quintet in order to stay with Sylvester.

After a three year lay-off, Braid and Ennis reformed the group without Kuhlke, who had opened a sandwich bar. With drummer John Ryan and guitarist Colin Manley from the Remo Four, they even released some shot-in-the-dark singles and an album movingly titled BRAND NEW AND FADED. In 1981, Ennis recorded a song called *I'm an Old Rock and Roller*, a statement he tacitly reiterates whenever the Swinging Blue Jeans close the show as always with *Hippy Hippy Shake*.

The Story of Them

The Emerald Isle's most famous pop group was easy-listening trio the Bachelors, who scored seventeen UK Top 50 smashes between 1963 and 1967. Their recorded output reflected roots in the continuing Irish Showband tradition founded on mainstream country and western, ranging from Jim Reeves sweetcorn to Frankie Laine cowboy pop, via rockabilly and singalong evergreens by the likes of Guy Mitchell and Ned Miller. Punctuating these were artefacts from the 'Auld Sod' itself which, depending on the mood of the hour, might vary from the quaking sentiment of *Rose of Tralee* to the lighthearted lilt of *Delaney's Donkey* to the bellicose rebel yell of *The Outlawed Raparee* (even if some unrepealed ballroom regulations in Ulster obliged the band to conclude the evening's entertainment with the British National Anthem).

With the advent of rock'n'roll, younger show bands aspired instead to be highly proficient copyists of American pop, a few even generating interest beyond the Irish sea. Other groups rejected the Showband ethos altogether, drawing inspiration from pure Gaelic sources, as purveyed by Cork's Na Fili and the McPeaks from Antrim, or from imported sounds. Many American bluesmen, for instance, found it worthwhile to include Belfast and Dublin on their European itinerary. Foremost among non-showband beat groups were the Creatures, the Fenlans, Rory Gallagher's Impact, and Bluesville, whose English vocalist, Ian Whitcomb, enjoyed some success in the States. However, apart from providing sanctuary for pirate radio vessels, Ireland's only direct intrusion into the main sequence of British Beat was that of Belfast R'n'B group, Them. Them's personnel consisted of local musicians and the remnants of an outfit called 'the Monarchs' who drank their pay principally in Germany, ploughing through up to seven sets a night in US military bases and the clubs of Cologne, Heidelberg and Frankfurt, concentrating mainly on the rock'n'roll end of R'n'B — Little Richard, Fats Domino, Ray Charles plus isolated highlights like *Hound Dog* (prefaced by a verse of *Que Sera Sera*) and *I Put a Spell on You*. An extrapolation based on a three note bass riff, *One Two Brown Eyes*, was the idea of the

Flashes from the Showband scene.

band's saxophonist and general factotum, George Ivan Morrison from Deanie Sands and the Javelins, a group whose repertoire had been divided between country, blues, and rock. Though barely 18 when the Monarchs cut their only disc in 1963, 'Van' Morrison had been playing music in public for seven years, encouraged by his father, himself a musician as well as possessor of an impressive jazz and blues record collection.

With Morrison, bass guitarist Alan Henderson, and a mutable pool of others, Them smouldered into form from jam sessions at an R'n'B club at the Old Sailors Maritime Dance Hall, a Belfast equivalent of the Ealing Blues Club or Newcastle's Downbeat rather than the Cavern or Twisted Wheel. From scanty rehearsals and loose, simple structures, Them plunged deeper into R'n'B than the Monarchs had done, attempting *Stormy Monday*, Sonny Boy Williamson's *Help Me* and selections from Muddy Waters to Chuck Berry. Later, they made concessions to popular taste by trying the likes of *Tobacco Road*, *Dancing in the Street* and *You've Lost That Loving Feeling*. A refinement of earlier compositions, Morrison's three chord monologue *Gloria* would often run up to twenty minutes in live performance. Singing like a more nasal, stentorian Jagger, he nonetheless gave Them a jazzy edge by incorporating scat singing and sax obligatos into the modus operandi. Like Manfred Mann, Them were not averse to using a vibraphone whenever one was available.

A four track demo taped by one of Them's many line-ups in an Ulster studio was the only musical archive of the band before they migrated to an uncertain London future in the winter of 1964, having signed to Decca a few months earlier. The group that made records attributed to 'Them' was more changeable in state than the most random Maritime band. With Henderson and Morrison the most constant factors, 'as another number passed, another member of the band would be substituted for by a session musician' commented Jimmy Page, who was among those hired as insurance against musical disaster.

The debut single, a bobsleigh ride through Slim Harpo's *Don't start crying now*, though it sold well in loyal Ulster, gave little indication that Them were any better than any other long-haired R'n'B group on the make. One such struggling musician with whom Them mixed socially was Rod Stewart, who was invited to Belfast for a blow at the Maritime. His first record was bound for deletion at the time.

Them, however, rose above the common herd with their second 45, a dynamic arrangement of Big Joe Williams' *Baby Please Don't Go* whose airplay reached its apogee when READY STEADY GO adopted it as a theme tune following Them's miming of it on the show in November 1964. Even then, Van cut a sullen figure, without the underlying humour of a Phil May or Eric Burdon. Backed by a severely-edited *Gloria*, *Baby Please Don't Go* deserved its Top 10 placing no matter how few bona fide Them members actually played on it. An ominous two-note bass line and whinging organ anchored the track, interspersed with rivetting guitar passages and Morrison's surging harmonica and clipped, stumbling vocal. Lapsing into incomprehensibility, one verse in particular sounded to unaccustomed ears like:

> 'Werp me a Dawg (thrice)
> An' gitcha way down here,
> I'll make yer walk the log —
> Baby please don't go.'

Them weren't destined to be one-hit wonders, as the contrasting *Here Comes the Night* cast its shadow at Number 2 in May 1965. A miss by Lulu the previous November, this Latin-slanted ballad of lustful envy was written by veteran New York showbusiness jack-of-all-trades Bert Berns who, in Britain in 1965, joined Them's movable feast of producers — Art Greenslade, Dick Rowe, Tommy Scott — as well as contributing further songs to their first L.P., THE ANGRY YOUNG THEM.

As well as Maritime die-hards like *Route 66* and *Bright Lights Big City*, this collection also embraced a hat trick of flop A-sides. The most surprising failure was *Mystic Eyes* which, though an atypical neo-instrumental, was an exciting streamlining of Them's R'n'B passion. Hidden on the flip of *Half as Much* was another tour de force, *I'm Gonna Dress in Black*, which might have done for Them what *House of the Rising Sun* did for the Animals.

With Decca flogging a 'New Stones' angle hard, Them's aggressive scruffiness adorned the sleeve of THEM AGAIN, rushed out within eight weeks of the first album. Among standout tracks were Bobby Bland's *Turn On Your Love Light*, *I Can Only Give You Everything*, revived a year later by the Troggs, and a more structured Morrison number, *Bring 'Em On In*. Eighteen years later, looking for all the world like Bradley Hardacre turned to agriculture, Van would remind a Dublin audience of one more THEM AGAIN item when he joined its composer, Bob Dylan, onstage for a heart-rending *It's All Over Now Baby Blue*.

In spring 1966, Them took off on a short, badly-organised US tour where *Here Comes the Night* had made Number 24 in the Hot 100. There had also

When Irish, Eyes aren't smiling — with Van 'Mystic Eyes' Morrison in pride of place. Alan Henderson stands immediately to his left.

been a more surrogate hit in the Shadows of Knight's cover of *Gloria* which subsequently became, with *Louie Louie*, an American garage band standard. A session at the Whiskey-a-Go-Go, during which Jim Morrison of the Doors clambered onto the boards to duet with his namesake on a rambling *Midnight Hour*, was a highlight of an otherwise harrowing expedition which was the last straw for Van as (in preference to one of his own songwriting efforts) Decca issued the absent Them's revitalisation of Paul Simon's *Richard Cory* in March 1966, the Animals' version being cancelled to give the ailing Irish band a break.

Withdrawing to his parents' Belfast home, Van maintained a few contacts within the business like Phil Coulter, another Ulster composer, whose *Puppet On a String* won the Eurovision song contest in 1967. Like Mr. Micawber, he was waiting for something to turn up.

Bearing in mind his disenchantment with his biographer Johnny Rogan, I was tempted to relate a smart alec story of Them without referring to Morrison at all. Turgid reading it would have made too, judging by the four L.P.'s — including a rehash of *Gloria* — that

Them, with a new singer, churned out as Henderson led them through another US trek — gluttons for punishment. Spending much of 1967 in Scandinavia, this final incarnation fell to bits before the year was out.

With even less to do with the turnover of town boys who sweated it out at the Maritime were 'the Belfast Gypsies', created by Kim Fowley taking advantage of Them's percolating American breakthrough. Giving this project an authentic sheen were two brothers named McAuley who had actually played organ and drums with Them in the early days. When their single *Gloria's Dream* sank into a coma, the Gypsies then mutated into 'the Freaks of Nature' who met a similar fate with *People Let's Freak Out*.

Meanwhile, something *had* turned up for Van Morrison when Bert Berns, sending an air ticket to New York, invited him to the Big Apple to resume his recording career. As well as producing a million seller in *Brown-Eyed Girl*, the sessions chronicled a period of transition for Morrison, best exampled by Them-style arrangements of *Beside You* and *Madame George* which were reworked when, following Berns' death in 1967, the impressionistic Astral Weeks album, recorded in two days flat, began Van's gruff, brooding climb to international stardom.

Hark at Unit Four Plus Two

The Hertfordshire group scene was as incestuous a game of musical chairs as anywhere else. From the Cheshunt-Hertford-St. Alban's triangle alone came the Hunters, Roulettes, Zombies, Argent, Daybreakers and Unit Four Plus Two. Here contents merged as personnel were swapped around and shared. Of them all, Unit Four Plus Two achieved most in the British charts with five Top 30 entries — one of which was a pop standard covered as recently as 1976 by Randy Edelman.

With his wholesome good looks and thick dark hair, Tommy Moeller had been a rival local attraction to another Cheshunt rock'n'roller, Harry Webb, who later adopted the stage name 'Cliff Richard'. Missing Cliff's boat Tommy was by 1962 singing in a modern folk quartet, Unit Four, in which he also played piano and guitar. Among the band's early members was Brian Parker, who had briefly tasted fame as guitarist with the Hunters, an instrumental act whose records included a minor classic in *The Storm*, which Parker had co-written, before the group broke up soon after drummer-leader Norman Stacey was killed in a car accident.

Despite only a short spell with Unit Four, Brian did not terminate the song-writing partnership instigated with Moeller. Among the first fruits of this was *Couldn't Keep It to Myself*, an odd hybrid of hootenanny and Merseybeat. The group's repertoire also mixed pop-folk items like *Cotton Fields*, *La Bamba* and *Wild is the Wind* with big ballads, such as *Climb Every Mountain* from THE SOUND OF MUSIC and Nat King Cole's *When I Fall in Love* which were draped in lush four-part harmony.

Unit Four Plus Two far away from Green Fields. Tommy Moeller is second from left.

The Hunters once backed Cliff at the London Palladium — the Shadows being tied up elsewhere. Sorrow and Pain harked back to the skiffle weepie All My Sorrows.

By 1963, it seemed the line-up had stabilised with Moeller, second vocalist Peter Moules, and guitarists Howard Lubin and David 'Buster' Meakle (who had once led the Daybreakers). At the suggestion of manager Johnny Barker, a sort of Hertfordshire Epstein, Unit Four broadened their scope by adding a rhythm section. With bass guitarist Rodney Garwood and drummer Hugh Halliday, Barker closed a deal with Decca on behalf of Unit Four *Plus Two*.

Though *Green Fields* irritated the lower regions of the charts, the soft ponderous accompaniment and pastoral lyricism of it and its follow-up *Sorrow and Pain*, though performed well, conjured an alien atmosphere to the Big Beat that dominated pop in 1964. The third single, *Concrete and Clay*, began life as a slow, soulful, semi-acoustic lieder much like the others. However, it was ultimately taped with a harder staccato edge and a pronounced Latin-American touch, possibly propounded when two old acquaintances were invited to help out. These were Russell Ballard and Robert Henrit, who had respectively pressed keyboards and drummed in Meakle's Daybreakers. Henrit was also a former Hunter. Both had since joined the Roulettes, who were another group on Parker's books. As well as backing Adam Faith, Russ, now a lead guitarist, and Bob continued to assist on the Unit's record dates. They were rewarded when Parker and Moeller (with Henrit) penned the Roulettes' single *The Long Cigarette*, which sold quite well though thwarted by a BBC ban. Tommy alone presented them with *To a Taxi Driver*, their final B-side. Before this, the Roulettes spent a long period in

*Ready Steady Win: the Bo Street Runners in triumph — (*left to right*) Gary Lewis (Gary Thomas), RSG presenter Gay Singleton, drummer Glyn Thomas (obscured), John Dominic and Dave Cameron in September 1964.*

Europe supporting French rocker Richard Anthony who was impressed with their excellent accompaniment for his Gallic interpretation of *Concrete and Clay*, unaware as he was of their part in the original, which had knocked the Stones from the top of the British chart in April 1965. Ironically, it was Cliff Richard who toppled them the week after.

Concrete and Clay solidified at a healthy Number 28 in the U.S. Hot 100, prompting the group to next update Jimmy Rodgers' aqueous *Woman from Liberia* purely for the American market. Unfortunately, they fell from grace in the USA in even less time than the year left to them in the home charts.

The Unit's next three UK releases refined the jerky style realised at the *Concrete* session but, though they gave a good account of themselves in the Top 30, they could not recapture the unique qualities of the blueprint. The more straightforward *Stop Wasting Your Time*, B-side of *Hark*, showed that they were able to branch out into other areas. If nothing else, the group were blessed with a talented though underrated source of original material in Tommy and Brian. The feverish tension of *Baby Never Say Goodbye*, for example, was every bit as engaging as *Concrete and Clay* if only

because a more legato approach belied the Costa del Hertford arrangements of earlier efforts. The song had been given originally to Harrow's Bo Street Runners, winners of a READY STEADY GO R'n'B contest in July 1965. A turntable hit on pirate radio, the Runners version rendered *Baby Never Say Goodbye* old hat by the time their benefactors' version reached the shops six months later.

The hitless Unit roamed an outer darkness of the college and dance hall orbit of Britain and Europe until their feet began to crumble in 1969. When they transferred to Fontana Records in March 1967, Halliday and Meikle cashed in what chips were left as Ballard and Henrit joined on a full-time basis. With Russ also casting his line into the songwriting pool, the group were buoyed by D.J. John Peel's belated advocacy of *I Was Only Playing Games* and other latter day singles. This only served to drag things out a bit longer.

Though a penchant for Pete Murray cardigans with mock-leather buttons gave them a vague uniformity in 1965, their image wasn't clear enough at a time when fans needed to identify distinctly with a group before committing themselves. Also, apart from Moeller (a devil with women, apparently), they were an unprepossessing bunch, resembling primary school teachers rather than pop stars. Nevertheless, sliding out of touch, at least in bypassing acid-rock and other trends, they were tenacious enough to mine a seam of British pop that, occasionally modified, still belonged only to Unit Four Plus Two.

IT SHOULD HAVE BEEN ME

Some Heroic Failures

In an industry where sales figures are arbiters of success, real and imagined pressures of pop stardom can be alleviated with the arrival of another massive royalty cheque. Much lower on the scale, a brief chart entry, a one-shot record contract, even an encore is sufficient to feed hope. Often, without vanity, mere awareness of worth in the teeth of ill-luck is enough, though with every passing day you are less likely to become the Beatles. You had the right haircut, clothes and accent at the wrong time. The drummer decides to leave. A band who used to support you turns up on TOP OF THE POPS. If only there hadn't been a power cut when Mickie Most was there; if only the singer hadn't had a cold at the Marquee; if only we hadn't lost our way.....

Of course, most groups *were* useless, though some were useless and lucky. A few, however, were blanketed by a mediocrity quite out of proportion to their talent. Brought to their knees, grubbing for whatever they could get, these Third Division bands, nevertheless, maintained flashback dignity, even grandeur. In fact, by retiming the truth and a certain logical blindness, some could even brag afterwards that they had indeed Hit The Big Time.

Liverpool Losers

Foremost among Liverpool losers were the Big Three, Undertakers, Mojos and Escorts. What went wrong? After all, they satisfied any qualifications required by grasping recording managers anxious to breathe the air round the Beatles. To a man they'd won their spurs in Hamburg and scored in the *Merseybeat* poll. The Big Three were managed by Epstein; the Escorts produced by McCartney. In Stu James (Stuart Slater), the Mojos had a rich stockpile of original songs into which other acts such as Faron's Flamingos, dipped. In August 1962, the Undertakers were compelled by rapturous Star Club patrons to reprise one song (*Speedy Gonzales*) *seven* times. The eminence of these bands at a time when a nation was crying out for Merseybeat allowed them to pick and choose amongst goods on offer by professional tunesmiths as well as their being one step ahead in rifling the vaults of the Americans, the best example being the Escorts' plunder of the elegant *The One to Cry* by Harlem vocal group the Solitaires.

*The Big Three, (*left to right) *Johnny Hutchinson, John Gustafson and Brian Griffiths, sweat it out down the Cavern.*

One way or another, they were each impressive onstage. Stu James and Undertaker Jackie Lomax were both exceptional lead singers, good-looking too, as was Terry Sylvester, main man of the Escorts, who cornered the female adoration market with their youth and dainty three-part harmonies. In the Big Three, departing heart throb Johnny Gustafson was replaced by Bill 'Faron' Russley (dubbed 'the Panda-footed Prince of Prance' in his previous group, Faron's Flamingos from whence also came the Mojos' agile guitarist Nicky Crouch). The Mojos were also blessed with the superb barrelhouse piano of Terence O'Toole, while the Undertakers were unusual in their employment of a saxophonist.

All four groups made the hit parade but only the Mojos breached the Top 10. A group collaboration from way back, *Everything's All Right*, despite a mundane lyric, was such an arresting piece with its unconventional verse form and arrangement and *Let's Twist Again* air of vivacious unpredictability, that nothing short of the sun going nova would stop it

selling. Less spectacular was the Big Three's *By the Way* at a tantalising Number 22, while the Undertakers and Escorts' gladness came too fast when their debut singles — and biggest hits — both faltered at a coincidental Number 49.

Accepting that the Beatles, Searchers and Gerry had a certain je ne sais quoi; what had, say, Billy J., the Fourmost, and the Swinging Blue Jeans got that the others lacked? Answer: they were more consistent in the choice and presentation of material. The Escorts were especially unfortunate when Fontana issued their pert emasculation of *Dizzie Miss Lizzie* with a built-in irritant factor in the defiantly flat guitar note curtailing each riff. This was followed by the better *I Don't Want*

*The 'Takers: (*left to right*) Brian Jones, Bugs Pemberton, Geoff Nugent, Jackie Lomax and Chris Huston.*

To Go On Without You, left at the starting post by a rival interpretation by the Moody Blues, fresh from a Number One.

More was expected of the Big Three than these mere striplings. A greater inspiration to other musicians and prototype of 'power trios' from Cream to Motorhead, the Three were a byword for instrumental attack and intuitive audience manipulation. Recorded in August 1963 before a packed Cavern, their live E.P. was a good representation of Merseybeat's subterranean excitement, the fans participation being almost as pronounced as that of the band. But though numbers like *Some Other Guy* and *Peanut Butter* went down a storm on the boards, they were executed with bland precision in the studio, making the Big Three sound uncannily like all the other groups who claimed droit de seigneur over these songs. The same applied when they tried new songs written to order such as *I'm with you*, the follow-up that didn't make it. Compared to the Cavern stomp of the E.P., they sounded like a different

group which, with their rapid turnover of personnel, wasn't far from the truth.

Theoretically taking care of their own product, the Mojo's failure was more complicated. *Everything's All Right* was all right but their next 45, James and O'Toole's *Why Not Tonight*, had the door slammed at a disappointing Number 25. As a holding operation, it wasn't in the same league as *From Me to You* was to *Please Please Me*. Too obvious was the transposed *Everything's All Right* intro (copying the hi-hat fill exactly) the jabbering rev-up on a dominant chord, and the 'no no no no no' catch phrase. For good measure, they'd subtracted the piano solo for a guitar break instead. Against this reverse came a change of style in a revival of Lonnie Donegan's trudging *Seven Daffodils* which was humiliatingly outpaced by the Cherokees, a hitherto unknown Yorkshire group, whose less fussy

Change your name . . . and loose out.

*The Mojos (*left to right*) Stu Slater, Keith Alcock, Terence O' Toole, Nicky Crouch and John Conrad.*

version was produced by one Mickie Most. With the Big Three, the Mojos had the added worry of indifferent promotional aid from Decca who tended to let all but its most reliable sources of profit fend for themselves.

Over at Pye, the Undertakers turned out best of the bunch as far as overall record quality was concerned. Like the Big Three, they cast aside any internal efforts to take first grabs at the R'n'B motherlode echoing round Matthew Street and Hamburg 4. Among these were sterling all-out ravers like *Stupidity*, *Think* and *Mashed Potatoes*. Though the teenagers couldn't have cared less, middle-aged promoters, agents and media executives were more than a little aghast when the band, true to its name, rolled up in a hearse to take the

stage in black frock coats, embalmers' trousers and top hats with black crepe. When subsequent discs fell short of *Just a Little Bit's* high of Number 49, they mothballed their morbid props and abbreviated to the 'Takers'. However, even these concessions and a THANK YOUR LUCKY STARS television plug in September 1964 for their tremendous *If You Don't Come Back*, a tale of lovesick insanity, won not even just a little bit more chart action.

This was virtually the last nail in Merseybeat's coffin anyway. With the almost overnight passing of Liverpool as a musical centre, groups all over Britain dropped the scouse slang before it was too late. Though they kept on releasing singles well into 1966, it was certainly too late for the Escorts. Apart from a compromising role in THE SOUND OF A CITY, with their fab shiny suits, boyish grins and Lennonesque small ads in Merseybeat, they were too blatantly winsome to

The original drummer with the Dennisons was Clive Hornby portrayed here in his later television thespian capacity as philandering Jack Sugden.

The unacceptable face of Merseybeat — though Denny Seyton (Brian Tarr) fleetingly tasted fame with a revival of the Lettermen's The Way You Look Tonight.

be more than would-be cabin boys on the Beatle ship of state.

The more gifted Mojos — 'the Liverpool Yardbirds' — were robbed of their inheritance by a botched plan for a tour of America where they had been seen in cameo in the movie SEASIDE SWINGERS. Another more insidious factor was the gaunt, bespectacled appearance of bass guitarist Keith Alcock. Probably a lovely bloke in himself, his ruminent, unsmiling stare pervading otherwise cheery Mojos publicity shots was a bit. . . . creepy at a time when groups had to be liked for their looks as well as their music.

The wiser Big Three, of which drummer Johnny Hutchinson was the only remaining original member, gave up the ghost by 1965. Taking their place on their aggravatingly more remote manager's files were the Koobas, for whom no amount of ligging in the Scotch and other fashionable clubs could eradicate their incriminating casting in FERRY ACROSS THE MERSEY.

Talent didn't come into it. Even at its height, there simply hadn't been room for all the 350 or so groups that infested Liverpool.

One that did squeeze in was the Dennisons, a scouse approximation of the Kingsmen, whose own Be My Girl and a perfectly-timed Walkin' the Dog left their visiting cards just beyond the Top 30.

Drummer Gibson Kemp played in both the Dominoes and Hurricanes, led respectively by Edward 'Kingsize' Taylor and Ringo Starr's old boss, Rory Storm (Alan Caldwell), who were each deprived of the acclaim their outstanding showmanship merited. Running down the list, other deserving causes included Mark Peters and the Silhouettes who improved upon Bobby Vee's Someday; Johnny Sandon whose Remo Four were led astray by Epstein to back his pretty Tommy Quickly; Ian and the Zodiacs; the Riot Squad; Lee Curtis and the All-Stars and, derived from them, the Pete Best Four, featuring the Robert Curthose of British Beat.

Bright Lights, Big City

By 1965, London once again held the whip hand and many scouse musicians boarded the Lime Street train to seek their fortunes there. Down south, many bands had veered from hard line R'n'B towards Motown and other black sounds, from which a few evolved characteristics that set them apart, as did the Action who, hitless, still had much Mod pulling power. Whenever they played Brighton, their van would be met on the outskirts by a vast convoy of scooters, who would escort them to the venue. Only the Prince Regent was treated better.

Other popular club acts were the T-Bones, fronted by boxer's son Gary Farr, and the Artwoods, who flowered from the alarmingly-named Red Bludd's Bluesicians. Ron Wood, younger brother of the Artwoods' vocalist, was guitarist with another Middlesex band, the Birds, who, in 1965, served a writ for infringement of copyright on the Byrds, but neither this publicity stunt or their part in horror film, *The Deadly Bees* lifted them above Number 45 with their second single, *Leaving Here*.

Joining them on their last legs, Ron again picked a dud in the Creation who had been, nonetheless, perhaps the most striking of later beat groups. In their pop art heyday, both their chart entries were lacquered

Though they enjoyed a minor hit with a version of Poison Ivy, *the Paramounts (*left to right*) Barrie Wilson (drums), Diz Derrick (bass), Gary Brooker (keyboards) and Robin Trower (guitar) really came into their own when Brooker formed Procol Harum in 1967, introducing Trower, Wilson and an earlier Paramount member, Chris Copping into the line-up by 1970.*

with the sound of a violin bow scraped across an electric guitar. This unprecedented gimmick was to be refined by Yardbird Jimmy Page as the Creation themselves had refined the fabricated feedback of the Who. Climaxing their stage act, singer Kenneth Pickett would create an action painting à la Tony Hancock on a canvas backdrop. One mischievous night, taking more time than usual, Pickett confronted onlookers with a messy exposition of the female nude. After their second Top 50 entry, *Painter Man*, dried up at Number 36, allegations of sharp practice at an executive level may have necessitated their touring Europe for a year until the scandal blew over — although they weren't alone in this sort of escapade. Returning in 1967,

The late Graham Bond, 1963.

A Bluesbreaker and a brace of Bondsmen: Cream make their TV debut on RSG in 1966 (left to right) Eric Clapton, Jack Bruce and Ginger Baker.

though the old 'red with purple flashes' of inspiration sometimes broke through still, most of their remaining output consisted of lightweight ballads and American covers. Somewhere along the autobahns they'd run out of ideas and assumed defeat.

Representing two more mainstream R'n'B extremes were the Downliners Sect and the Graham Bond Organisation. From a blues core, the Sect covered many other fronts — country, rock'n'roll, soul, bad taste (the 'Sick Songs' E.P.) and self-referential originals (*Sect Appeal* — suspiciously like Bo Diddley's *Mona* — *Sect maniac*, *Leader of the Sect*, *Insecticide* ad nauseum). An abundance of material was issued from an independent E.P. to three Columbia albums and a pestilence of singles. Yet, apart from a Swedish Number One with a gleeful *Little Egypt*, they missed everywhere else. Nevertheless, they had a devoted following and could utilise an audience's time interestingly but their confusing mixture of styles did not reconcile easily on disc. Also guitarist Johnny Sutton's deerstalker didn't have the idiosyncratic appeal of Manfred's beard, Hank's glasses or Johnny Kidd's eyepatch. With the Sect, versatility was no virtue as it blurred a simpler image that might have worked wonders. The market had to take its medicine neat.

At least they had a more overt sense of humour than Bond's Organisation who, though they'd all been through Blues Incorporated, were also hardened jazz veterans. Drummer Ginger Baker had served Bilk and Terry Lightfoot, but Bond's pedigree was more cultivated through his blowing alto sax with Don Rendell. Jack Bruce had been with the Scottsville Jazzman before trading his double bass for a Fender six-string. With saxophonist Dick Heckstall-Smith, Baker, Bruce and Bond had all played together in the Johnny Burch Octet before forming the Organisation. An earlier member, Yorkshire guitarist John McLaughlin, later recorded with Miles Davis. Bond himself was quite at ease playing sax and organ simultaneously. Open-minded about new instruments, he was patiently demonstrating the mellotron to Cathy McGowan on READY STEADY GO as early as 1964.

They took pot shots at the hit parade with A-sides like *Tammy*, dripping with sentiment and piano triplets but, though Jack was a handsome rustic, the teenagers wouldn't have stood Graham's moustachioed pipe smoking, skeletal Ginger, or receding Dick. A hit would have been pleasant but a small hip audience based in London supported their jazzy approach to R'n'B until Bond broke up the band after the release of the formidable SOUND OF '65 L.P. and left for the USA, though he returned briefly for a final Organisation 45 in 1967 with Dick and drummer Jon Hiseman. Containing the ablest musical technicians of the era, the Graham Bond Organisation could, at any given moment of their existence, have wiped the floor with a joke band like the Downliners Sect.

It Should Have Been Zoot

The most fondly remembered London club act was, perhaps, Zoot Money's Big Roll Band whose *Big Time Operator* was their only Top 30 entry. George Bruno Money acquired his nom de théâtre at his Dorset secondary school through his verbose worship of saxophonist Zoot Sims. However, his jazz purity polluted by rock'n'roll, young Money became a fixture at pop presentations at the Pavilion on Bournemouth pier as the South Coast answer to Elvis, though reports suggest he had more in common with the Big Bopper. An excellent showman, his outrage often extended after hours. Dave Dee once witnessed him ritually hurling a faulty amplifier into the sea after one gremlin-troubled performance.

The Big Roll Band that Zoot took to London in 1964 included future Police man Andy Summers on guitar, Johnny Almond on baritone sax, drummer Colin Allen and bass player/second vocalist Paul Williams. With a blues and soul set stretching from Marvin Gaye smoothness through James Brown panic to Rufus Thomas clowning, keyboard pumping Zoot and his band were better live entertainers than Georgie Fame, Geno Washington and other draws at the Flamingo where their management, the Gunnell brothers, established them. However, as journalist Brian Hogg described him, Zoot's stage presence was akin to 'a psychotic Bud Flannagan' which with his face-pulling, trouser-dropping, dressing up (*e.g.* army gear to promote *Let's Run For Cover*) and comedy routines like *Zoot's Sermon* and *Self-discipline*, lost him the credibility of a Georgie Fame or even wretched Geno. Zoot was a laugh, yes, but he wasn't cool. Like the Big Three, he was also unable to live up to his potential in the studio. Often dogged by lacklustre material such as *Please Stay*, a muggy afternoon special by Burt Bacharach, even a live L.P. without the visuals lost out.

Ironically, the reverse was the case in 1967 when, disbanding the Big Roll combo, Money and Summers formed Dantalion's Chariot which, despite the light show, robes and change of venue to Middle Earth, didn't really come off in concert though their single, *Madman Running Through the Fields* was a psychedelic classic granted another lease of life when re-recorded by Eric Burdon's New Animals, whom Andy and Zoot, best man at Burdon's wedding, joined the following year. Zoot's later supporting roles in Ellis, Grimms, and the Kevin Ayers Band intimate that under the roguish, hard-drinking, gossip column lunacy he was, like many so-called extroverts, quite a shy, self-effacing person. However, some old madness was

delivered when, on an ITV mock-up of a 1940s dance band show in 1982, he took the stage for a lip-smacking *Closer to the Bone* during which a few thousand viewers may have affectionately recalled a wild evening down the Flamingo.

Zoot Money, 1964.

The Celtic Fringe

Of a more original bent were the Poets, who concocted an unlikely blend of their own mordant folk ditties with Mod sensibility. A Glaswegian songwriting trio, singer George Gallagher with guitarists Tony Myles and Hume Paton were destined for folk clubs before courage and ambition took command when they hired a bass player and drummer to enable them to work dance halls. It came to Andrew Loog Oldham's notice that not only did tough city gangs not beat up the Poets but also actually liked their music. Signing them first to Decca,

The Poets breathe the air round a bust of Robert Burns.

Oldham then transferred them to his own Immediate label.

Their output varied from the acoustic misery of *I'll Cry With the Moon* to a reluctant all-electric cover of *Baby Don't Do It* — produced by Paul Gadd 'Gary Glitter'. Their only hit, *Now We're Thru'*, best combined all vital Poetic ingredients, flickering 12-string chording against single note electric runs framing Gallagher's Lanarkshire brogue — a sort of agitated Celtic Herman — rounded off with a rock rhythm section and wordless backing vocals borrowed from the Kinks. Unhappily, craving for popular appeal, this distinctive sound was modified and, though their unique charm could still be discerned by true fans, to John Citizen, they ended up sounding like all the rest.

They Should Have Known Better

Among All The Rest was a competent Kentish quintet, Bern Elliott and the Fenmen, who adapted what they learned over two years in German clubland to their own devices. Theirs was, apart from the Flying Lizards 1981 tinpot monologue, the best-selling single of that Reeperbahn warhorse *Money* simply because, Barrett Strong's original apart, it was the first. With their next three discs tailing off as regards sales, Bern discorporated from his Fenmen for a solo career, which included a *Make It Easy On Yourself* totally eclipsed by the Walker Brothers version, using the Klan band for live dates. The Fenmen split up in 1968 when half their number were swallowed into the Pretty Things.

Playing it less safe were the Sorrows from Coventry who, composing much of their own material, functioned in a mean R'n'B mode. Aided by pirate radio, their atmospheric *Take a Heart* almost made the Top 20 in 1965 but the failure of their other six singles led to fragmentation two years later. Nonetheless, *Take a Heart* was a stunner — drummer Bruce Finlay's suitably throbbing tom-toms welding Philip Witcher's unsettling guitar interjections and Don Maughn's moody vocal.

A less attractive noise was emitted by the Migil *Four*

The Migil Five at the height of their fame: Red Lambert (guitar), Alan Watson (sax), Mike Felix (drums), Lenny Blanche (bass) and Gilbert Lucas (piano).

who took over the Dave Clark Five's residency at the Tottenham Royal in January 1964, though the vexation of Clark fans had spilled over into very real street riots. The Four, with a drumming vocalist in Mike Felix, contrived to become externally more like their predecessors by adding a saxophonist, Alan Watson, at Kenny Ball's suggestion. Earlier, as a North London pub trio, they had likewise sniffed the wind and, hiring balding, Bilk-bearded guitarist Red Lambert, transferred their allegiance to pop which they partly interpreted as jumping-up moonglow ballads like *Glad Rag Doll* and *Lucky Old Sun* as well as apologetic glances back at their jazz origins. Anyway, their luck held when, at the apogee of the Blue Beat craze, they underpinned their revival of Ronald Ronalde's *Mocking Bird Hill* with a hiccupping Blue Beat lope which, issued by Pye, leapt to Number 10. They cashed in as best they could but, by 1967, they had reverted to the jazz cabaret style in which they felt most comfortable. The best epitaph for the Migil Five was that, like the Portsmouth Sinfonia, they were incomparable.

Other lost bands that made the hit parade by fair means or foul included some who, in the view of Overlander Paul Friswell, 'did the Beatles a favour' with unsolicited covers of Lennon-McCartney songs. Among these philanthropists were the Naturals, pride of Harlow, at Number 24 in 1964 with *I Should Have Known Better*; Manchester's St. Louis Union who, though cursed with winning a *Melody Maker* band contest, still enticed *Girl* to Number 11 and, finally, Friswell and his Overlanders who, topping the charts with the bi-lingual *Michelle*, kept Northern Songs off Skid Row. From Rugby, the Mighty Avengers dashed to the rescue of Nanker-Phelge Music by allowing Andrew Loog Oldham to produce three Jagger-Richard A-sides for them of which only *So Much in Love* wooed the charts.

Another Rugby team, Pinkerton's Assorted Colours, formerly the Liberators, brought greater honour to the town when their debut 45, *Mirror Mirror* got a look in at Number 9 while the second saw them out at Number 50 for one week. All Colours discs shimmered with the amplified autoharp of Sam'Pinkerton' Kemp and, though the Downliners Sect had used one occasionally, it was this innovation that was the group's contribution to the rich tapestry of British Beat.

From Cheshire came the Lancastrians. Their Top 50 entry *We'll Sing in the Sunshine* was a pleasant amble that contradicted an arrogant attitude towards romance in the lyrics. Less opinionated were the Trendsetters, formed mainly from staff at a Bedford R.A.F. station. Becoming the Hedgehoppers, from air force slang, the word 'Anonymous' was tacked on in 1965 on the advice of manager Kenneth 'Jonathan' King, an owlish, teetotal Cambridge graduate whose *Everyone's Gone To the Moon* had rocketed to Number 4 that same year. He wrote Hedgehoppers Anonymous's *It's Good News Week*, a multi-purpose protest song broadcast by Decca as Barry McGuire was poised to blow up the charts with *Eve of Destruction*. Though the group scrambled likewise into the Top 5, the remainder of their five singles were grounded.

The first one-hit-wonder of the era was Danny Peppermint and his Jumping Jacks who sprang to

The Peddlers put one over on Danny Storm.

Number 26 in January 1962 with a cover of *Peppermint Twist*. Three months later, Hampshire's Danny Storm and the Strollers sauntered in at Number 42 with an orchestrated ballad, *Honest I Do*. To be honest, the Strollers were not invited to their own recording sessions until their clean cut leader continued his plea with the uptempo *Say You Do* in 1963. In this attempt to move into the Big Beat, Danny and his Strollers tripped up in not pushing the B-side, *Let the Sun Shine In*, thus putting one over on the Peddlers and Georgie Fame who both recorded this Teddy Randazzo number a year later.

The Peddlers were an amalgamation of two ex-Tornados, singing organist Roy Philips and seated bass guitarist Tab Martin, with Trevor Morais, who had drummed with both Faron's Flamingos and — like Ringo, Keith Hartley and Gibson Kemp — Rory Storm's Hurricanes. In 1965, their *Let the Sun Shine In*, delivered by Roy in a kind of blues-tinged snort, rose to Number 48 giving cause for celebration. When it sank without trace the following week, the trio once again felt obliged to get beastly drunk. It was a long wait but the Peddlers came up trumps again in 1969 when *Birth* put them into the Top 10. This meant that they could

now ask an even greater fee on the cabaret circuit where, like many of their contemporaries, they found most work.

Another bite at the cherry was also granted to certain individuals in the other groups, notably the Sorrows' Don Maughn who as 'Don Fardon' whooped it up to Number 3 in 1970 with *Indian Reservation*. Others, with lost business innocence, speculated in the executive side of showbusiness as managers, producers and jobbing tunesmiths. From the Creation, Kenny Pickett's Christmas of 1970 was made when his composition, *Grandad* sung by Clive Dunn, doddered its way to Number One. Boney M also boosted the bank account of Pickett and guitarist Eddie Philips with their revival of *Painter Man* in 1976.

Most participants in the British Beat Boom, however, went back to the securer anonymity of Straightsville via application form or supplicatory telephone call. Like National Service, your old job was often waiting for you when you got back, as butchers Kingsize Taylor and Brian Poole discovered. At Garston Job Centre in 1983, it was possible to be interviewed by Pete Best. Cushioned by secret relief at returning to the fold from the more shabby aspects of the record business, some thick-skinned musicians reappeared at the local venues from whence they came, still craving after all these years.

The End of one Era . . . .the Start of Another.

PAPERBACK WRITER

How Dare You Write What Your Wrote about My Favourite Group! — A Sort of Epilogue

After 1967, most groups that still carried any weight began concentrating on L.P.'s rather than the Top 50. Some had already become pseudo-mystics, dictating a shift in parameters of musical consciousness, as unsettled in state as a hangover if a P.R.S. cheque arrives. It was feasible to operate ambiguously, with good old rock'n'roll singles to keep investors sweet and experimental concept albums to indulge more personal artistic whims. Many groups no longer merely passed time by providing entertainment. Superficially boring, public attention was still demanded because, like Hercules' Twelve Labours, repeated listening was necessary to comprehension — no matter how puerile the underlying perception proved to be.

Nevertheless, the spirit of the first flush of British Beat has almost but not quite returned at various times since its passing, most overtly in the punk explosion of 1976 and its aftermath, though its more subtle influences are incalculable. Sometimes it takes a conscious effort for me to prevent once habitual tastes — that I've never really outgrown — from asserting their old power. Over the past few years, I've met several old heroes from the 1960s in the course of my work. This has been perhaps not as profoundly disturbing as finding the Pope using an adjacent kiosk in a row of pay phones, but I have, nonetheless, felt vaguely in awe of them no matter how mundane their present day activities or circumstances.

An article I wrote for *Record Collector* led to my being made an honorary member of the World-Wide Dave Clark Five Fan Club centred in Holland. When the quarterly newsletter is delivered, it is rather like receiving a tract from the Flat Earth Society, but I always read it from cover to cover with avid interest though, God knows, I've no time to listen to their records these days.

INDEX